Banking and Finance Series

The Practice of Banking, Part 1

Banking and Finance Series

The Practice of Banking, Part 1

by

Michael Marsden
Bank of Credit and Commerce International, London

Graham & Trotman

First published in 1985 by

Graham & Trotman Limited
Sterling House
66 Wilton Road
London SW1V 1DE

Graham & Trotman Inc.
13 Park Avenue
Gaithersburg
MD 20877, USA

ISBN 0 86010 563 6 (softcover)
0 86010 580 6 (hardbook)

British Library Cataloguing in Publication Data

Marsden, Michael
The practice of banking.——(Banking and finance series)
Pt. 1
1. Banks and banking——Great Britain
I. Title II. Series
332.1′0941 HG2988

ISBN 0–86010–580–6
ISBN 0–86010–563–6 Pbk

Typeset in Great Britain by Castlefield Press, Northants

Printed and bound in Great Britain

Contents

Series Foreword

The *Banking and Finance Series* has been written for students who are preparing for the Associateship of the Institute of Bankers. The structure of the series follows the syllabus closely. Although the emphasis is on the Institute of Bankers' examinations the series is also relevant to students for the kinds of other professional examinations such as the different Accountancy Bodies, Chartered Secretaries, Diploma in Public Administration, undergraduate business course, B.T.E.C., B.E.C., H.N.D., D.M.S., Stock Exchange courses, Association of Corporate Treasurers, Institute of Freight Forwarders, Institute of Export.

July 1985

Brian Kettell
Series Editor

Preface

This book covers a broad range of topics relating to banking but aims primarily at the aspects of banking which comprise the syllabus of the Institute of Bankers examination in Practice of Banking — 1 (Banking Diploma — Stage 2). Although the textbook should be of particular interest and assistance to students engaging upon a study of the relative Institute of Bankers subject, the book will, due to the wide range of technical banking information it contains coupled with the practical guidance it affords, provide a useful general reference book for practising branch bankers and for students in educational institutes who are studying financial and business courses.

A separate publication of "Questions and Answers" has been produced in conjunction with this textbook which is structured similarly to the textbook, and which is cross-referenced to the relative section of the textbook. Those readers who are studying for the Institute examination should benefit from using that manual in conjunction with this book, particularly since it contains a considerable number of questions with specimen answers. The questions and answers in each chapter of the "Questions and Answers" manual involve topics covered in the corresponding chapters of this book, and thus the student reader is able to test his knowledge of the various banking topics as he goes along.

The Practice of Banking examinations for the Banking Diploma of the Institute of Bankers are practical ones and require candidates to identify the banking issues involved, set out the relevant principles and then, based upon an appreciation of these together with the application of common-sense, state what action is needed in the particular circumstances set out in a question.

The contents of this book should provide students with the knowledge they require for this type of examination question and the "Questions and Answers" manual referred to earlier, which is available as a separate publication, gives students ample opportunity to practice their approach to such questions and then assess their efforts by reference to the specimen answers provided.

Michael Marsden
July 1985

Chapter 1

Banker and Customer Relationship

INTRODUCTION

There is no really adequate definition of the term "banker", neither is there a statutory definition of a "customer." Nevertheless it is important for a banker to know what constitutes a customer, especially bearing in mind the purposes of Section 4 of the Cheques Act 1957. The length of association is not now considered to be an essential feature, but the customer must have an account, although the intention to open an account may suffice. A series of isolated transactions carried out by a banker for a person (e.g. the collection of cheques for someone who has no account and the payment to the person of the proceeds after clearance) does not make that person a customer. A reasonable definition of a "customer" may therefore be: "a person who has an account or an account in contemplation", and where the banker has agreed to open an account if so requested. When someone walks into a bank and asks to open a banking account, he is making an offer to enter into a contract. When the banker agrees to open the account, he is legally accepting the offer and thus a binding contract is created. However, before committing himself, the banker will want to be satisfied that the person will be a suitable customer, either by personal introduction, by taking and following up references or making some form of enquiry (see later).

Before considering the nature of the relationship between banker and customer, it is perhaps useful to revert to the question of what a "banker" is in the light of the changes introduced into the system for regulating "banks" by the Banking Act of 1979.

THE BANKING ACT 1979

The United Kingdom has had a highly developed banking system for centuries which, unlike the banking systems of most countries, was until recently not comprehensively regulated by statute. Regulation was nevertheless present, by way of the control exercised by the Bank of England by informal means, supported by the provisions of the Bank of England Act 1946. Other statute law has played a part in governing certain aspects and activities of banks and other financial institutions, e.g. the moneylenders Acts, the Protection of Depositors Act and the Consumer Credit Act.

Due to a variety of reasons (such as the growth of institutions on the fringe of the established banking system, and the fringe banking crisis which came about in 1974, the tremendous influx of overseas banks into the UK, the growth and development of newer and larger international capital markets with the added complication and sophistication these brought about) the task of domestic regulation became far more difficult than it had been when the banking system was less developed and less diverse. However, the factor primarily responsible for the Banking Act of 1979 was the UK's European Community obligations and the directive which required the UK to have an official licensing system for banks and similar financial institutions. Nevertheless, the need for a banking act had been recognised due to the awareness of the dangers of inadequate supervision of fringe institutions and the need to remove confusion on the part of the public as to what were and were not banks. The banks themselves were also, in general, probably receptive to the introduction of tighter controls; certainly the English and Scottish clearing banks would have seen and supported the need for some change, in the light of the extent to which they collectively had to safeguard the fabric of the UK banking scene, under the leadership of the Bank of England, by means of the "lifeboat" they provided to preserve confidence and underwrite public deposits when the fringe banking crisis emerged.

The Banking Act 1979 does not set out to control and regulate detailed aspects of banking. Its main purposes are:

(1) to stop any bank or financial organisation, whether existing or newly formed, accepting deposits without having obtained covering authority from the Bank of England;
(2) to lay down the criteria which it is necessary to satisfy in order to obtain and retain such authority;
(3) to provide a statutory framework within which the Bank of England will supervise the activities of all the relative institutions;
(4) to monitor and control banking names, with banking names being restricted largely to recognised banks (see later);
(5) to safeguard depositors' money in licensed institutions by way of a Depositors' Protection Scheme.

The Act brought in two types of authorisation for deposit taking institutions, these being:

(a) Recognised Bank; or
(b) Licensed Deposit Taker.

The requirements of the EEC banking directive did not contain such division and the two categories were devised by the Bank of England with the intention of limiting the use of banking names and descriptions and enabling close control to be exercised over licensed deposit takers, with the more informal measure of control being retained as far as recognised banks were concerned.

The Act came into operation in October 1979 and all relevant institutions had to apply by April 1980 to the Bank of England for recognition or a licence to enable them to continue accepting deposits thereafter. After that time, any new institution could not legally commence business to take deposits without first obtaining a licence to do so from the Bank of England.

Certain institutions which take deposits are specifically excluded from the requirements of the Banking Act. The Bank of England does not require a licence, neither do the National Savings Bank, the Trustee Savings Banks, the National Giro and local authorities. For one reason or another these institutions are all regarded as not being subject to the risks that prevail in the private sector. Although the building societies are huge takers of deposits, they are not, at present, governed by the Banking Act but by separate legislation, and they have for many years been under the control of the Chief Registrar of Friendly Societies.

Any institution seeking recognition or a licence will be required to satisfy the criteria laid down by the Act. The applicant will have to satisfy the Bank of England as to its solvency and also on the question of whether or not its management is competent and sufficiently experienced. Over and above this, an institution seeking recognised status has to provide a sufficiently wide range of banking services and must satisfy the Bank of England that it is of high standing and enjoys a good reputation in the financial community.

Under the terms of the Act, a recognised bank has to provide the following five services:

- the acceptance of deposits;
- granting loans and other credit facilities;
- foreign exchange dealing;
- bill finance and the handling of documents relating to overseas trade;
- corporate finance and investment management.

However, the Act grants discretion to the Bank of England to accept the absence of one or two of the last three services where it considers this appropriate, and the Bank of England can also award recognised status to institutions who may not provide these services in full but who demonstrate to the satisfaction of the Bank of England that they provide what in the Act is referred to as a "highly specialised banking service."

The Banking Act of 1979 has removed some uncertainties which may have existed about the scope of the Bank of England's powers and has clarified where responsibility for banking supervision rests; whereas prior to its introduction there was an element of confusion caused by divided responsibilities on some aspects such as between the Bank of England and the Department of Trade. Additionally the Act has made redundant certain provisions which previously existed under sections of the Protection of Depositors Act and the Companies Acts.

The banking industry and the markets seem to have settled down with the Banking Act which has now been in operation for almost six years. Although the system of supervision has undergone change as a result of the legislation, with authorisation being derived from statute, the requirements of the Act nevertheless are part of a broader and balanced supervisory role performed by the Bank of England, which seems successful in achieving a good balance between the respective merits of statutory and non-statutory methods of supervision. Whilst basic criteria are applied to all authorised institutions on an individual basis to allow for any particular circumstances, the supervisory system still relies considerably upon regular, close contact being maintained between the Bank of England and the management of the individual institutions, together with the monitoring capacity afforded by the submission to the Bank of England of quarterly statistical returns from all authorised institutions.

There are currently some 600 plus authorised institutions, split almost equally between recognised banks and licensed deposit takers. Around two thirds of the institutions supervised are foreign-owned or foreign-controlled and the developments which have come about in international supervisory co-ordination and co-operation over recent years have had an influence on the UK system of control.

As to the future, it would seem reasonable to assume that some changes in the supervisory system will be brought about by the various influences which will impact on markets and thus create the need for supervisory responses. Technological changes, the emergence of new types of institutions, competitive pressures and a continued increasing involvement in international banking may all play a part, as will further European integration. Due to the spread of automated teller machine networks and the likely early introduction of electronic funds transfer at point of sale, the use of paper in payments' systems could virtually be eliminated and this would enable institutions other than banks (e.g. building societies) to provide increasingly cash dispensing and money transmission services in competition with banks but without the heavy operating costs of the present paper-based system. Links between institutions providing similar financial services could be made and this could well spread beyond mere collaboration between banks and building societies, should "financial supermarkets" be created providing a very wide range of financial services and perhaps embracing banks, building societies, insurance companies, multiple retail chains and possibly others. Such changes would certainly raise the question of the suitability of many of the capital and liquidity ratios and the other monitoring tools currently regarded as appropriate for banks; furthermore if considerable diversification does take place the matter of ownership would need to be considered in a supervisory context.

Thus both international and domestic developments in banking and other institutions will affect the way in which banks are supervised in the future, and the Bank of England and other authorities may well face difficult judgments in dividing what sort of balance should be struck between their providing a lead and allowing market forces to operate.

Indeed, after a relatively calm period since the introduction of the Banking Act, there have recently been disturbing instances within the banking community which have again raised the thorny problem of bank regulation. This, together with the continued concern internationally over the pressures now applying to commercial banks, means that the whole question of the supervision of banks will remain an active one for the foreseeable future.

THE NATURE OF THE BANKING CONTRACT

As with any contract, the banking contract involves rights and duties and over the years the terms of the contract have gradually been clarified by means of decided cases. The main terms of the contract are however implied and there is no statute which covers the subject and (at least in the UK) there is no precise written or even oral notification of the terms of the contract. The relationship of banker and customer has several facets and the terms relating to these are given consideration from time to time in the courts and in this way the terms are tested, clarified and perhaps defined as time goes by.

The CONTRACTUAL aspects of the banker/customer relationship are examined more fully below. As a customer must be an account holder, the basic relationship between banker and customer is that of DEBTOR AND CREDITOR, the banker being the debtor with regard to funds deposited with him, and being the creditor in respect of money lent by him. However, a banker is not an ordinary debtor as a banker is liable to repay only when demand has been made on him whereas under Common Law an ordinary debtor has a duty to seek out his creditor and repay the debt. Although in past years efforts have been made to get the courts to rule whether a banker was a trustee for his customer, an agent of the customer or bailee of his customer's property. These all involve to some extent the holding of money or property by one party for another. Nevertheless, so does a debtor since he is holding money of his creditor and, although different roles arise in an overall banker and customer relationship, the fundamental relationship can be regarded as that of debtor and creditor. In providing ancillary services for the customer the question of other relationships arises and the PRINCIPAL AND AGENT relationship rears its head where the banker acts for his customer where a third party is involved. The law relating to Agency is therefore relevant to bankers because they will act on occasions as agents on behalf of their customers and also because many of their normal business transactions will involve their having dealings with other agents, e.g. company directors, partners and attorneys. The other important relationship which arises is that of BAILOR AND BAILEE in instances where bankers are holding for safe keeping their customers' valuables and securities.

It is therefore necessary for bankers to understand the principles involved in these different types of relationship so that they can conduct their banking business and transactions in full knowledge of the various rights and obligations which may apply. The various relationships are explained in more depth below.

THE CONTRACTUAL RELATIONSHIP

The implied terms and conditions of the contract between banker and customer were mainly defined in *Joachimson v. Swiss Bank Corporation* (1921):

(a) the bank undertakes to receive money, and
(b) to collect bills for its customers' account.
(c) The proceeds received, under (a) and (b) are not held in trust but borrowed by the banker, who undertakes
(d) to repay them at the branch where the account is kept and during banking hours, and
(e) to repay any part of the amount due against the written order of the customer.
(f) As such written orders (cheques) may be outstanding for some days the banker undertakes not to cease business with his customer without reasonable notice.
(g) The banker is not liable to repay until demand has been made by the customer. (Notice that this is the opposite of the ordinary rule that a debtor must seek out his creditor and that, as a result, the Limitation Act does not commence to run against the **customer** until demand has been made).
(h) The customer undertakes to exercise reasonable care in drawing his cheques so as not to mislead the bank or to facilitate forgery.
(i) The banker owes a duty of secrecy.

BANKER'S DUTY OF SECRECY

This is an important topic and one which can rear its head in practice in a variety of ways. Failure to observe this obligation on the part of a banker can cause serious problems and involve loss by way of damages, and it is therefore an area with which the banker needs to be fully familiar. Breach of the duty of secrecy will give a claim for nominal damages or, where it can be shown that the customer has suffered injury, for substantial damages. Quite apart from any monetary cost which could thus be incurred, there is also the danger of the banker's reputation being seriously harmed by the bad publicity that could be generated should the bank be seen to fail to observe its duty.

A banker's duty of secrecy to his customer is a legal duty implied in the contractual relationship between banker and customer. Secrecy should be maintained not only in relation to the actual state of the customer's account, but also, and often more importantly, in relation to any information derived from the account.

A leading case on this duty of secrecy is *Tournier v. National Provincial and Union of England Bank* (1924) which involved the bank, who were becoming concerned about their customer's overdraft, disclosing to the customer's employers that he was thought to be gambling. As a result of this, the customer lost his job and successfully brought an action against the bank for damages. The judgement in this case qualified the banker's duty of secrecy and stated that disclosure was justified in the following four instances:

(a) Under compulsion of law.
(b) Where there is a duty to the public.
(c) Where disclosure is necessary in the interests of the bank
(d) Where disclosure is made with the express or implied consent of the customer.

Disclosure under Compulsion of Law

Bankers can be obliged to produce copies of banking accounts for the courts under the Banker's Books Evidence Act 1879 but normally would not disclose until required to do so by subpoena. In *Barker v. Wilson* (1980) it was held that a microfilm which records a customer's account could be a banker's book for the purpose of the Act.

This decision is reinforced by the Banking Act 1979 which provides that bankers' books for the purposes of this Act include records used in the ordinary cause of business by the bank, whether in written form or a microfilm, magnetic tape or some other form of mechanical or electronic data storage and retrieval mechanism.

In *Bankers Trust Company v. Shapira* (1980) the Court of Appeal required the bank to disclose information that was subject to the bank's duty of confidentiality to the customer. In the judgement it was stated that the court would not let the duty of secrecy be used to conceal a fraud but an order for disclosure should be restricted to information needed in relation to the transactions in question.

Under the Companies' Act 1985, a banker is required to give all the assistance it reasonably can to an Inspector appointed by the authorities to investigate the affairs of a company; or, in the winding up of a company, to the Director of Public Prosecutions if proceeding against a member or official of the company.

A banker may also be required by statute to disclose certain information to the authorities by Treasury direction.

Under the Taxes Management Act 1970 Section 17, (re-enacting earlier legislation) banks are required to supply, when requested by the Inland Revenue authorities, a return of the names and addresses of all persons to whom interest has been allowed without deduction of income tax, over and above a level specified by the Inland Revenue from time to time.

Public Duty to Disclose

Some confusion sometimes arises under this heading, and it should be noted that this heading does not imply that a bank must disclose to the Inland Revenue if tax evasion is suspected or to the Police who are seeking information about a customer who they may wish to charge for fraud. In such situations, the authorities can take the appropriate steps under the Bankers' Books Evidence Act. This heading is aimed at matters of greater general significance such as where subversive activities are suspected or involved. For example, the disclosure of funds held or transferred to finance illegal arms dealing.

Disclosure in the Interests of the Bank

This heading covers those instances where it is necessary for the banker to disclose the balance of a customer's indebtedness in order to progress some legal action the bank may be taking or to enforce security the bank is holding. For example, when issuing a writ against a customer for repayment of the customer's debt to the bank, the amount of the indebtedness would have to be stated. Similarly, where the bank is making demand on a guarantor, the banker necessarily has to state the balance of the principal debtor's bank debt, or at least indicate, where the guarantee is for a limited amount, that the bank borrowing is in excess of the limit on the guarantor's liability. It must be appreciated that disclosure is not justified under this heading merely where disclosure on the bank's part would provide material gain for the bank. Thus, for example, where a company customer, intending to pay its employees by crediting their bank accounts, asks the bank to confirm which employees have accounts at that bank this information cannot properly be divulged without the customers' authority.

Disclosure with the customer's Express or Implied Consent

Where express consent is given, this should give precise instructions to the bank, signed by the customer. For example, where the bank is asked to confirm balances and/or give other information to the customer's accountants.

Implied consent is not so clear cut and the case *Sunderland v. Barclays Bank Ltd.* (1938) should be noted in this connection. A cheque in the sum of £2–15 shillings drawn by a doctor's wife had been returned unpaid by the bank as her account was only 8 shillings in credit. She telephoned the bank to complain about such a small cheque being dishonoured and after a lengthy discussion her husband took over the conversation with the bank. In explaining his action in returning the cheque, the bank manager explained to the husband that the wife regularly drew cheques in favour of bookmakers and the doctor, who had not been aware of this, subsequently stopped his wife's allowance. The Court, when giving judgement for the bank, stated that the manager was justified in the circumstances in thinking that the wife did not object to his offering to the husband the explanations which were intended to satisfy him that his wife's complaint was unjustified.

A banker would be unwise to rely upon an implied authority to disclose and should always be wary about releasing information about any customer's account without proper authority. Nevertheless, as seen in the above case, the necessity to assume and rely upon an implied authority could arise in practice.

JUSTICE AND CONFIDENTIALITY

In the provision of services to customers, bankers are not entitled to discriminate on grounds of sex or race. In *Nasse v. Science Research Council* and *Vyas v. Leyland Cars Ltd* (1978) the Court of Appeal analysed powers of discovery under the Sex Discrimination Act 1975 and the Race Relations Act 1976. In both actions, decided by one judgement, the allegations were that, on the grounds of sex in one case and colour in the other, opportunities for promotion were denied. The parties making the allegations sought production of the relevant papers concerning the other staff who were promoted. The Court of Appeal stated that tribunals should not order or permit the disclosure of reports or references that had been given or received in confidence except in very rare cases where, after inspection of a particular document, the chairman decided that it was essential in the interests of justice that the confidence should be overridden. The Court stated that "the prospect that an applicant who alleged discrimination by a bank by the refusal of an overdraft might be able to compel the bank to disclose the confidential documents relating to every customer who had been granted an overdraft is appalling." The decisions were confirmed by the House of Lords in 1979.

STATUS ENQUIRIES AND BANKER'S CONFIDENTIAL REPORTS

In answering status enquiries on a banker's customer, the banker is to a large extent relying on implied consent since this service is not yet a clear term of the banking contract. It is however generally accepted that the practice of banks replying to enquiries from other banks and certain approved bodies is so well established that the opening of an account constitutes an implied authority to the bank to answer such enquiries. The banker does not in practice seek and obtain the customer's consent before replying but would not normally open an account where the prospective customer was trying to stipulate that the bank must not reply to status enquiries concerning him.

There are two risks involved for the banker. These are action either by the customer because the reply is too unfavourable, or by the party making the enquiry because the reply is too favourable.

Action by the customer: This could involve a claim of libel or slander, but it is very difficult to envisage circumstances in which a banker would, without justification, report adversely on the credit standing of a customer. The risk therefore is a very small one although confusion of customers due to similar names is a situation which could possibly lead to a successful action against a bank.

The other risk is an action for breach of contract by unauthorised disclosure which could succeed if the Court held that the authority to give reports is not an implied term in the contract between banker and customer.

Action by the party who received the information: This could involve a charge of Fraud, but this is a small risk as no banker is very likely to give fraudulent information, although it should be borne in mind that even recklessly given information will count as fraud for this purpose. If an action arose involving a claim of fraudulent misrepresentation, the Statute of Frauds Amendment Act 1828 (Lord Tenterden's Act) is relevant, which states that a banker giving information to a customer or third party about the credit and standing of an individual or business concern would not be liable for any loss arising due to the information being false unless the representation was in writing and signed by the party being charged. Thus in practice, bankers do not sign or initial their replies to status enquiries, although these are of course given in writing. The case of *Banbury v. Bank of Montreal* (1918) involved a manager giving advice on investments to a customer, with an unsuccessful outcome, and the customer sued the bank who claimed a defence under Lord Tenterden's Act and also claimed that the advice given was not within the scope of the manager's authority. The House of Lords gave judgement in favour of the bank stating that there was no evidence to show that the giving of advice as to investments was within the scope of the manager's authority and duties, and therefore the bank was not bound. However, it was laid down that Lord Tenterden's Act applies only in the case of fraudulent misrepresentation (not innocent misrepresentation as in this case) and therefore liability can arise even in the absence of writing. In *Commercial Banking Co. of Sydney Ltd. v. R.H. Brown & Co* (1972), an Australian case, the court held that an express disclaimer of liability (such as banks include by way of a "without responsibility" clause) was ineffective where a reply is so recklessly and unjustifiably given as to amount to a fraudulent misrepresentation.

The more likely charge to be brought against a bank would be alleged negligence on the banker's part. Until 1964 the usual defence argued successfully was that there was no duty of care owed by a banker to a party making an enquiry since there was no contractual relationship or other link between them; therefore if there was no duty to exercise care there could be no remedy for breach of this, i.e. failure to take care, which is negligence. In *Hedley Byrne & Co. Ltd. v. Heller and Partners Ltd.* (1964) the House of Lords held that a bank replying to an enquiry from the customer of another bank (i.e. where there was no contractual relationship) owes a duty to exercise care unless there is a specific and precise clause disclaiming liability.

However, the Unfair Contract Terms Act 1977 has removed some of the protection afforded by the *Hedley Byrne* case as the Act limits the degree to which a business can exclude liability for its own acts or defaults. Generally, the Act states that such exclusions will not be upheld unless they satisfy a "reasonableness" test. The Act (which despite its title is not confined to contractual situations) therefore invalidates the "disclaimer" clause in a reply to a status enquiry, except to the extent that the disclaimer is held to be reasonable.

SOME PRACTICAL CONSIDERATIONS WHEN MAKING OR RESPONDING TO ENQUIRIES

Making an Enquiry

Enquiries should be channelled through the enquirer's bankers and not direct since these are made and answered on a confidential and privileged basis as between bankers. (Nowadays, however, it is not uncommon for the enquirer, usually a supplier company or retail store, to enquire direct to the customer's bank but asking the banker to reply to their bank. This obviously saves time and is generally accepted as reasonable practice. A banker should however never reply to anyone other than another banker, a customer, or a recognised trade protection society.)

Enquire for the actual amount under consideration where possible. If a larger amount is mentioned to "give a margin" the banker receiving the enquiry will be misled and have an inaccurate picture of his customer's commitments.

Replying to Enquiries

Exercise great care in drafting the reply; facts are better than opinions. Have regard to other facts within knowledge as well as to those available from the account. In *Parsons v. Barclay & Co. Ltd.* (1910) it was held that there was no need to make **outside** enquiries.

Do not disclose the actual state of the account unless expressly authorised by the customer — in such circumstances it is not a normal banking practice to do so; this would be a breach of the implied contract.

It is preferable to confine the remarks to general statements.

If the reply concerns a company and it is known that debentures are issued it is advisable to mention the fact notwithstanding that the information would be revealed by a search of the Register of Charges kept by the Register of Companies. If the debenture is given to the **bank** it is essential to disclose that fact.

The reply should be unsigned to guard against action for **fraud**. Remember that a statement made recklessly without caring whether it is true or false may be fraudulent.

As an action for **negligence** may be brought even though the reply is unsigned, ensure that the reply is honest and justifiable, and contains a clear and sufficient disclaimer of liability.

As a branch manager is normally authorised to reply to enquiries he will incur no personal liability for he is acting within the scope of his authority. If however, a cashier, for instance, who was not so authorised replied to an enquiry, personal liability would result in the event of negligence, and he could not rely on any disclaimer clause in favour of the bank.

A careful record should be kept of all replies, whether in respect of trade enquiries or guarantee liabilities: such a record will prove of assistance in dealing with subsequent enquiries and renewals as well as giving an indication of the customer's liabilities outside the bank.

In the latter respect, however, care has to be taken insomuch that the cumulative effect of enquiries received on a particular customer may mislead and may not genuinely reflect the customer's actual liabilities. An example of this is a civil engineering company which may well not be awarded many of the contracts in respect of which it had status enquiries made on it.

There is within the banking community a fairly well-recognised set of replies to status enquiries which has developed over the years. Care and tact is needed whenever phrasing replies and consideration must always be given to what the recipient banker will read into the reply and pass on to his customer. When a straightforward favourable reply is justified, there should be no difficulty in wording this. Where the response has to be qualified to some degree or other, it is not so easy. For example a reply to an enquiry about a party's suitability and creditworthiness "as guarantor for £5000, without supporting security" could state "undoubted for your figures." This would be interpreted by the enquiring bank as a sign of considerable strength and indeed such a positive favourable reply would not be given lightly. "Good for your figures" is a lesser answer but still satisfactory, "Should be good for your figures" introduces an element of doubt, and "we regret we cannot speak for your figures, but do not think that our customer would enter into a commitment which he could not see his way clear to fulfil" conveys a quite clear impression. At the other extreme, wording such as "we recommend caution" would be seen as a red warning sign and should put the enquiring banker on guard.

THE DEBTOR/CREDITOR RELATIONSHIP

As stated earlier, the basic banker/customer relationship is that of debtor/creditor and there are several aspects which need to be considered in relation to this heading.

APPROPRIATION OF PAYMENTS

The rule generally is that the person who pays the money has the right to stipulate which debt, if he owes more than one, shall be repaid by the money he pays to the creditor. In the context of the banker/customer relationship it is important to know how appropriation takes place and the strict order of by whom appropriation may be made is as follows:

To whichever debt the debtor indicates

- This usually occurs when an overdrawn account is not being conducted regularly and the customer, when paying in a credit, earmarks the credit to meet certain cheques which he has issued. When this occurs, the banker must appropriate the payment as instructed by the customer irrespective of the state of the account unless the bank has previously given notice to the customer, which has now expired, that the account is to be closed. In practice, a customer often makes a similar type of appropriation to cover debit interest which the bank applied to the account so that the customer has paid the interest and thus can apply for a Bank Interest Certificate for tax purposes.

Appropriation by the creditor

- If at the time of payment, the debtor does not make any specific appropriation then the creditor may do so at any time. The payment may be applied to any debt owing by the debtor (*Simson v. Ingham* (1823)) and can be appropriated to a statute-barred debt. Once the creditor's appropriation has been notified to the debtor the creditor cannot then retract what he has done.

Appropriation by the law

- In the case of a continuous, unbroken running account where there is no specific appropriation by either the debtor or the creditor, then the law appropriates and the earlier payments in are appropriated to the earlier payments out, and so on in regular sequence. In other words, it is the first sum paid in that is first paid out and this rule is known as the Rule in Clayton's Case — *Devaynes v. Noble* (1816). This rule will apply to all current accounts whether in credit or overdrawn although the banker will usually be more concerned with the impact of the Rule on debit accounts. The Rule in Clayton's Case can be of great practical significance to the banker, and if the operation of the Rule is to be prevented, the account must be broken (i.e. "ruled off") and all further transactions put through a new account. It may be necessary to take such action in the following instances:
    - On receipt of notice that a second or subsequent charge has been given on the security held to secure the bank's advance. Failure to do this would result in all subsequent credits being appropriated in reduction of the bank's lending against that security, with the subsequent debits constituting fresh advances which would rank behind the further charge that has been executed. The relevant case is *Deeley v. Lloyds Bank Ltd.* (1912).

- On the death of a party to a joint account where the banker wishes to preserve recourse against the deceased's estate and where joint and several liability obtains.
- On the determination of a guarantee (although most bank forms of guarantee bind the deceased's personal representatives, thus avoiding the need to break the account).
- On the bankruptcy of a guarantor.
- On the change in constitution of a firm.

The following example shows the effect of the Rule. Suppose there is a joint account in the names of Andrews and Stephens. Andrews is undoubted whereas Stephens has no means whatsoever. Andrews dies when the account is £3000 overdrawn. Unless the bank breaks the account any subsequent credits will be appropriated to repay the £3000 advance, thereby releasing Andrews' estate, whilst any further withdrawals, although not increasing the amount of the debt, will constitute a fresh advance for which only Stephens is liable.

When a customer's account contains partly his own money and partly trust money and he draws out amounts by cheques in the usual way, the customer must be taken to have drawn out his own money and deemed not to have touched the trust money until all his own money has been drawn out. Therefore in this particular set of circumstances the Rule in Clayton's Case does not apply — *Re Halletts Estate* (1880). However, if trust monies belonging to separate beneficiaries are paid into the account, then the Rule will apply as between the beneficiaries.

SET OFF

Set off is the legal right whereby a debtor is entitled to take into account a debt owing to him by a creditor when being sued for a debt due from him to the creditor. As part of his contractual relationship with the customer, and as stated in the Joachimson case referred to earlier in this chapter, the banker undertakes to repay "on demand". Where a customer has several accounts, some overdrawn and others in credit, difficulties may arise in that the banker has to decide the amount of the available balance. In other words, the banker needs to determine whether or not he can combine or "set off" the accounts to arrive at the balance due to or from the customer. In practice, the difficulty arises when a cheque is presented by a third party and, although the account upon which the cheque is drawn is sufficiently in credit to stand being debited with the amount of the cheque, the credit balance on that account has been regarded by the banker as covering another account which is overdrawn. The danger is that if the cheque is returned for lack of funds and the drawer successfully challenges the bank's action in setting-off the accounts, the drawer will have a claim against the bank for damages.

No difficulties are experienced when the accounts are stopped by reason of death or bankruptcy, the winding-up of a company, or the service of a

Garnishee Order because the banker's right of set-off is determined automatically. In these cases no question arises as to risk of action by the customer for wrongful dishonour — if cheques are presented for payment they will be returned whatever the state of the accounts: the funds are to be accounted for elsewhere.

The legal right of set-off exists in respect of debts due from and to the same **parties** in the **same right** unless there is an agreement, express or implied, to the contrary.

In *Greenhalgh v. Union Bank of Manchester* (1924) it was inferred that the mere fact that separate accounts existed constituted an implied agreement to keep them separate. However, this case was much criticised in *National Westminster Bank Ltd. v. Halesowen Presswork and Assemblies Ltd.* (1972) and now has to be regarded as doubtful. In the Halesowen case the court analysed the legal issues involved in a banker's right of set-off (or right of lien). Basically this right arises whenever a customer owes money to a bank but the right of set-off or lien can be modified by express or implied contract between the banker and customer. The banker cannot exercise the "right" in breach of any agreement with the customer. The lien is exercisable on all securities coming into the possession of the bank in its capacity as banker (but not in any other capacity) and the securities must belong to the customer in the same right as that in which the customer is indebted to the banker. Such securities include cheques and their proceeds. The Court of Appeal also considered the effect of Section 31 of the Bankruptcy Act 1914 (which follows through into the winding up of companies by Section 317 of the Companies Act 1948). Under these sections in the liquidation of a company balances must be set-off against each other if there are mutual debts, credits or dealings between the company and one of its creditors. The House of Lords eventually held that the dealings in this case involving the two accounts were mutual and that the parties could not contract to exclude the operation of Section 31.

Therefore, whilst it has always been considered that bankers have an automatic right to combine accounts without notice in a bankruptcy or liquidation, the Halesowen case now indicates that to so do is not in fact a right but an obligation as the provisions of Section 31 are mandatory and cannot be contracted out of. Instances could arise in practice where a banker would not wish to set-off a balance, perhaps where a moratorium had been agreed or where a bank had agreed to hold sums on separate account for the benefit of creditors. The only safe way to prevent such funds being set-off would be for such an account to be with a different bank which would successfully guard against an undesired set-off.

Crown Right of Set-off: In Re H.H. Curtis (Builders) Ltd. (1978) it was established that set-off is not limited to mutual contractual claims. In this case it was held that the Crown was entitled to set-off monies owed by the company to the Inland Revenue against monies owing to the company by the Commissioners of Customs and Excise. The possible practical effect of this case should be appreciated particularly where the banker is trying to assess his likely position under a floating charge in relation to preferential creditors: e.g. a bank could be expecting to receive under its floating charge the proceeds of a VAT refund only to find that in liquidation the Crown set-off those monies against, say, unpaid PAYE. Indeed, such instances of Crown right of set-off being exercised have been arising increasingly over the past year or so in line with the higher numbers of bankruptcies and liquidations, and bankers should always be alive to this possibility and the impact it could have on their positions, particularly where companies are having financial problems and where it is known or suspected that the company could both owe money to and be owed money by the State, albeit involving different departments.

Although the Halesowen decision threw light on some aspects of set-off, it did not tidy up once and for all the law relating to the topic and the subject remains a problematical one for the banker. It is reasonable to summarise the legal position on the following general basis:

Once something has occurred to stop the account as, for example, the death or bankruptcy of the customer, the bank's right of set-off comes into operation without restriction, but so long as the accounts are active the banker cannot set-off the debit balance of one account against the credit balance of the other except after reasonable notice given to the customer, unless (a) there is a definite agreement giving the banker the right, or (b) such a right can be inferred from the course of business between the bank and its customer. This all applies whether the accounts are at different branches or not.

No right of set-off exists nor can be acquired when there is express or constructive notice that the credit balance represents trust monies. e.g.

- Trust Accounts against the Trustee's personal indebtedness. (*Re Gross, Ex Parte Kingston* (1981)).
- Solicitor's Clients Accounts against overdrawn office or private accounts.
- Insurance brokers' I.B.A. (Insurance Broking Accounts) balances against borrowings on other accounts of the brokers. (Separate accounts have to be maintained under the provisions of the Insurance Brokers (Registration) Act 1977 and brokers are required to obtain written confirmation from their banks that the bankers are not entitled to any charge, incumbrance, lien, right of set-off, compensation or retention against monies in these accounts.)
- Accounts designated in such a way that they clearly indicate an element of trust against differently or non-designated accounts, e.g. P. Jones — Cricket Club Account; M. Phillips — Churchwardens Account.

In *Barclays Bank Ltd. v. Quistclose Investments Ltd.* (1968) the company made a loan of £209,719 to Rolls-Razor Ltd. to enable it to pay a dividend which had been declared, and sent its cheque to the bank with a covering letter stating this fact. The cheque was credited to an Ordinary Dividend No. 4 a/c. Soon afterwards Rolls-Razor went into liquidation and the bank set-off this credit balance against other debit balances. The House of Lords gave judgement for the company against the bank because as between the company and Rolls-Razor Ltd. the money was impressed with a trust in the company's favour in the event of the dividend not being paid, and the bank had sufficient notice of the trust to make it binding on them.

In *Re Kayford Ltd. (in liquidation)* (1974) the problem of a trust account which did not bear any special designation was highlighted. Although the case did not involve bankers, it is of interest to bankers. A mail order company had paid into a deposit account with the bank sums it had received from its customers as payments in advance for goods ordered. As goods were sent off to customers, the appropriate sums were transferred from the deposit to the current account. When the company went into liquidation the question arose whether the deposit account balance was held in trust for the customers or formed part of the company's general assets. It was held that on the evidence, including clear evidence of intention, the deposit was a trust account. In such circumstances a banker would lose his right of set-off if he had notice of the existence of the trust (as in the Quistclose case) as he most probably would on the facts of the Kayford case.

Accounts opened in connection with **VAT** and **PAYE Income Tax** present some difficulty and there are no decisions by way of guidance. The safest course appears to be to regard them as **not** available for set-off in any circumstances. There would almost certainly be no right to set-off without notice but, having regard to the fact that such funds need not legally be placed to a separate account and may be employed in the business until actually paid over to the Customs & Excise or Inland Revenue, it may be that if the account were stopped on liquidation of a company for instance, a right of set-off would accrue.

A right of set-off arises after due notice where the accounts are those of the same parties (not representing trust monies) in the same right, e.g.

Current account and loan, (reasonable notice is required, *Rouse v. Bradford Banking Co.* (1894)).
Credit current account and overdrawn current account.
Credit balance on partner's account against overdraft on firm's account, **provided he has agreed to be severally liable**.
Private account against overdrawn joint account provided the parties to the joint account have agreed to be severally liable.

There is, however, no right, without special arrangement, to set-off the credit balance of a partnership or joint account against an overdraft of one of the partners or parties.

A right of set-off exists immediately between:

All accounts, including loans, on

Death;
Bankruptcy;
Liquidation.

There is apparently a right to set-off the Dividend account of a company upon liquidation, but an account in the name of the liquidator cannot be set-off against an overdraft in the name of the company, neither can the account of a Receiver be set-off against an overdraft in the name of the company. (The Quistclose case involved a dividend account but the funds put into this had been provided by the third party for the payment of the dividend and the resulting trust was in favour of the third party providing the monies.)

All **current** accounts but **not** between current account and **loans**.

When a Garnishee Order is served;
On notice of a second charge.

On the principle that the loan having been made and the amount credited to current account reasonable notice is required to combine the accounts.

Set-off can always be acquired by express agreement (except in respect of trust monies) e.g., where there is an agreement for a net limit between two or more accounts, or a letter of set-off is taken. Indeed the fact that in many instances letters of set-off are taken might make it more difficult for the banker to exercise a right of set-off in the absence of such an agreement.

Deposit Account: Possibly a deposit account which is subject to notice is not available as a true set-off for the amount is not **due** until notice has expired — the debts are not in the same right. Nevertheless it may be regarded as such for if the customer gave notice to withdraw the bank could immediately give counter notice to set-off. There is no difficulty with regard to outstanding cheques and a short notice would, presumably, be "reasonable".

General: In practice, although bankers should be fully aware of the law and current legal thinking on set-off, there is nevertheless room for a practical approach in many instances whereby the banker, if facing problems on the availability of credit balances as set-off, should initially set-off such balances. The banker can always face up to any challenges made at a later stage and concede or dispute fully as appropriate. The real test may well be if the banker is faced with presentation of a cheque on one of the credit accounts having a credit balance in excess of the amount of the cheque. In such circumstances the banker will have to consider carefully the strength of his right to dishonour the cheque and take such legal advice as he requires.

JOINT AND SEVERAL LIABILITY

Joint accounts are covered in a later chapter but an early understanding of what is meant by "joint and several" liability is called for.

In the case of "joint" liability:

(a) a creditor can bring only one action and is debarred from successive actions. If he sues some but not all of the debtors and obtains a judgment which is not satisfied he may not then sue the remainder.
(b) The death of one debtor leaves the creditor with sole recourse against the survivors.
(c) No right will accrue, without special arrangement, to set-off the credit

account of an individual against a joint debt to which he is a party.

Where liability is "joint and several":

(a) the creditor has as many rights of action as there are debtors: an unsatisfied judgment against one will not bar action against the others.
(b) The estate of a deceased joint debtor remains liable but the account must, of course, be stopped to prevent the operation of the Rule in Clayton's Case.
(c) Private accounts in credit can be set-off against the joint debt but adequate notice would normally be considered necessary.

PASSBOOKS AND STATEMENTS

The law concerning passbooks and bank statements is not particularly satisfactory from the point of view of the banker. Passbooks contained the record of the transactions on a customer's account, the name referring to the fact that the book "passed" between customer and the banker periodically so that the entries could be brought up to date by the bank in the passbook from the bank's own ledger. Nowadays, although passbooks exist for certain types of account, they have very largely been superseded by computer-produced loose-leaf statements. Where a customer returned a passbook to the bank without raising any objections to its contents, debit entries were prima facie evidence against him and when a balance had been struck this was regarded as evidence of a settled account — *Blackburn Building Society v. Cunliffe Brooks & Co.* (1882). Nevertheless, it is considered that the customer owes no duty to his bank to examine his passbook or statement and even when he has done so, this does not prevent him from subsequently disputing entries and recovering against the bank — *Chatterton v. London and County Banking Co. Ltd.* (1891).

Despite this rather doubtful area of law as far as the banker is concerned, the practical benefit aimed at in sending out statements as regularly as possible is that hopefully most customers will check through their statement and get in touch with the bank to query any entry they cannot reconcile with their own records.

Inevitably, mistakes will occur resulting in items being wrongly debited or credited to a customer's account and a very significant point which should always immediately be established is whether or not the resultant incorrect position has been communicated to the customer. In *Holland v. Manchester and Liverpool District Banking Co.* (1909) it was held that where the customer acts, in good faith, upon a wrong entry made in the statement or pass book, so altering his position, the banker is estopped from claiming to have the error adjusted. Similarly in an earlier case, *Skyring v. Greenwood and Cox* (1825), the defendants, who were paymasters of the Royal Artillary, had by mistake overpaid major Greenwood over a period of years. When this subsequently came to light, the defendants tried to debit the plaintiff with the amount with which they had over-credited him, but judgement was given in favour of the plaintiff. In *British and North European Bank Ltd. v. Zalzstein* (1921) it was stated that where the customer knows that the passbook or statement is wrong, the banker is not estopped from correcting the error. However, although in this case it was known that the customer knew that the credit in question was wrong, it could be difficult in other circumstances to prove that a customer knew that he had been over-credited. *Lloyds Bank Ltd. v. Brooks* (1950) produced a judgement in favour of the recipient of amounts wrongly credited to her but in *United Overseas Bank v. Jiwani* (1977) the defendant's claim that the bank was estopped from trying to recover the sum incorrectly credited to his account was rejected, because the defendant failed to show that he had altered his way of living in a manner which he would not have done but for his reliance on the mistake. In the judgement given in this case, the three conditions which the defendant has to satisfy before he can resist repayment were outlined:

(a) that the bank had misrepresented the state of his account;
(b) that he had been misled by the misrepresentation; and
(c) that as a result "he changed his position in a way which would make it inequitable to require him to repay the money."

In the case itself, the first condition was satisfied whereas the defendant's evidence as regards the second condition was not accepted. However, more importantly from the banker's viewpoint generally, even if that evidence had been accepted, the third condition was held not to have been met. This was due to the fact that the defendant would have gone ahead with the purchase of the hotel he had negotiated and which in the event was partly financed by his drawing the wrongly-inflated balance on his account-following the bank's error, and thus it was regarded that since he would have had to raise funds to do that, had the bank not over-credited him, he could raise the funds to enable him to repay the bank.

Some Practical Points to Watch

(a) Customer overcredited

Customer may, if he is unaware of the error, rely on the balance shown and draw cheques against this. Such cheques must be honoured.

(b) Cheques not debited

This would not usually be so serious, for the customer should know whether cheques, which he has drawn, are outstanding. However, if the mistake occurred some considerable time before it was discovered, it would be courteous and prudent for the customer to be advised.

(c) Undercredited

The danger is that cheques may have been returned unpaid due to the balance being less than it should have been. This would be a difficult and possibly serious position for a banker to find himself in and steps would need to be taken to correct the matter speedily and take whatever steps seemed necessary to minimise any damage caused to the customer's credit. Before returning cheques, it is always a good idea to look back some way through the customer's account to see whether any regular credits are missing; if so, they could perhaps have been posted wrongly to someone else's account.

(d) Cheque wrongly debited

Here again the important question is whether any subsequent cheques were dishonoured due to the balance having been depleted by the error. Wherever possible, it would be a useful safeguard to check through a customer's paid cheques and other debit vouchers to make sure there had been no error, when confronted for the first time with having to consider dishonouring a cheque for that customer.

LIEN

A lien is the right to retain property which belongs to someone else until a debt due from the owner of the property to the possessor of the property is paid.

A particular or specific lien is when it is a right to retain the specific goods in connection with which the debt arose (e.g. a garage proprietor's lien over a car which he has repaired). A general lien is when it is a right to retain goods not only for the debt relating to those goods, but for the general balance outstanding from the owner of the goods to the person exercising the right of lien (e.g. a warehouse keeper's right to retain an article until his charges for storage relating to several other articles have been paid).

Lien is a right of retention only and with an ordinary lien there is no power of sale. A lien arises essentially by implication of law and must be differentiated from a "pledge" which is the subject of an express agreement.

Various types of lien can exist such as ship owners' liens, brokers' liens, solicitors' liens and agents' liens, and a banker himself may have a lien. A Banker's lien is a general lien on all securities or property coming into the banker's hands in the ordinary course of his business as banker in respect of any balance that may be due to him from that customer, unless there is an implied or express contract to the contrary. Unlike other types of lien, a banker's lien gives the banker the right to realise and repay himself from the proceeds of negotiable securities, thus making a banker's lien on negotiable securities an implied pledge.

The usual type of property over which a general lien arises in the case of a banker comprises negotiable securities such as bills of exchange, coupons and promissory notes. Cheques paid in for collection can also be subject to lien.

From a practical point of view lien can be rather a nebulous matter, arising as it does from implication of law, and whether or not lien exists could depend very much on the particular circumstances surrounding each case where an effort is made to establish a lien. Sometimes a letter of set-off is called a "lien letter" and is signed by a customer where a credit balance on one account is to secure an overdraft on another account. The letter does not however itself raise a lien, for this already exists (subject to the rules of set-off as discussed earlier in this chapter) but it does dispense with the banker having to notify the customer when he proposes to set-off the accounts.

Lien is excluded:

(a) Where there exists a contract, express or implied, which is inconsistent with lien. For example, if securities are specifically charged or if they are informally deposited without charge by way of security, lien is excluded. In the latter case, the bank would have an equitable mortgage by deposit.

(b) Where the securities are lodged for a special purpose. Therefore, when the property is handed to the banker for a particular purpose — e.g. security handed over for the purpose of selling it through a stockbroker — the banker has no lien. Similarly when security or goods are handed to the banker for safe custody lien does not arise as the contract is one of bailment.

No implied lien, general or specific, arises in the case of property left casually or by mistake.

It is likely that securities deposited for specific advances can be claimed by the customer when those specific advances have been repaid, even though the customer may owe the bank money on other accounts. The securities could not be retained by right of lien. However, on the sale of securities by a banker, a right of set-off would accrue in respect of other debts due to him by the customer concerned.

(c) Where the securities are not those of the customer, except in the case of fully negotiable securities where the bank has no notice of any equitable trust. The banker would have a lien over bearer bonds where the coupons were cut and collected by the bank even though those bonds were trust property, provided the bank had no notice of the trust.

In practice lien is not something which is in itself often looked to as formal comfort since a disadvantage of lien is that so much depends upon the facts of the particular case which may of course be disputed. Nevertheless, a banker's knowledge that he should have a lien over a customer's securities for example, may in some instances be useful when lending to a customer who resists the idea of giving the bank a formal charge over the security, but where the bank does not feel sufficiently strongly about this to risk falling out with the customer by insisting on formal security.

INJUNCTIONS AND GARNISHEE ORDERS

Garnishee Orders

A Garnishee Order is an order of the Court, obtained by a judgement creditor, attaching funds in the hands of a third party who owes the judgement debtor money.

In relation to the banker's contractual obligation to repay on demand, this is determined by the service of a garnishee order which itself is deemed to operate as a demand for repayment.

There are two stages in Garnishee proceedings:

(a) Service of a Garnishee Order **Nisi**. This is served on the garnishee (the person holding the attached funds) by the creditor and requires him to hold, to be applied in discharge of the debt and costs, **all** funds in his hands and owing to the judgement debtor. It also requires the garnishee to appear before the Court.
(b) Making of an Order **Absolute**. This directs actual payment from the funds over which the order nisi gave the creditor an equitable charge. The order nisi gives no authority to make payment and none should be made until the order has been made absolute or the rights of the Trustee in Bankruptcy may intervene.

There is another form, a **Garnishee Summons**, which is similar in effect to the order nisi except that it gives the garnishee the option of paying into Court, eight clear days before the date of the hearing, a sum sufficient to satisfy the debt and costs or the amount of the garnishee's debt to the judgement debtor, whichever is the lesser. Payment in this way frees any surplus funds in the garnishee's hands.

A Garnishee Order attaches:

(a) Only debts that are actually due or accruing due (i.e. debts payable at a **definite** future time) **at the time of service** of the Order of Summons.
(b) The entire credit balance except where a **specific amount** is claimed by the Order.

In *Rogers v. Whitely* (1892) which went to the House of Lords, it was held that a bank was correct in returning cheques drawn against a credit balance after being served with a garnishee order nisi attaching "all debts owing or accrued due." In this judgement however the inconvenience which could be caused by attaching a large sum for a small debt was recognised and the limited order was devised. A limited order is issued for the amount of the judgement debt plus an estimated sum for costs, enabling the banker recipient to isolate the stated amount onto a suspense account leaving the balance on the customer's account available to him and the main account able to be operated normally.

The balances attached are as follows:

(a) *Current Accounts:* the whole of the balance is attached unless a specific (and lesser) amount is claimed but uncleared effects, against which the customer has no right to draw, may be deducted. The banker is entitled to first combine all balances which he previously could have set-off without notice to the customer, but cannot transfer the credit balance(s) to any loan account so as to defeat the garnishee order unless a letter of set-off is held. The banker also cannot retain moneys to meet a contingent liability unless such funds were previously specifically set aside for this purpose and would not therefore have been at the disposal of the customer. The order is effective from the moment it is served and only funds in the hands of the banker at the time of the service of the order are attached. Credits paid in later (even on the same day) are not attached and are usually placed to a separate account. Cheques already in the bank on the day of service and paid are unaffected. With regard to credits, the crucial time is when the credit reaches the bank and thus bank giro credits may have been paid in elsewhere previously and still be in transit. When such an item arrives it will be affected by the order, unless it was paid in at another branch of the same bank before the service of the order.

(b) *Deposit Accounts:* under the Administration of Justice Act 1956 deposit accounts are attached, but small savings deposit accounts from which small sums may be withdrawn without notice at any branch of the bank were excepted. However, savings accounts are now attachable under the Supreme Court Act 1981.

(c) *Joint Accounts:* a joint account is not attached unless all parties to it are named as judgement debtors in the order — *Hirschorn v. Evans* (1938). Whether or not either or any of the parties can sign alone on the account is immaterial as the balance on a joint account is not a debt due or accruing due to any one of them; it is a debt due to them jointly. If they are all included in the garnishee order their individual accounts are attached as well as the joint account.

(d) *Trust Accounts:* even though an account may clearly indicate a trust, the debtor/creditor relationship between the bank and the customer is maintained and in *Plunkett v. Barclays Bank Ltd* (1936) it was held that a solicitor's Client's Account was attached. The bank has a duty to inform the Court of the nature of the account where a trust is involved and to tell the customer immediately that an order has been served and that cheques on the account cannot therefore be honoured. The Court will not include trust money when making the order absolute so that the trust funds would not be paid over to the judgement creditor. In *Lancaster Motor Co. (London) Ltd. v. Bremith* (1941) it was held that an order naming a company as the judgement debtor did not attach an account in the name of the liquidator of the company. Similarly, in *Pritchard v. Westminster Bank Ltd* (1969) where a garnishee order was obtained against a bank which was executor of a deceased's customer whose estate was insolvent (and therefore where the bankruptcy rules apply) the Court set aside the appeal because of the overriding rule that all creditors should be treated equally and a garnishee order would have given the plaintiff preference over the other creditors.

Practical Steps on receipt of Garnishee Order:

(a) Stop the accounts and advise the customer, making the customer aware that all the accounts are frozen or, if it is a limited Garnishee order, that the relevant amount has been earmarked against the garnishee order and is not therefore available to the customer. Cheques will not be charged to the account until the debt and costs are satisfied. If the order is for a lesser amount than the balance (e.g. £120 against a balance on the account of £800) and the banker remains satisfied as to the overall means and standing of the customer and thus does not want to return cheques, the banker could pay cheques to the debit of a new account, permitting an overdraft in anticipation of funds becoming available from the old account when the proceedings are over. However, an allowance for costs should be borne in mind. Nowadays it is more common for the order to be a limited one, attaching only a fixed sum and limiting the claim to this amount, in which case the customer can transfer the surplus on the account to a new account. Where cheques have to be returned unpaid the answer should be "Refer to Drawer" or "Unavailable balance."

(b) Any credits received after service of the order may be placed to the new account.

(c) The balance to be attached should be calculated by deducting:
- any uncleared effects
- any amount for which the bank is committed (e.g. settlement for Stock Exchange securities bought on the customer's instructions)
- any debit balances which can be set off by the credit balance.

(d) If the account is a trust account, the Court should be advised of this but the balance is nevertheless attached.

(e) The order should clearly indicate who is the judgement debtor, otherwise the bank can refuse to accept it.

(f) Where no funds are available to be attached, the creditor's solicitors should be so advised so that the proceedings can be withdrawn.

(g) An account in a business name (e.g. "Premier Motors") where the business is a sole proprietorship would be attached by an order naming the sole properietor as judgement debtor, since the balance on the account would be due to him.

"Mareva" Injections

A "mareva" injunction is a remedy conferred by the courts upon a claimant in litigation before the court has adjudicated on the merits of the case; by it the defendant is restrained from disposing of his assets pending the hearing and thus becoming unable to meet the claim if judgement is given against him. Banks can be served with copies of these injunctions with the intention that they shall observe the injunction with respect to credit balances, the use of any facility or to deeds or other documents.

This type of injunction has been granted by the court increasingly since the mid-seventies and the courts have over the last few years recognised the practical burden facing banks served with copies of them. Basically problems arose because sometimes the notices received by banks did not identify the bank account(s) in question and did not state any account-holding branch. The court recognised that when an account was not identified, it was not proper for the bank to have to incur expense in ascertaining whether the alleged account existed (e.g. by circulating all branches and devoting management and staff time to searching for the relevant account(s)) without being reimbursed by the plaintiff — *Rahman (Prince Abdul) bin Turki al Sudairy v. Abu-Taha* (1980). In *Searose Ltd. v. Seatrain UK Ltd.* (1981) the injunction granted conditionally restrained Seatrain UK Ltd. from disposing of assets and in particular from disposing of any funds in its bank account. The order was restricted to such assets or monies up to a value of £44,000 which was the amount claimed for breach of contract. The injunction was granted only on condition that the plaintiffs undertook to pay any reasonable costs incurred by any party other than the defendent to whom notice of the order was given in establishing whether or not any assets to which the order applied was within that party's possession and control. A subsequent case (unreported) sets out clear principles relating to mareva injunctions insofar as they affect bank accounts, and sets out to prevent the continuance of the type of order which had increasingly been served on bankers restricting their customers from disposing of or dealing with any assets save in excess of a stated value. Prior to this case and decision, several banks had made it known to the High Court that they were encountering difficulties with that type of order with resultant problems arising with the banker/customer relationship. In a subsequent case — *Fidelity International Bank v. International Finance and Exchange Corporation* (1982) — it was held that a plaintiff who obtained a mareva injunction must pay all reasonable costs of an innocent third party who successfully intervened in the proceedings to have the injunction varied, providing the costs are regarded as reasonable in amount and reasonably incurred. This strengthened the rights of banks who are third parties to mareva injunctions in respect of claiming costs.

Mareva injunctions have extended into criminal law and the courts can now freeze credit balances where the police are able to satisfy the courts that the funds represent the proceeds of an alleged crime — *West Mercia Constabulary v. Wagener and Others* (1982). On the same grounds, credit monies in bank accounts were successfully frozen in *Chief Constable of Kent v. V. and another* (1982).

THE BANK GIRO, STANDING ORDERS AND DIRECT DEBITS

The English and Scottish clearing banks' money transfer service is named Bank Giro and primarily relates to credit transfers and direct debits.

The credit transfer system has developed from the traders' credits system which operated for many years after being introduced some forty years ago. Credit transfers are now increasingly known as Bank Giro credits, and basically are initiated by the payer. In its most simple form, the system entails individuals paying at any branch of any bank for the credit of an account at a bank other than one where the credit is paid over the counter. Nowadays, many concerns send out bank giro credits with their bills for the use of their customers, e.g. electricity and gas boards, rating authorities, mail order companies and the telephone authority. The system also enables a person, or more often a business customer, to make out several credit slips and hand these into their own bank together with one cheque drawn on their account for the total amount of the credit slips. The bank then will put these through the credit clearing system on the due date.

Standing orders are orders given by a customer to his bank instructing the bank to make periodical payments on stipulated days. These are frequently used by customers for payment of items such as club subscriptions, insurance premiums, mortgate or hire purchase instalments.

Direct debiting is a system which entails a debit entry being initiated by the creditor who sends this direct instruction via his own bank to the debtor's bank. This system requires the debtor's prior agreement which takes the form of an authority the debtor gives to his bank authorising them to accept the direct debits for the debit of his account. The system is especially useful where the amounts payable are variable and direct debiting is increasingly used by insurance companies, clubs and societies, professional bodies and some charge card companies. However, an organisation can only use the system if it indemnifies all the clearing banks against any claims arising from debiting under the system and authorises any bank to settle a debtor's claim without reference to the creditor. In practice, this takes the form of the organisation's bank sponsoring the organisation in its application to come into the system.

The increasing use of computers has meant that many aspects of these systems are now automated, and in particular the BACS system (The Bankers' Automated Clearing Service Ltd.) provides for the processing, distribution and collection of large volumes of payments. Where volume warrants it and the customer's computer facilities are appropriate, a customer can now deliver computer tapes to the bank containing the instructions relating to the payments the bank is asked to make, and these automated credit transfers systems are used by many companies for payment of salaries and pensions.

Obviously any system whereby entries are made on customers' accounts, needs the facility on the part of a banker, to be able to refuse to allow a debit to an account where either the account is not sufficiently in funds to stand the debit or, of course, where the banker is not prepared to permit an overdraft (or an increased overdraft if the account is already overdrawn). Standing orders can be withheld by the banker if the customer's account is not in a position to stand the item being debited, and direct debits can be refused and returned, in a similar way to cheques being dishonoured, the appropriate answer being "Refer to Debtor."

LIMITATION OF ACTIONS

The Limitation Act 1939 (as amended and consolidated by the Limitation Act 1980) limits periods within which legal action must be taken:

(a) To 6 years after the cause of action accrued for actions founded upon a simple contract.
(b) To 12 years after the cause of action accrued in the case of a speciality

contract (i.e. one under seal).

(c) To recover the principal sum secured by mortgage or other charge on real or personal property (except a ship) to 12 years from the date when the right to receive money accrued.

These limitations are limitations on the right of legal action i.e. proceedings in a court of law. In other words they prevent enforcement of the debt even though the debt still exists. They are not however bars to rights, which may continue to be exercisable when no legal action is needed, e.g. recourse can still be had against security. Thus securities could be realised where a power of sale exists and therefore where title can be transferred without having to go to court.

Right of action is revived by part payment of the debt, part or full payment of interest or an acknowledgement in writing signed by the person liable or his agent. Any type of acknowledgement in writing by the debtor will restart the statutory period running and a reference to a debt in a company's balance sheet is sufficient acknowledgement for purposes of the Act — *Re Gee & Co (Woolwich) Ltd.* (1973). When an acknowledgement takes place, then the statute will run from the date of revival and not from the original default.

Practical Effect on Banking Transactions

(a) Simple Contracts

As stated earlier, the relationship between banker and customer is that of debtor and creditor but the banker is not liable to repay until demand has been made by the customer. With accounts that are in credit, the Limitation Act has little significance since a banker is not likely to set up the Statute against a valid request for withdrawal of a balance. In the case of unclaimed balances, there is a legal liability to repay a current account balance even if no demand has been made. Even if the account has been dormant for 6 years it is not statute barred. The position is very much the same with deposit accounts although there are views to the effect that where notice has been given the Statute will run from the date of expiry of the notice. However, this raises two other factors, one being that if interest continues to be credited to the account this could be construed as an acknowledgement of the debt and prevent the running of the Statute in favour of the bank. Secondly, if the return of the deposit or savings book or receipt is a condition precedent to repayment, non-production of the book could be sufficient to prevent the Statute from running. This latter point is probably not now particularly relevant since with many deposit accounts, the customer receives computerised statements in the same form as those issued for current accounts.

With accounts that are in debit, the statute starts to run from the date upon which demand for repayment is made. The 1980 Act stated that the limitation period for actions for debts with no specified repayment date will run from the date of demand. However, as mentioned earlier, part repayment or payment of interest will revive the right of action so that any credits which are not otherwise appropriated could be treated as part repayment or towards covering interest and thus would restart the Statute running. Therefore the effect is that the debt is statute barred 6 years from the time the account became dormant or from the last acknowledgement of the debt by the customer. It should be appreciated that the mere debiting of interest will not revive the debt; there has to be a credit or credits to the account which are able to be appropriated by the banker towards the payment of the interest charged.

As far as guarantees are concerned, most bank forms of guarantee provide that the amount is not "due" from the guarantor until the bank has called upon the guarantor to substantiate his liability. Therefore a guarantor, in the case of a guarantee under hand which is a simple contract, cannot claim that the debt is statute barred until 6 years after he was formally called upon by the bank to pay up. Any payment made by the principal debtor will revive the bank's right against the guarantor but an acknowledgement by the principal debtor does not have this effect. A payment made after the expiration of the 6 years would not bind the guarantor although it would be binding as far as the principal debtor was concerned.

(b) Specialty Contracts

In the case of contracts under seal, these are not statute barred until 12 years after the right of action. In the case of bank security, if the contract is by deed it will not be statute barred for the 12 years. Most bank security documents contain a personal covenant to repay on demand and if the security is under seal, the right of action can be commenced at any time within 12 years from the date demand for repayment was made. Where third party security under seal is concerned, and both the surety and the principal debtor have given their personal covenants to repay on demand, the Statute runs separately against each party as from the date of demand on him and the right of action is not barred for 12 years. In the case of a guarantee under seal, the amount due from the guarantor will not be statute barred until 12 years from the date upon which demand was made on him whereas the debt due from the principal debtor would in the normal way be statute barred 6 years after the right of action arose.

(c) Security comprising a mortgage on real or personal property

When a debt is secured in this way it will not be statute barred until 12 years after the right to receive the money accrued. This will apply to most charges taken by a banker as security — e.g. land, stocks and shares, produce, life policies — but does not apply to guarantees since these are not charges but are in effect promises to pay. On a practical note, the danger of overlooking the effect of the Statute in the case of a dormant but well-secured advance should be guarded against.

Where interest is in arrears, action cannot be brought to recover the arrears after the expiration of 6 years from the date interest became due and this applies even if the charge is by way of deed. Part payment of the interest, although reviving the principal debt, would not extend the period for claiming the remainder then due.

It is important to remember that the Statute of Limitations limits the creditor's remedy to bring a legal action against his debtor. It does not bar any rights against the security and even where it is necessary to go to court (say to enforce equitable charges) this remains so since the bank is not taking legal action within the terms of the Act. Note however that an exception arises in the case of charges over land where both the right and the remedy can be lost after 12 years even though legal action to realise the security is not necessary.

(d) Negotiable Instruments

The period of 6 years will commence to run:

(a) in favour of the drawer of a cheque or of the acceptor of a bill payable on demand, as from the date of the instrument, since no demand is necessary to enable a person to sue.
(b) in favour of the acceptor of a bill other than a bill on demand as from the date of maturity. If such a bill is dishonoured by non-acceptance the Statute begins to run as in (c).
(c) In the case of parties liable on a bill other than the acceptor, or liable on a cheque other than the drawer, the Statute begins to run in their favour from the time when notice of dishonour was received.

PRINCIPAL AND AGENT

An agent is a person who is employed to enter into contracts on behalf of his principal.

Knowledge of the rules of agency are important to bankers in the context of the banker/customer relationship as banks often act in the capacity of agents for their customers. Furthermore, many of a bank's normal transactions are with agents which again makes it important that the banker understands the principles involved.

There are different types of agent as follows:

(a) *Universal agent* — is authorised to act for the principal in any capacity.
(b) *General agent* — authorised to do anything but with certain constraints.
(c) *Special agent* — authorised to act for a specific purpose.
(d) *Del credere agent* — an agent who accepts responsibility for payment by the parties he introduces to his principal.

A partner acts as a general agent of the firm for the purpose of the business carried out by the partnership. A person authorised to sign on another person's account would be a special agent for this purpose.

As the agent does not contract on his own behalf it is not necessary that he should have full contractual capacity. From this it follows that a minor can act as agent although the contract might be void or unenforceable if entered into by him as **principal**. By the Infants Relief Act 1874, all contracts by minors for the repayment of money lent are absolutely void, but, if so authorised, he could borrow money on behalf of his principal and bind the principal.

Note, however, that a minor cannot act as **Executor**, nor can he be appointed as **Trustee**. He may be a **Partner** but is not personally liable for partnership debts incurred during minority.

Similarly an **undischarged bankrupt** may act as an agent, but note two exceptions:

(a) He may not as a general rule act as a Company Director without leave of the Court. Section 187 Companies Act 1948.
(b) He may not act as **Receiver or Manager** for a debenture holder unless appointed by the Court or unless he was bankrupt and appointed prior to 1st July, 1948.

There are different ways in which an agency may be created. An agent may be appointed by deed and the appointment must be by deed (in the form of a Power of Attorney which is covered later in this chapter) if the agent is authorised to contract under seal. As opposed to being by way of deed, an appointment may simply be in writing. Although generally this is not necessary, a banker would always require suitable written authority before carrying out transactions on the instructions of someone acting as agent for the banker's customer. However, an agency can legally be created orally.

Agency may arise by implication or estoppel. When a bank collects cheques for a customer, the bank, by implication, is acting as the customer's agent for collection since there is no written agreement to this effect. Agency by estoppel arises where a person has acted in a way which prevents him from subsequently denying that another person was his agent. An example of this is where a customer regularly sends another person to collect his bank statements. He could not afterwards successfully challenge the bank's action on one occasion as he would be estopped from denying that the person was his agent for that special purpose. When a person acts on someone else's behalf but has no authority or exceeds the authority he has, the principal will not be bound (unless by implication or estoppel) but may afterwards confirm and adopt the contract thus retrospectively creating an agency. To be effective the following conditions have to be met:

(a) The "agent" must have contracted as an agent.
(b) The principal must have existed and had contractual capacity when the contract was made. In *Kelner v. Baxter* (1866) it was held that a company which had not been incorporated at the time the contract was made on its behalf by its promoters could not subsequently ratify that contract. However, in such circumstances, those contracting would now be personally liable as a result of the European Communities Act 1972.
(c) The whole of the contract must be ratified to prevent a principal taking over the benefits of it and rejecting any liabilities.

Finally, an agent can be appointed by necessity where circumstances create an emergency in which case an agent may bind his principal without prior authority or subsequent ratification.

An agent's authority may be set out in the terms of his appointment or implied by the circumstances of the case. The acts of a general agent will bind his principal if they are within the scope of his apparent authority, albeit outside the scope of his actual authority, provided the other party to the contract is unaware of the limitation.

It is an agent's duty to perform the acts he has agreed to do with reasonable competence and diligence. He should not delegate his authority as a general rule and must render an account to his principal when so required. There are exceptions to the rule of non-delegation which were stated in *De Bussche v. Alt* (1878). Work can be delegated if specifically agreed so and delegation is permitted where necessary to achieve proper performance. For example a banker may use the services of a stockbroker when shares are being purchased or sold for a customer.

As far as the agent's rights are concerned, he is entitled to his agreed remuneration when he has performed. The principal must indemnify the agent for all acts lawfully done and against any losses incurred whilst the agent was acting for him (unless they were caused by the agent's own fault).

Where an agent borrows money on behalf of a principal without authority or in excess of his authority, a lender acting in good faith will in equity have a right to recover against the principal to the extent that the funds were applied in paying the principal's debts. This right to stand in the shoes of the creditor is called "subrogation."

Thus where a bank, contrary to instructions, honoured the cheques of a company on the signature of one director only, the cheques having been drawn in favour of and proceeds received by trade creditors, so that its liabilities were not thereby increased, the bank on being sued by the company for the amount of the cheques was held entitled to take credit for such payments — *Liggett (Liverpool) Ltd. v. Barclays Bank Ltd.* (1928).

A banker who has paid a cheque on insufficient mandate may therefore, having failed to get the customer as principal to ratify which should be the first step, claim the right of subrogation where the customer's debts have been paid.

When acting in the capacity of agent for a customer, a banker must exercise care to ensure that he is acting strictly within his authority. When buying or selling investments on behalf of a customer, the banker needs to make certain that in the first place he takes the instructions from the customer carefully and accurately, and thereafter that he acts strictly in accordance with them.

Any instructions given by a customer as to which signatories shall be operative on a bank account also need to be rigidly observed, and failure to do this will usually mean the banker having to stand any loss arising from his not having obeyed instructions.

When acting as agent for his customer, the banker will be able to charge the customer the appropriate commission charge for any specific task performed for the customer. For example, having collected a cheque drawn on an overseas bank or having transferred funds abroad acting on the customer's instructions, the banker will normally pass on the respective charge to the customer.

Bankers are often asked to give bonds of one sort of another on behalf of customers and this type of service has increased over recent years. Nowadays bankers can be faced with requests from different customers to give various types of bond or guarantee including performance bonds, bid and tender bonds, warranty or rentention bonds, advance payment guarantees and customs and excise bonds. Although an agent is entitled to be indemnified by his principal if he suffers loss whilst engaged on his principal's business (except where the loss is caused by the agent's negligence), a banker will take a specific indemnity from his customer relating to each bond given, thus placing the indemnification on a contractual basis.

A banker also will act as agent for another bank, such as when one bank cashes cheques for a customer of another bank under a credit-open arrangement. In these circumstances, there is no legal relationship between the paying bank and the customer and if the customer has any complaint he must pursue this through his own bank — who nominated the other bank as agent — who may in turn then try to recover from the agent bank. Agency arises also where a bank which is a member of the Clearing House handles cheques for a non-clearing bank.

MANDATES AND POWERS OF ATTORNEY

A mandate does not itself delegate powers but is usually in the form of an advice that power has been delegated together with a request to accept the instructions of the principal for the purpose indicated. When a customer wishes his account to be operated by delegated authority, the banker will require a mandate from the customer expressing precisely what powers have been delegated to the mandatory. For example the form of delegation confirming authority for a third party to operate on an account may comprise the following type of wording:

> "Will you please note that I have authorised Mr. ...... to draw, sign, accept or endorse cheques, bills of exchange on my behalf etc. etc."

A Power of Attorney on the other hand is an instrument embodying the authorisation to a person (the attorney) to act on behalf of the principal. It is the actual authority itself and the traditional form commences with the wording "Know all men by these presents that I ...... do hereby appoint etc. etc." The deed then elaborates the powers given to the attorney and usually ends with a "general" or "omnibus" clause authorising the attorney to do any act the principal himself could do. Such a clause, however, refers only to acts incidental to those specifically covered. The Powers of Attorney Act 1971 brought about considerable changes and provided for a short and simplified general power of attorney in a form prescribed in the Act. Thus a power of attorney either in the form prescribed or similar to it but expressed to be made under the Act, operates to confer on the attorney authority to do on behalf of the principal anything which the principal can lawfully do by an attorney.

When acting for a customer under the terms of either a mandate or a power of attorney, the banker needs to exercise care that he is acting strictly within the terms specified. A power of attorney, particularly if prior to the Powers of Attorney Act 1971, will usually be a quite complicated document and contain considerable matter which is not relevant to the banker, and therefore this form of authority is not as satisfactory from the banker's viewpoint as the bank's own specially-drawn up form.

BAILMENT

Bailment is a contract whereby goods belonging to one person (bailor) are delivered to another (bailee) on the express or implied terms that they shall be returned when the bailor wants them. Whilst they are with the bailee he is responsible for their safe keeping.

It is arguable whether or not bailment is implied in the banker/customer relationship since there is perhaps no obligation on the part of a banker to accept goods for safe custody. Nevertheless, banks do receive and hold deed boxes, securities, sealed packets and parcels and valuables belonging to customers.

The extent to which a bank is liable in the event of an item being stolen, lost or delivered to the wrong party is not particularly clear cut but it used to be felt that the degree of care necessary on the part of a bailee varied according to whether the bailee was a gratuitous bailee or a paid bailee. The former was expected to take such care and exercise such skill as would a careful person in handling their own affairs, whilst the latter was expected to exercise such care and take such precautions as were exercised in the ordinary and proper course of carrying out a business of this nature for which the bailee was paid. The difference in practice as far as a banker is concerned becomes somewhat academic since whether he makes a specific charge or not, the goods will be kept in the strongroom and the facilities thus used by the bank will be similar to those used by people in the business exclusively of safe custody. Some banks make specific charges for the safe custody service they provide and quite clearly are therefore paid bailees. What became unclear, however, was whether any normal bank commission charged would be regarded as embracing a safe custody service so as to make the bank a paid bailee. In *Houghland v. R.R. Low (Luxury Coaches) Ltd.* (1962) it was stated that the standard of care required by a paid or gratuitous bailee is the standard called for by the circumstances of the particular case. However, the general view now held is that in practice the bank's position would not differ according to whether it was regarded as a paid or gratuitous bailee. Where items held in safe custody are surrendered to the wrong person, the question of negligence would not normally arise as the bailee would be guilty of conversion whether or not he had been negligent. In *Langtry v. Union Bank of London* (1896) the bank delivered valuable jewellery it had been holding to a thief against a forged order. Although the case was settled by judgement for the plaintiff by consent for a fairly substantial sum of money, it clearly showed the distinction between a situation in which valuables were by mistake delivered to the wrong person and the very different situation where goods are destroyed, lost, stolen or fraudulently abstracted whether by a bank officer or some other person. The former is a question of conversion, irrespective of whether or not necircumstances of the particular case. However, the general view now held is that in practice the bank's position would not differ according to whether it was regarded as a paid or gratuitous bailery until he can satisfy himself fully. In *Roberts v. Tucker* (1851) it was held that a refusal to deliver up goods in such circumstances was not conversion. If a banker was shown to have wrongly detained the delivery of goods, he could be liable for "detinue" but there again if he could show that he was trying to act equitably in the interests of all concerned this should not provide a real threat.

The whole question of a banker's responsibilities and possible liability when holding goods for safe keeping is a matter of great importance to bankers. Whilst the matter of the different standards of care depending on whether the banker is a paid or gratuitous bailee is perhaps academic because banks have to have strongrooms and safes for their cash and documents, the utmost care is needed on the part of the banker. Strongrooms been have known to be flooded causing customers' goods to be damaged and ruined, and criminals show from time to time that what are thought to be completely thiefproof facilities can be successfully breeched by the increasingly sophisticated tools available to and methods adopted by present day thieves.

Most banks' forms of receipts issued to customers when accepting their property state that the bank, although it will take the greatest possible care of such property, is not responsible for it and that if it is valuable then the customer should insure it.

The question of liability arising out of the provision of night safe facilities for customers has to be considered. Bankers almost invariably will charge customers for this service but the facility should be afforded only to customers of sound integrity and usually the customer acknowledges in writing that the normal banker/customer relationship shall not arise until the contents of the night safe wallet have been paid in in the ordinary course of business the following day, and that the wallet when placed in the night safe is deemed to be held for safe custody only and without further responsibility.

Chapter 2

Bankruptcy

INTRODUCTION

Bankruptcy is the legal machinery whereby the estate of a person who cannot pay his debts is compulsorily wound up and equitably distributed amongst his creditors. Subsequently, and subject to certain conditions, the person who was made bankrupt can receive his discharge which means that he will no longer have any liability for the debts incurred before his bankruptcy.

The law relating to bankruptcy is presently laid down in the Bankruptcy Act 1914 but some changes, albeit of a relatively minor nature, were introduced by the Bankruptcy (Amendment) Act 1926. The Insolvency Act 1976 revised upwards the monetary limits to make these more realistic, and also provided for a system of automatic discharge to try to cope with the very large number of undischarged bankrupts which had by then accumulated. It has been recognised for some time that the existing bankruptcy system is in many ways inadequate to cope with the vast number of bankruptcies which have come about each year for several years, in particular the many small bankruptcies which nowadays occur, and the whole subject of Insolvency has been the subject of investigation over the past few years by a committee under the chairmanship of Sir Kenneth Cork. This Review Committee has now published its final report which covers a wide range of topics surrounding insolvency, bankruptcy, liquidation and receivership. A white paper on insolvency reform was issued and a bill subsequently introduced. The recommendations which are very far-reaching include a fundamental rationalisation of the present cumbersome procedures covering both the bankruptcy of an individual and the winding-up of a company. The proposals suggest that there is a need to distinguish in practice between an "incompetent" debtor and a "dishonest" one, and recommend a revised system which encourages and assists an insolvent debtor to meet his liabilities without the present traumas and disabilities of bankruptcy procedure in its existing form. (Further comment on this Report is made at the end of the chapter.)

However, reverting to the existing law, it should first be appreciated who may be made bankrupt. Any person who has the capacity to contract may be made bankrupt.

- **A minor** may not normally be made a bankrupt but there is a possibility that he could if the debt was incurred for necessaries, or is a judgement debt founded on a "tort" (i.e. a civil wrong which is independent of contract, e.g. assault, libel, negligence or trespass).
- **A Married Woman** may, since the Law Reform (Married Women and Tortfeasors) Act 1935, be made bankrupt so far as her separate estate is concerned.
- **An Alien** is subject to our bankruptcy laws if within a year previous to the presentation of the petition (i) he was living or had a place of residence in England or (ii) he carried on business in England, whether personally, by agent, or as a member of a firm.
- **A mentally disordered person** can be made bankrupt for debts contracted while sane or if the Court consents.
- **An imprisoned person** may be made bankrupt.
- **A Partnership** may be made bankrupt and this will involve the bankruptcy of all the partners.
- **One Partner** may be made bankrupt without including the others.
- Although a **deceased person** cannot be made bankrupt his estate may be administered in bankruptcy.
- **A Joint Stock Company** cannot be made bankrupt but it may be wound up under the Companies Act.

The various steps of the bankruptcy process are:

- The commission of **an available act of bankruptcy;**
- The presentation of **a petition;**
- The making of a **receiving order;**
- The **meeting of creditors;**
- The **public examination;**
- The **order of adjudication;**
- The **discharge.**

STAGES OF BANKRUPTCY

ACTS OF BANKRUPTCY

Bankruptcy proceedings must be founded on an Act of Bankruptcy as defined by Section 1 of the Bankruptcy Act 1914, (Nos. 1 to 8) and extended by the Administration of Justice Acts 1965 and 1970, Criminal Justice Act 1972 and Insolvency Act (1976):

1. Assignment of **whole** of debtor's property for benefit of creditors generally.
2. Fraudulent conveyance of any part of debtor's property.
3. Fraudulent preference.
4. Debtor keeping out of the way of creditors with intent to defeat or delay. This is known as "keeping house".
5. Seizure of goods by the sheriff after execution has been levied.
6. Bankruptcy petition presented by the bankrupt against himself.
7. Bankruptcy notice to pay a judgement debt served on a debtor.
8. Notice to creditors of suspension of payment of **debts** — but the notice need not be in writing.
9. The making of an Administration Order.
10. The making of a criminal bankruptcy order under the Criminal Justice Act, 1972.
11. The order to a debtor by a County Court to supply a list of his debts in certain circumstances.

These various acts of bankruptcy ought to be well-known by bankers since when a banker becomes aware that one of his customers has committed an act of bankruptcy, he must restrict operations on the customer's account as explained later in this chapter.

The following points enlarge upon certain of these acts.

Assignment

The assignment must relate to the entire property of the debtor and must be assigned for the benefit of all the creditors.

Fraudulent Conveyance

"Fraudulent" has a special meaning in bankruptcy law. If the effect of the conveyance is to delay or defeat creditors, even if it has been made in good faith by the debtor, it will be deemed a fraudulent conveyance.

The case of in *re Simms* (1930) is of considerable importance to bankers. A builder had creditors for £28,000 and an overdraft of £6,500. He converted his business into a private Limited Company and assigned his assets to the Company for £17,000, satisfied in shares, the Company assuming responsibility for his liabilities. Bank accommodation was then arranged **for the company**, the bank taking a debenture on the Company's assets. An unsatisfied creditor petitioned against the debtor in **his personal capacity** on the grounds that the conveyance to the Company was fraudulent. It was held that the assignment was void as the substitution of shares for substantial business assets resulted in delaying the creditors. As the assignment to the Company was void the bank lost its debenture security. Note that there was no deliberate intention to defraud but that as the effect of the conveyance was to delay creditors it was fraudulent for purposes of the Bankruptcy Act.

In *Lloyds Bank Ltd. v. Marcan & Others* (1973), the defendant had charged his property to the bank and when the bank claimed possession he granted a lease to his wife (following legal advice he had taken) to defeat the bank's claim. It was held that the transaction was invalid as a fraudulent conveyance with intent to defraud the Bank. The transaction was thus covered by the Law of Property Act 1925 S.172 (which covers conveyances with or without consideration provided that actual intention to defraud creditors is shown) and the bank could therefore ignore the lease. With agricultural land (as in the *Marcan* case) leases can be granted notwithstanding a contrary provision in the mortgage (Agricultural Holdings Act 1948), but since the bank was entitled to disregard this lease because of the fraudulent conveyance, the wife could not claim protection under the lease.

Fraudulent Preference

Fraudulent Preference is very different from the two classes described above since it involves a creditor having his debt paid or property has been conveyed to him to the same effect. It therefore, at first sight, seems perhaps strange that the discharge by a debtor of some of his liabilities should be a ground for other creditors taking action.

The point is, however, that although it is expected that a debtor should pay his debts, it is not fair that he should pay any creditor to the exclusion of others, knowing that those others cannot be paid in full. It is the intention to prefer (and not the payment itself) which is fraudulent. This is very different from the situation where a debtor in the ordinary course pays some of his creditors out of funds he has available at the time, if he reasonably believes that he will be able to pay the other creditors.

Fraudulent Preference therefore is a payment or transfer of property made by a debtor when insolvent in favour of a creditor with a view to giving that creditor, or any surety or guarantor for the debt to such creditor a preference over other creditors. This is defined similarly in Section 44 of the Bankruptcy Act 1914 and extended to companies' winding up by Section 320 of the Companies Act 1948 (now Section 615 of the Companies Act 1985). In practice, it is difficult for a creditor to prove that a fraudulent preference has occurred, so that rarely is such an act used to base a petition upon. However, fraudulent preference is very important and can have great significance should bankruptcy follow if the trustee in bankruptcy can recover money paid or avoid transfers of property in circumstances constituting fraudulent preference.

Fraudulent Preferences are void as against the trustee but the trustee must prove:

(a) that the payment was made voluntarily with the intention of giving preference **to the creditor or any surety or guarantor for the debt due to such creditor;**

(b) that it was made within six months of the petition; (note that the period has been increased from three months by the Companies Act 1948);

(c) that the debtor was insolvent **at the time the preference was made.**

The mere fact that a creditor has been preferred is not enough to constitute fraudulent preference; there must be an intention to prefer. In *Re M. Kushler Ltd.* (1943) the guarantor and co-director of a company were professionally advised that the company was insolvent. Between that date and the date two weeks later of the resolution for voluntary winding up, the company's overdraft was further repaid although only two trade bills were paid during the same period and they had been under pressure from a major trade creditor for some months. The Court of Appeal held that the credits paid into the bank were made with a view of giving the bank preference over other creditors, and the bank had to refund to the liquidator the amount of the credits concerned.

In *Re William Hall (Contractors) Ltd.* (1961) a bank had held memoranda of deposit over title deeds for several years (containing the usual power for the bank to be given legal mortgages on request) and then took legal mortgages just before the company went into liquidation. It was held that the giving of the legal mortgages was not fraudulent preference, but merely the carrying out by the company of its pre-existing obligation under the memoranda of deposit. In *Re F.L.E. Holdings Ltd.* (1961) the execution of a legal charge in favour of a bank was held not to be a fraudulent preference, as the evidence showed that the prime intention at the time was to keep on good terms with the bank in the hope of future facilities, rather than confer an advantage on the bank.

The preference must be voluntary and will not therefore be fraudulent when made as a result of real pressure by the creditor on the debtor. There is no fraudulent preference where payment is made:

(a) under such pressure as amounted to duress, or
(b) in the belief that there is a legal obligation to pay, or
(c) to save the debtor from exposure or a criminal prosecution, or
(d) to prevent an undisputed debt becoming statute-barred, or
(e) in meeting trade acceptances as they fall due in order to be able to continue trading.

Although the payment must be made with the intention of giving preference to the creditor or any surety for a debt due to him, the trustee is entitled to recover from the person to whom payment has been made, even if this is not the person preferred. In *Re T.N. Barling & Co. Ltd.* (1932) and in *Re Joseph Johnson Lyons* (1934) there was the question of a guarantor of the debtor's banking account being preferred by payments into the account, but it was held that the bank and not the guarantor was liable for refunding the trustee. The decision in *Re Conley (Trading as Caplan and Conley)* (1938) confirmed this and it was also held that the deposit of security to secure the indebtedness of a third party, even if not accompanied by any personal undertaking by the depositor, makes him a surety or guarantor within the meaning of Section 44 of the Bankruptcy Act 1914.

Where third party security for a customer's debt was held (and where the third party giving the security did not undertake personal liability for the customer's debt and the banker, having released his security, consequently found himself liable to the trustee as in the Conley Case, the banker could not recover from the third party who was actually preferred. This hardship was eventually mitigated by the Companies Act 1948 which provides as an amendment to the Bankruptcy Act:

(a) That the person actually preferred (the surety) shall be subject to the same liabilities as though he had undertaken personal liability for the debt to the extent of the charge or the value of the security charged if less.
(b) That the Court has power to order repayment by the surety to the extent of his liability; the banker not needing to bring a separate action for this.

Nevertheless, the banker remains liable to the Trustee (or a liquidator in the case of a company) and the revival of a personal liability of the surety does not give the banker any right against the security previously released to the surety.

The Court of Appeal's decision in *Re F.P. & C.H. Matthews Ltd.* (1981). provided a salutary reminder of the dangers which exist when a company's borrowing is reduced or extinguished as a result of the decision of the company's directors who have guaranteed or secured in some other way that borrowing. In this case, the Company, owned by Mr. and Mrs. Matthews, had an overdrawn bank account which was secured by a guarantee and a charge over the matrimonial home. The company ran into financial problems and the directors decided it would have to stop trading. Two cheques were then received which were credited to the company's account, clearing the overdraft. The company then went into liquidation. The bank had not been pressing for repayment and, at the time of paying in the cheques, Mr. Matthews had genuinely believed that the company would be able to repay all its creditors within six months.

The Court of Appeal held that the payments to the bank constituted a fraudulent preference within the meaning of Section 44 of the Bankruptcy Act 1914 because Mr. Matthews was aware that the company could not pay its debts as they arose and the bank had deliberately been paid ahead of other creditors. The following factors were considered:

(a) the Section does not require any enquiry as to whether the debtor's intention when making a payment is to affect the *pari passu* distribution of the debtor's assets amongst his creditors;
(b) the question instead is whether the payment was made "with a view of" giving the creditor a preference over the other creditors;
(c) a payment is made with such a view if at the time it has the effect of a creditor receiving payment prior to other creditors;
(d) the Section is concerned only with the ability of the debtor to pay his debts as they fall due;
(e) a genuine belief held by the debtor (at the time the payment is made) that he can then pay all his debts as they fall due must negative any intention to prefer.

Seizure of Goods by a Sheriff

This Act of Bankruptcy is not committed until the sherriff has held the goods for 21 days or has sold them.

Bankruptcy Notice to Pay a Debt Served on a Debtor

This is often the Act of Bankruptcy upon which proceedings are taken. The creditor obtains judgement and then has a bankruptcy notice served on the debtor requiring him to pay or secure the debt. The consequences of the debtor not complying are set out and if the debtor fails to comply within 10 days, he has committed an Act of Bankruptcy.

Notice to Creditors of Suspension of Payment of Debts

If the wording of the notice or the language used is such that a reasonable person would be led to suppose that the debtor intends to suspend payment, then this is sufficient.

The Making of an Administration order

This involves, as an alternative to bankruptcy, the court making an administration order following its approval of a scheme proposed by the judgement debtor for settling his debts. Under such an order, the liabilities are settled under the supervision of the court and creditors are precluded from taking independent action. If the debtor does not observe the terms of the order, the court will revoke it and make a receiving order against him. In this event, the debtor will be deemed to have committed an act of bankruptcy on the date on which the receiving order is made.

The Making of a Criminal Bankruptcy Order

Where a person has caused damage or loss to the property exceeding certain amounts, the court may make a criminal bankruptcy order against the person, who is then regarded as a debtor who has committed an act of bankruptcy on the date which the order is made.

An Act of Bankruptcy is said to be "available" if it is one committed within three months previous to the date of presentation of a petition.

THE PETITION

Bankruptcy proceedings are commenced by a petition being presented asking that a receiving order be made against the debtor. A debtor can present his own petition or a petition may be presented by one or more of his creditors.

When a debtor presents his own petition he commits an act of bankruptcy; the petition has to allege that the debtor is unable to pay his debts whereupon the court forthwith makes a Receiving Order.

Any creditor who becomes aware of the commission by the debtor of an act of bankruptcy can present a petition providing the debt due to the petitioning creditor, or to two or more creditors joining in a petition, amounts to £200 or more. The Act of Bankruptcy on which the petition is founded must have occurred within three months before presentation of the petition.

If the petitioning creditor is secured, he must in his petition either state that he is willing to surrender his security for the benefit of the creditors in the event of the debtor being made bankrupt, or give an estimate of the value of his security. It should be remembered that a creditor holding security given by a third party is not a secured creditor within the meaning of the Bankruptcy Act. A petition once presented (by either the debtor or a creditor) cannot be withdrawn without leave of the court. Shortly after the presentation of a petition, the petition is given a court hearing and is either dismissed or a receiving order is made.

RECEIVING ORDER

This is in a sense an interim order; it does not have the effect of making the debtor bankrupt, nor does it deprive him of the ownership of his property. He is however deprived of the possession and control thereof, in order for it to be preserved for equitable distribution amongst his creditors. The receiving order prevents creditors from taking further action against the debtor since, when matters have reached this stage, it is essential that no one creditor should seek to obtain an advantage over the others. Notice of the receiving order, giving the debtor's name and address, a description of the debtor, the date of the order, the court making the order, and the date of the petition, is published in the London Gazette and advertised in a local newspaper. The Official Receiver is an officer who is appointed by and acts under the direction of the Department of Trade, and who is also an officer of the court to which he is attached. The official receiver of a district (the number of districts and official receivers are fixed by the Department of Trade) always acts until a trustee is appointed (see later under "Adjudication") and will in some cases act as trustee himself. Upon the making of a receiving order the debtor is given seven days in which to prepare a statement of affairs. The statement of affairs must be lodged with the official receiver within three days upon the debtor's own petition, or within seven days upon a creditor's petition, and is in a prescribed form setting out the debtor's assets and liabilities, and is submitted to the meeting of creditors.

CREDITORS' MEETING

This meeting has to be held within fourteen days after the making of the receiving order unless this time is extended by the court. Six days' notice of the meeting must be given and advertised in the Gazette and a local newspaper.

The debtor may submit a Scheme of Arrangement and the creditors have to decide whether the debtor should be adjudged bankrupt or whether his composition or scheme of arrangement should be accepted. The scheme should normally offer at least 25p in the £ and must be approved by a majority in number and three quarters in value of the creditors. If the court sanctions the scheme, the receiving order will be rescinded. If the creditors do not accept the scheme, or if none is offered, a Trustee in Bankruptcy will be appointed (usually a chartered accountant who specialises in insolvency work, or the Official Receiver himself may be appointed) and in some cases a Committee of Inspection (to supervise the Trustee) may also be constituted.

PUBLIC EXAMINATION

As soon as convenient after the making of the receiving order, the court will, on the application of the official receiver, fix a time and place for the public examination of the debtor. In some cases the court may dispense with a public examination under Section 6 of the Insolvency Act 1976. The purpose of the public examination is to ascertain the cause of the debtor's failure and when the examination is closed the court makes an adjudication order.

ADJUDICATION ORDER

The adjudication order makes the debtor bankrupt and the whole of his property is now vested in the Trustee who is authorised to sell or otherwise dispose of the assets for the benefit of the creditors as a whole. However, even after adjudication a scheme of arrangement may be submitted and, if sanctioned, the court will annul the adjudication order.

It is important to distinguish between the Receiving Order and Order of Adjudication and their respective effects.

A Receiving Order is a warning to all persons dealing with the debtor that all sums owing to him must be paid to the Official Receiver and not to the debtor himself. A Receiving Order gives the Official Receiver power to **receive** all monies due to the debtor, but does not give him any power to dispose of any of the debtor's property. After the Order of Adjudication has been made, the Official Receiver, or Trustee, as the case may be, is given power to sell or dispose of the debtor's estate in the interests of the general body of creditors; consequently, until a debtor has been adjudged bankrupt, the Official Receiver has no power to surrender a policy, but should the policy have produced a claim, then the Official Receiver is in a position to give a valid discharge for monies arising under the policy.

DISCHARGE IN BANKRUPTCY

In the past a large number of bankrupts failed, for some reason, to apply for their discharges. Whilst a person remains an undischarged bankrupt he is subject to many disabilities (see later) but nevertheless the growing number of undischarged bankrupts was recognised as a problem by the Insolvency Act 1976 which provides for automatic discharges by the court after five years where it thinks fit on the circumstances of each case.

PROPERTY DIVISIBLE AMONGST CREDITORS

By Section 38 of the Bankruptcy Act 1914 the trustee is entitled to claim:

(a) All goods which at the commencement of the bankruptcy were in the possession, order or disposition of the bankrupt. These would comprise goods of which the bankrupt is the "reputed owner."
(b) Certain property that the bankrupt has paid or given away for his own benefit at the commencement of the bankruptcy;
(c) All property belonging to the bankrupt at the commencement of the bankruptcy or that may be acquired by him before his discharge.

The following are exceptions:

(a) Necessaries to the value of £250.
(b) Property held in trust for other persons;
(c) Personal earnings so far as they are necessary for the maintenance of the bankrupt and family;
(d) Rights of action to recover damages for personal injury;
(e) The benefit of contracts requiring the personal skill of the bankrupt; if the bankrupt elects to perform the Contract, the Trustee may enforce it as against the other contracting party.

There are also circumstancs in which the trustee can seek to disclaim onerous property, such as land with onerous covenants or partly paid shares, but any party who suffers injury from a disclaimer has the right to prove against the estate in respect of the injury suffered.

GOODS IN BANKRUPT'S REPUTED OWNERSHIP

It is not unusual that a person carrying on a trade or business has in his possession at the commencement of his bankruptcy goods belonging to others. If this is so and the circumstances are such that he can be regarded as the reputed owner of those goods, his trustee is entitled to claim them as part of the estate (Section 38(c)). This provision of bankruptcy law is known as the "order and disposition clause" or the "reputed ownership" clause.

To be within this clause goods must, at the commencement of the bankruptcy, be in the bankrupt's possession or at his **"order or disposition"**:

(a) in the trade or business; (*Lamb v. Wright & Co.* (1924))
(b) by the consent (which may be implied) of the true owner;
(c) in such manner as to make the bankrupt the reputed owner of them.

The word "goods" includes all personal goods and chattels but not fixtures attached to the freehold or "choses in action" when they are other than debts due in the course of the bankrupt's business.

The presumption of ownership may be rebutted by the custom of trade, e.g. goods hired, cattle taken in for grazing, etc., but the usage or custom must be proved and it must be so general as to be within the probable knowledge of the persons likely to have dealings with the bankrupt.

The true owner's only remedy is to prove for the value of the goods.

The **object of the "reputed ownership" clause** is to protect creditors from the consequences of the false credit which a person may acquire by being allowed to have in his possession, as apparent owner, property which did not really belong to him. Property held by the bankrupt as trustee and goods and chattels in the hands of an executor or factor will not commonly fall within the doctrine of reputed ownership.

Possession by a banker of a warehousekeeper's certificate and a delivery order will not take the goods out of the order and disposition of the bankrupt unless the goods have been registered in the banker's name.

If the true owner demands possession of goods before the bankruptcy and from no fault of his own fails to get them, they are not in the bankrupt's possession with his consent. And if, without notice of an act of bankruptcy, he obtains possession before the receiving order is made, his title will prevail against that of the trustee.

A trade debt which has been assigned by a person who becomes bankrupt will remain in the disposition of the bankrupt unless notice of the assignment has been given to the debtor and is a **general** assignment of book debts unless the assignment is registered as an Absolute Bill of Sale.

The doctrine of Reputed Ownership does not apply in the case of the Winding-up of a Company.

RECOVERABLE PROPERTY

The Trustee in Bankruptcy may reclaim property in the following instances which are void against the Trustee:

(a) **A Voluntary Settlement** made within two years of the bankruptcy; if made within **ten** years it is void unless it can be proved that the assignor was then solvent apart from the property concerned. A Voluntary Settlement is a transfer of property without valuable consideration.

(b) **A General Assignment of Book Debts** as regards debts not paid at the commencement of the bankruptcy, unless it has been registered as a Bill of Sale.

(c) Rights of **Execution Creditors** which have not been exercised. If a creditor has issued execution against the land, goods or debts of a debtor he must give up the property so taken if a receiving order is made, or the creditor has notice of a bankruptcy petition or an act of bankruptcy before the execution is completed, or whilst the goods or the money produced from the sale is in the hands of the sheriff. The court could, however, set aside the rights of the Trustee in favour of execution creditors.

(d) Fraudulent Preference.

RELATION BACK

If the Trustee obtained merely what belonged to the bankrupt at the date of **adjudication** it is obvious that the debtor would take good care to divest himself of as much of his property as he possibly could when the pending crash was imminent and that the Trustee would get very little and the creditors less.

For this reason Section 37 of the Bankruptcy Act 1914, stipulates that the bankruptcy is deemed to have commenced at the time of the **first provable Act of Bankruptcy** within **three months** preceding the presentation of the **Petition**.

The title of the Trustee to property available for distribution is not limited by the date of his appointment, or after the date of the Receiving Order or of the adjudication but it **relates back** to the **commencement of the bankruptcy**.

It should be noted that the Trustee's title does not necessarily relate back to three months before the presentation of the petition. The three months period is the maximum period; the Trustee must ascertain the first available act of bankruptcy within this period and it is the date of that which will be the date from which his title is derived.

PROTECTED TRANSACTIONS

If the doctrine of "relation back" were applied without any alleviation, although the interests of creditors would be fully protected, considerable hardships would be inflicted upon others who had no knowledge that an act of bankruptcy had been committed and who had entered into transactions of one sort or another with the debtor. For instance, a banker who, in all innocence, had paid away a credit balance after the commencement of the bankruptcy would be faced with a claim by the Trustee for reimbursement.

Therefore the doctrine of relation back has been modified by Sections 45 and 46 of the Bankruptcy Act 1914 and these sections are of practical significance to bankers.

Section 45 protects bona fides transactions with the bankrupt in the ordinary course of business provided that the following conditions apply:

1. Without notice of an **act of bankruptcy**, and
2. Before a Receiving Order has been made.

It should be noted that this section of the Bankruptcy Act would not give protection against a fraudulent preference.

Section 46 protects any payment or delivery to a bankrupt or his assignee provided:

1. Without notice of the presentation of a Petition, and
2. Before a Receiving Order has been made.

Therefore until a banker receives notice that his customer has committed an act of bankruptcy, payments may be safely made and received on the account so long as a receiving order has not been made (Section 45).

When notice of an act of bankruptcy has been received before notice of presentation of a petition, payments or deliveries of properties are protected only if they are made to the debtor or to a person claiming by assignment from him. The transactions must additionally be in the ordinary course of business and otherwise bona fides. A payment to a creditor made on the instructions of the debtor by a third party in possession of funds of the debtor (as in the case of a banker paying a cheque drawn by a debtor in favour of a creditor) may be protected as a payment "to the bankrupt" under either Section 45 or Section 46, as appropriate, provided that, in the latter case, the payment is made in good faith which boils down to having regard to the interests of the general body of creditors, or in the ordinary course of business. The relevant law case here is *Re Dalton, ex parte Herrington & Carmichael v. the Trustee* (1963). Despite the interpretation in this case (which concerned a solicitor paying away money belonging to the debtor who was his client) the safest course is not to pay any cheques payable to third parties. Nevertheless, the question of protection under this Section was further confused by the decision in *Re Clark* (1975) where the official receiver's claim for the amount of two third party cheques paid after the date of the receiving order was refused on equitable grounds.

SUMMARY OF CONDUCT OF ACCOUNTS IN THE LIGHT OF SECTION 46 BANKRUPTCY ACT 1914

CREDIT ACCOUNTS

Payments should be made only to the customer against the existing balance.

Where the act of bankruptcy comprises the assignment of the whole of the property for the benefit of creditors generally (e.g. to a Trustee under a Deed of Arrangement — see later), a banker will be protected in paying over the balance to the Trustee under the Deed.

Cheques payable to third parties should not be paid (despite possible protection by relying on *Re Dalton* as mentioned earlier).

Any credits received should be credited to a suspense account, under advice to the customer, for three months since they could be claimed by the Trustee. Section 46 does not cover payments in at all and if the bank allowed the customer to deal with those funds it would be guilty of conversion, since the amount of the credits would be the property of the Trustee if bankruptcy followed.

OVERDRAWN ACCOUNTS

In the case of an **overdrawn** account a banker on receiving notice of an available act of bankruptcy, **will not pay any cheques** since if the overdraft is unsecured the additional debt created after notice of the act of bankruptcy is not provable against the estate, and if the overdraft is secured the surplus security relied on may become the trustee's by virtue of the doctrine of "Relation Back".

The restrictions imposed due to notice of an act of bankruptcy remain until the last act no longer is "available" which is three months after its date.

DELIVERY OF SECURITIES

Articles held for safe custody can safely be delivered to the customer himself but not to third parties on his request.

Where the act of bankruptcy is the assignment of the whole of the debtor's property for the benefit of creditors generally, the assignment would include such securities which could safely be handed over to the trustee under a Deed of Arrangement.

Notice of an act of bankruptcy means either actual formal notice or knowledge of facts which may constitute an act of bankruptcy. It must be distinguished from notice of an **intention** to commit an act of bankruptcy which may be ignored until the act of bankruptcy is committed. The notice need not be official, but if in doubt it is advisable to make enquiries as to the accuracy of the information. The mere statement of the customer or of others that the customer is in a state of insolvency would not constitute notice. The mere calling together of a debtor's creditors and the offer to them of a composition does not in itself constitute an "act of bankruptcy".

When a banker regards himself as being on notice that the customer has committed an act of bankruptcy, he should formally advise the customer that third party cheques will not be paid and that only cheques payable to the customer himself can be debited to the account.

AFTER NOTICE OF PRESENTATION OF PETITION

The banker should permit no transactions on the account nor release any securities until the petition has been dismissed. If the bank is committed on the customer's behalf such as where Stock Exchange securities have been purchased but not delivered, the account may be debited but the securities themselves must be accounted for to the Trustee.

AFTER THE MAKING OF A RECEIVING ORDER

When a receiving order has been made against a customer, the Official Receiver, or Trustee in Bankruptcy who follows, alone can give the bank an effective discharge for the balance of the account(s) and any securities held belonging to the debtor.

PROOF IN BANKRUPTCY

A "proof" is the actual claim made by each creditor for the amount he asserts is owed to him. The debt may be "proved" by delivering or posting to the official receiver (or to the trustee if one has been appointed) an affadavit verifying the debt, if the official receiver requires this, or merely an unsworn claim. Under the Insolvency Act 1976 an unsworn claim will suffice unless an affadavit is insisted upon by the Trustee or Official Receiver. The Trustee will check and verify each proof, and will either challenge it or admit it as eligible for dividends in the bankruptcy.

RIGHTS OF CREDITORS

SECURED CREDITOR

A secured creditor is a creditor who holds a mortgage, charge or lien upon any of the DEBTOR'S PROPERTY.

It should be appreciated fully that third party security (i.e. property not belonging to the debtor or guarantees by third parties for the debtor's account) may be disregarded for purposes of proof. In *Re Rushton* (1971) property was jointly charged by the bankrupt and another in favour of a bank. On sale this property did not realise enough to discharge the debt completely. It was held that the bank could not prove for the full amount of the balance owing, but for half the balance only since it must give credit for the other half as secured.

A **Secured Creditor** may:

(a) Give up his security and prove for the whole debt;
(b) Realise the security and prove for the difference;
(c) Value the security and prove for the deficiency, but in this case the trustee may redeem the security at the assessed value if the proof is for purposes of dividend, and at the assessed value plus twenty per cent if it has been used for purposes of voting; or
(d) Rely on his security and waive his rights to prove.

Normally a banker would choose to value the security and prove for the deficiency (c) for there may not be time to realise the security as in (b). If his security were ample he might choose (d), but he will very rarely, if at all, choose to give up his security (a).

With regard to (c): If the trustee is dissatisfied with the valuation, he may require the property to be sold. Under certain circumstances, the valuation may be amended. The creditor, however, may at any time, by notice in writing, require the trustee to elect whether he will or will not redeem the security or require it to be sold, and if the trustee does not within six months signify in writing his intention to exercise the power, he loses the right to exercise it.

Where the security consists of goods which have been pledged, the Official Receiver or Trustee, after giving notice in writing, has the right to inspect the goods, and after receipt of such notice the secured creditor is not entitled to realise the security until he has given the trustee a reasonable opportunity of inspecting the goods and of exercising his right of redemption if he thinks fit to do so.

A bill holder is not a secured creditor.

PREFERENTIAL CREDITORS

Section 33 of the Bankruptcy Act, as amended, provides that the following debts must be paid in priority to all others:

1. Local Rates due and payable within twelve months prior to date of Receiving Order.
2. Income Tax and other assessed taxes assessed on the bankrupt up to the 5th April before date of Receiving Order, with a maximum of one year's assessment (the Inland Revenue can select the year).
3. VAT due within twelve months before Receiving Order.
4. Employer's liability for PAYE Tax due within a similar period.
5. Wages and salaries in respect of services rendered to the bankrupt during the four months prior to the Receiving Order with a maximum of £800 per claimant.

   "Wages" is deemed to include remuneration for holiday period or absence through sickness and any accrued holiday pay. The following also must be treated as wages:

   (a) a guarantee payment;
   (b) remuneration on suspension on medical grounds;
   (c) any payment for time off;
   (d) remuneration under a protective award arising under the Employment Protection Act 1975.

6. Contributions payable under Social Insurance Acts by the bankrupt as an employer within the twelve months prior to the Receiving Order.

Employers' contributions under the Redundancy Payments Act 1965 are treated in the same way as social security contributions, but payments made out of the Redundancy Fund to the employees of an insolvent employer, although recoverable by the Secretary of State by right of subrogation, are not preferential claims in the insolvency.

DEFERRED CREDITORS

The undermentioned debts are not payable until all other creditors have been paid in full:

1. Loans by wife to husband or husband to wife for purposes of trade or business.

2. Loans for business purposes where the rate of interest varies with profits.

ORDINARY DEBTS

All debts proved in a bankruptcy (except those having legal priority as mentioned earlier or conversely those which are deferred — see above) must be paid *pari passu* and an agreement between the debtor and certain of his creditors which aims at settling their debts in a manner inconsistent with this rule is contrary to public policy and can be set aside — *British Eagle International Airlines Ltd. v. Compagnie Nationale Air France* (1975).

DISCHARGE IN BANKRUPTCY

A bankrupt can apply for his discharge at any time after adjudication but in any event the position will be reviewed automatically after five years. A person may be discharged either with or without conditions or the order of discharge may be suspended for a certain period or until a certain level of dividend has been paid. In some instances, when adjudicating a person bankrupt, the court will specify that a discharge will be granted automatically after a certain period.

Until an order for discharge is made, however, the person remains an Undischarged Bankrupt and thus subject to certain restrictions.

It is a punishable offence for him (1) to obtain credit to the extent of £50 or more without disclosing his bankruptcy (2) to trade under an assumed name without disclosing his other name. He cannot become a director of a company without the consent of the Court (Companies Act 1948, Section 187 — now Section 302 of the Companies Act 1985).

Under the Insolvency Act 1976, a person who has been a director of two insolvent companies which have been wound up within five years of each other is disqualified for a period of five years from taking part in the management of a company without leave of the Court.

A bankrupt's dealings with **after-acquired property** of any kind (i.e. acquired by him after adjudication) are valid, if bona fide and for value, unless the trustee has already intervened. (Bankruptcy Act 1914, Section 47).

But it is only people dealing **directly** with the bankrupt who are protected. This enables people to deal with him in respect of after-acquired property with security to themselves but it does not prevent the trustee from claiming, at any moment, money or goods from the bankrupt himself.

If a bankrupt customer deals with assets **not** after-acquired, the banker has no protection at all, and may have to account to the trustee for their value.

The receipt of money, security or negotiable instrument from, or by the order or direction of a bankrupt by his banker and any payment and any delivery of any security or negotiable instrument made to or by the order of a bankrupt by his banker are specially declared to be a "dealing with the bankrupt for value" and the banker is protected accordingly. It applies to real as well as personal property. Knowledge of the bankruptcy is immaterial and therefore property acquired after adjudication, although it belongs to the trustee if the trustee chooses to claim it, does not belong to him until he does claim it. Hence title to after-acquired property dates from the time the trustee intervenes. However a duty is imposed upon a banker when he has established that a customer is an undischarged bankrupt.

ACCOUNTS WITH UNDISCHARGED BANKRUPTS

When a banker ascertains that a customer is an undischarged bankrupt he should inform the Trustee in Bankruptcy or the Department of Trade of the existence of the account and make no more payments for a month except under instructions by the Court or the trustee. If the banker omits to do this he will be liable to the trustee for all money paid out of the account (S. 47).

Although the Act is silent on the point, it would appear preferable to take the same action with accounts for persons who are obviously acting as mere nominees of an undischarged bankrupt, e.g. his wife. No action is required if the account of the undischarged bankrupt's wife is clearly private and personal.

After the period of one month has elapsed the account may be continued provided no directions have been received from the Trustee.

The bank should advise the customer that the account must be stopped. If thereupon he states that he has obtained his discharge he should be asked to produce a copy of the Order of Discharge. In any case a bank may discover whether or not a customer is an undischarged bankrupt by searching the Bankruptcy Register in London (a personal search, as there is no provision for official ones). Alternatively, most banks nowadays use the services of one or more of the leading credit reference bureaux who have on their register details of bankruptcies, county court judgements, bills of sale etc.

BANKRUPT PAYEE OF CHEQUE

A cheque payable to a person known to be an undischarged bankrupt should not be paid since it may belong to the Trustee in Bankruptcy and the payee's title may therefore be defective. The cheque would not be discharged by payment to the payee, and the customer would still be liable on it to the trustee. Therefore the bank should safeguard the customer by returning the cheque "Payee Bankrupt."

If it were proved that the money belonged to the estate but the banker had paid away to the bankrupt payee, the banker would not be able to debit the customer's account and would be responsible to the Trustee. A banker is under no obligation to pay a cheque if doing so involves him in personal risk, and if he paid to the bankrupt payee, the Trustee may sue him for conversion. If the banker paid the cheque without knowledge of the bankruptcy, the Trustee would not be able to sue for conversion. Obviously, care needs to be taken that the answer on the cheque does not damage the drawer's credit and it would be appropriate to advise the drawer that the cheque is not being paid and the reason for this.

PROOF BY THE HOLDER OF A BILL

The drawer and endorser of a bill stand in the position of surety for the acceptor. If the holder releases the acceptor he will lose his right of proving against the drawer and endorsers unless he expressly reserves his rights against them. If however, he has not in any way released them, he will have a right of proof against all such parties to the bill, provided he has not failed to give proper notice of dishonour.

Where the bill is not due at the time of the bankruptcy the holder is entitled to prove subject to a rebate of interest at 5 per cent per annum from the time when the dividend is declared to that at which the bill would have become due. If the holder has received a dividend out of the estate of any one of the parties (or, indeed, if any such dividend has been declared) he can only prove for the balance as against the estate of any other party. Generally speaking he is entitled to prove for the full amount against all the parties to the bill, until he has been paid to the full 100p in the £.

When a bill accepted for the accommodation of the drawer is deposited by him as security for a debt less than the amount of the bill, the holder is entitled to prove in the bankruptcy of the acceptor for the full amount of the bill, though he cannot receive dividends in excess of the debt due to him by the drawer.

A surety who has paid the creditor prior to the bankruptcy of the principal debtor may prove for such amount on the latter's bankruptcy, and if the creditor has tendered his proof the surety is entitled to stand in his place. Where, on the other hand, it is the surety who becomes bankrupt, the creditor is entitled to prove for the sum due to him even before the principal debtor has made default.

The discount of a bill must be distinguished from the pledge or deposit of a bill as security. A discounter is a holder for value. The position of a pledge is this — if he sues a third party he sues as trustee for the pledgor as regards the difference between the amount he has advanced and the amount of the bill. If the pledgor could have sued on the bill the pledgee could recover the whole. If the title of the pledgor is defective the pledgee can recover the amount of his advance provided he took the bill without notice.

When proving in bankruptcy for a debt secured by a bill or note the liability of persons antecedent to the debtor must be treated as a security and the value estimated, and for voting purposes deducted from the proof, **but not for the purpose of dividend**.

A bill holder is not a secured creditor. A secured creditor is one who holds a mortgage, charge or lien ON ANY PROPERTY OF THE BANKRUPT. A bill holder has a right of action against any party to the bill but that does not give him a special charge on some portion of the bankrupt's estate. He must prove for his debt like any other unsecured creditor. But the holder of a bill accepted payable against delivery of bills of lading who holds the bills of lading is a secured creditor.

BILLS OF EXCHANGE AND RECEIVING ORDER

A Creditor cannot prove for a debt contracted after a receiving order has been made but a distinction must be made between a debt contracted after the receiving order and a debt contracted before the receiving order has been made and for which a bill has been drawn. In such a case, the Bills of Exchange Act says the bill may be presented either to the bankrupt himself or to the trustee. Hence the acceptance of the bill by the bankrupt is quite in order. It is merely an acknowledgement of an existing debt and the holder can prove against the estate for the amount of the bill.

RIGHTS OF DRAWER

Apart from special contract, where goods sold are to be paid for by the buyer's acceptance of the seller's draft and the acceptor fails or dishonours the bill, the lien of the drawer as unpaid vendor thereupon revives if he has not parted with the possession of the goods or he can stop them being delivered and it is immaterial that the drawer has negotiated the bill.

If the drawer of the bill remits goods or securities to the drawee as cover for the bill and in consequence of the drawer's failure is obliged to take up the bill, he is entitled to the return of any such goods or securities as the drawee may hold unrealised at the time of his failure.

RIGHTS OF DRAWEE OR ACCEPTOR

If the drawer of a bill of exchange remits goods or securities to the drawee as cover for it and the drawee accepts, he thereby acquires a lien upon or right to the goods or securities. If the drawee does not accept he has no right to or lien upon them. If the acceptor fails during the currency of the bill or dishonours it at maturity, his lien upon or right to the goods is thereby determined and he holds them at the disposition of the drawer. If the drawer, by a collateral agreement, has assigned his rights to a particular holder, the acceptor holds the remittances for the benefit of that holder.

RIGHTS OF HOLDER

A bill does not operate as an assignment of funds. Such an assignment can only be effected by agreement, extraneous and collateral to the bill. When a bill of exchange is on the face of it expressed to be drawn against specific goods or securities the holder does not obtain thereby any charge upon the goods or securities except in case of double insolvency. Where the estates of two insolvent parties, both liable to holders of bills of exchange, are administered under the control of a court of justice and one of those parties holds goods or securities of the other as cover for the bills, the holders are entitled to have the proceeds of those goods and securities applied in payment of the bill provided the remain unrealised at the time of the failure of the party holding them. If the proceeds do not equal the amount of the bills, the holders are entitled to prove as creditors for the balance. It is not necessary that the insolvent estates should be administered in bankruptcy. It is sufficient that they are both administered for the benefit of creditors under the control of a court of justice. This rule is generally known as the doctrine of *Ex Parte Waring* (1815).

DISCOUNTED BILLS

A banker who has discounted bills (which are not yet due) for a customer who becomes bankrupt may set-off the contingent liability of the bankrupt on the bill (a proveable debt) against any credit balance he may hold, paying over to the trustee any surplus only. (Bankruptcy Act 1914, Sect. 31.)

Where a banker has discounted a bill for a customer and during the currency of the bill a receiving order is made against the acceptor, the banker is unable to compel the customer to take up the bill and he has no right to retain any current account balances to cover the contingent liability on the bill. At maturity the banker can recover from the drawer or endorsers. The banker can, however, prove on the acceptor's estate for the full amount of the bill subject to a rebate of interest at five per cent per annum from the time when the dividend is declared to that at which the bill would have become due.

BANKRUPT FIRM (i.e. PARTNERSHIP)

On the firm's becoming bankrupt the partners also become bankrupt. The firm's creditors are paid first out of partnership assets; private creditors out of private assets. Any surplus on a private estate is added to the partnership estate; any surplus on the partnership estate is distributed pro rata amongst the partners to help to pay their private creditors.

Notice that security deposited by a partner to secure the firm's account is "collateral" security and that the banker may prove for the full amount of the debt against the firm, making up any deficiency from the security. Any surplus must be paid over to the trustee of the depositor of the security.

ADMINISTRATION IN BANKRUPTCY OF THE ESTATE OF A PERSON DYING INSOLVENT

A creditor of a deceased debtor may, if his debt would have been sufficient to support a bankruptcy petition, petition to the Court for an Order for the

Administration of the Estate according to the law of Bankruptcy; the Court, if satisfied, and on prescribed notice being given to the legal personal representative of the deceased debtor, will make such an Order, which will operate in the same way as an order of Adjudication and will override a Grant of Representation (Probate, etc.); Administration of Estates Act 1925, First Schedule, Part 1 and Bankruptcy Act 1914, S. 4(1)(a).

DEEDS OF ARRANGEMENT

A Deed of Arrangement (sometimes known as a Deed of Assignment) is an alternative to bankruptcy and it is an agreement under which creditors agree to accept a composition (i.e. a payment of so much in the pound in full and final settlement of their debts); and an assignment by the debtor of all his assets to a trustee for the benefit of his creditors as a whole.

Although the execution of a Deed of Arrangement is an act of bankruptcy, the provisions of the Bankruptcy Act 1914, do NOT apply; deeds of arrangement are executed under the Deeds of Arrangement Act 1914, and are not part of the machinery of bankruptcy nor should they be confused with **Schemes** of Arrangement.

As the execution of the deed is an act of bankruptcy the practical steps previously outlined must be taken but no payments whatever can be permitted from the account if the deed relates to the property of the customer **generally** or refers specifically to the banking account. The Trustee under the deed may, however, give a valid discharge for the bank is protected by Section 46 of the Bankruptcy Act (the deed being an assignment) so that any balance in the hands of a banker belonging to a customer who executes a deed of assignment can safely be paid to the trustee named in the deed, **provided payment is made before the actual date on which a receiving order is made and without notice of the presentation of a bankruptcy petition**.

Where the trustee opens an account with a banker it must be in the name of the estate (Section 11, iv, Deeds of Arrangement Act 1914) and the banker should not permit withdrawals until there is no longer any possibility of bankruptcy proceedings based on the execution of the deed, i.e. until three months have elapsed.

If, therefore, the trustee named in the deed opens an account in the name of the debtor's estate and pays into that account the sums that represent the collection of debts and the realisation of the assets, then cheques should not be drawn on the account or be paid out of it for three months from the date of the deed. Until that time such an account is purely a paying-in account and not a current account. It is opened for the purpose of keeping the assets for the Trustee in Bankruptcy in the event of bankruptcy supervening on the petition of the dissentient creditors within the allotted period.

The Deed must be registered with the Registrar of Deeds of Arrangement within seven days and unless it is assented to by a majority in number and value of the creditors within 21 days after it has been registered it becomes void. It only binds those who assent to it and dissenting creditors may present a petition in bankruptcy against the debtor any time within the next three months. But if the trustee gives written notice to any creditor of the execution of the deed and an intimation that the creditor will not after one month be entitled to present a petition then the creditor will not be allowed to present after that time.

Should the deed become void through want of adequate assent then any creditor may use it as the basis of a bankruptcy petition.

The Trustee appointed under a Deed of Arrangement may be solicitor, accountant, one of the creditors or some other party. In any event he is nothing to do with a Trustee in Bankruptcy and will be called the trustee under the deed of assignment. In practice the trustee will often be a chartered accountant with experience in insolvency matters.

INSOLVENCY LAW REFORM: THE CORK REPORT: THE INSOLVENCY BILL

The Review Committee which was chaired by Sir Kenneth Cork produced its final report around the end of 1983 and a Government White Paper was issued in February 1984 on the various changes recommended.

In December 1984 the Government introduced into the House of Lords the bill to give effect to the proposals in the White Paper. Response to the White Paper itself had been very mixed and it seemed that revised legislation would be many years away; however the Bill has progressed through the House of Lords but several amendments have been made. Implementation of many of the proposals in the Bill will be effected by way of statutory instruments yet to be drafted.

Chapter 3

Types of Accounts

THE ACCOUNTS OF PRIVATE INDIVIDUALS

Until fairly recently banks would always seek references before opening an account for an individual and each reference would often involve two letters being sent by the bank; the first being to the referee and asking for his confidential opinion of the new "customer" who has given his name. The letter should include a specimen signature of the prospective customer (*Marfani & Co. Ltd. v. Midland Bank Ltd.* (1967) and should ask the referee to state the name and address of his bankers. When the reply to this is received, the second letter will be written and this is to the referee's banker asking for his opinion of his customer as a suitable person to act as referee for the opening of a new account (*Guardians of St. John's, Hampstead v. Barclays Bank Ltd.* (1923)). When the whole of this exercise has been carried out, then can the reference be said to be complete. Where the new customer is newly arrived from overseas, the bank should see his passport (*Lumsden & Co. v. London Trustee Savings Bank* (1971)).

In view of the decision in the Savory Case, if the customer is an employee the name of his or her employer should be ascertained. Additionally, in the case of a married person the name of the spouse's employer (if the spouse is employed) should be obtained.

If the account is to be worked in any particular way, full details should be given and recorded.

There are many risks in opening an account for a stranger without first obtaining references or an introduction. The person may be an undischarged bankrupt and there are several risks, especially for a banker, in having business relations with such persons. The person may be a minor in which case any overdraft will not be enforced against him. If the banker has any doubts about a person being of age, he must enquire.

The banker too, runs risks in collecting cheques and if the account is opened by the payment in of cheques the risk is greater still. Formerly it was held that the first transaction did not make a customer and that the banker could not claim his statutory protection in such a case. Legal decisions have now established the fact that the relation of banker and customer begins with the first payment to credit and thus the banker is relieved on that score and is entitled to protection as having received payment for a customer. But he may lose it by want of due care and in one of the cases he was held to be guilty of negligence in not making the usual enquiries before opening the account (*Ladbroke & Co. v. Todd* (1914)).

A cheque book should not be issued to a stranger until the bank is satisfied that the prospective customer is a responsible person.

To some extent some banks are now relaxing their rules on the matter of insisting on a reference in all cases and are adopting a commercial approach to this in the full knowledge that on occasions they could be caught out.

In not obtaining a satisfactory reference and introduction, a bank could run the risks outlined above, in particular through losing its statutory protection due to its negligence. However, most banks now have access to one or more of the credit reference companies and bureaux, and the facility to make a speedy search through this medium which would usually immediately bring to light any published information against the subject of the enquiry, such as County Court Judgements, Bankruptcy Notices and Petitions, Receiving Orders, etc. Additionally, the service may include reference to the most recent Voter's Roll from which confirmation of an address may be available. Whilst obviously providing some protection, such searches reveal only published and recorded adverse information; they do not give the fuller assurances which may be forthcoming from obtaining the more conventional type of reference.

Certainly when the prospective customer is giving his personal details etc. to the banker he should be asked to produce satisfactory means of identification.

When a banker wishes to **close an unsatisfactory account** he should **give notice** to the customer in writing of his intention.

The notice must be sufficient to enable the customer to make arrangements for meeting outstanding cheques or bills so that there may be no injury to his credit (*Joachimson v. Swiss Bank Corporation* (1921)).

After the expiration of notice by the bank no more credits should be received and the customer should be asked to return all unused cheques and to withdraw the balance. If the customer refuses to draw out the balance, the account should be closed by transfer to a branch suspense account, and the bank could send its own cheque to its ex-customer. Any cheques presented after expiry of the notice shold be returned "Account Closed." There are different views on the practice of sending a cheque for the residual balance to the ex-customer since he could behave awkwardly and choose not to present the cheque. However, on the basis that the bank is not prepared to pay any cheques presented, irrespective of whether he is paying in at other banks or branches, it seems likely that the ex-customer will come to his senses and presumably make other banking arrangements, resulting in the branch cheque representing the closing balance being presented. In the event that credits arrive in the credit clearing after the customer's account has been closed, these should be credited to the suspense account and thus included in the amount of the branch cheque sent to him, or if subsequent to this, retained under advice to him pending his making arrangements to withdraw the relative sums.

In *Prosperity Ltd. v. Lloyds Bank Ltd.* (1923) it was held that a month's notice was not adequate due to the wide ramifications of the customer's business and clearly a banker wishing to close an unsatisfactory account should carefully consider the circumstances of the particular customer. If a customer refuses to have his account closed, and attempts to keep it open by paying in at other branches or other banks, such credits should be credited to a suspense account if received after the nominated day for closure of the account, and left there until the customer accepts the position and arranges to withdraw the funds. Obviously, when considering closing an account, the banker should ascertain how many cheques remain in the customer's possession since clearly it would be foolish to advise a customer of the bank's wish to close his account just after issuing the customer with a fresh cheque book. The banker should also check whether the customer has a cheque guarantee card and, if so, ask that this be returned to the bank along with any unused cheques.

Care needs to be exercised where tolerance has been permitted by the bank in paying a troublesome account up to overdrawn figures in excess of formally agreed limits or where no formal limit exists. In such cases, and when the banker wishes to dishonour cheques with a view to ceasing the relationship, due attention must be given to the question of whether there is an implied agreement on the bank's part to support the customer to the extent of the figures previously permitted on the account. Obviously a practical approach will be adopted according to the particular circumstances of any one situation, but this factor is one which has to be borne in mind.

There are many reasons why a bank should desire to close an account. No bank can be expected to continue an account which involves them in risk or loss. Neither can they be expected to encourage trading on false credit, rash speculation without capital or fraudulent dealings. An account may give endless trouble and be quite unremunerative. Cheques may have to be frequently dishonoured, the account may be frequently overdrawn without security, worthless credits may be received, the customer may be engaged in illicit dealing, innocent persons may be frequently defrauded, securities deposited or guarantees given may become worthless or many circumstances may arise which make it desirable that the account should be no longer continued.

DEATH OF CUSTOMER

The account should be stopped and cheques presented after notice of death returned marked "Drawer deceased". If the account is overdrawn the personal representatives must be advised of the liability; if in credit, they alone can give valid discharge **after** Probate or Letters of Administration have been taken out.

All mandates are cancelled so that if a third party has been authorised to sign on the account that authority is revoked on the death of the Principal.

A practical difficulty often arises when securities are held in safe custody for the deceased, possibly in a locked deed box which also contains the will. It is customary to permit the solicitors of interested parties to examine the securities so that a Schedule may be prepared for Probate purposes. The will is released to the named Executors or to their solicitor and a suitable acknowledgement taken. Release of the securities is not made until Probate has been produced.

MENTAL DISORDER OF CUSTOMERS

Contracts of persons of unsound mind are generally voidable if the other contracting party is aware of the fact.

However, a banker can find himself in a difficult position when notice is received of a customer's mental incapacity, the difficulty arising because it may be hard to ascertain whether the degree of mental illness is sufficient to preclude the patient from operating the account. The question of mental incapacity comes under the Mental Health Act 1959 and under this Act, a patient may be compulsorily admitted to a hospital or recognised nursing home on a certificate signed by two doctors. An application supported in this way may be made to the local health authority asking for a guardian to be appointed.

Where either of these two occurrences happen, the banker can regard the customer as mentally incapable but a further possibility could be that the customer may enter a hospital voluntarily for mental treatment. Mere entry to a hospital is not really sufficient justification to stop an account as it is the medical certificate which is conclusive evidence.

Once a banker regards himself as being sufficiently on notice that a customer is mentally incapacitated, the account should be stopped. Whilst all mandates should be regarded as rescinded, a banker would normally exercise discretion and standing orders for the payment of life policy premiums, and any similar payments clearly in the best interests of the customer, would be paid. Under the Mental Health Act, the Court of Protection, Royal Courts of Justice, can appoint a person to act as receiver for the patient, and such an application is usually made by a near relative and often a near relative (possibly the applicant) is appointed receiver. When the banker is informed of the appointment of a receiver, the banker should inspect the receiver's authority, stop the patient's account and open an account in the name of the receiver. Should the account be overdrawn, the receiver must be informed of this immediately. The authority of the receiver terminates with the death of the patient and any balance on the account of the receiver vests in the personal representatives.

THE ACCOUNTS OF LIMITED COMPANY CUSTOMERS

It is of fundamental importance to recognise that a company is a separate legal entity; it has a separate existence quite apart from its directors and shareholders, with a distinctive name and the capacity to sue and be sued in that name (*Salomon v. Salomon* (1897)).

Companies are formed by compliance with the statutory formalities under the various companies acts. At present companies are governed by the Companies Acts of 1948, 1967 and 1976 which have replaced earlier acts, but the more recent Companies Act 1980 and Companies Act 1981, which implement various EEC directives, have brought about some significant changes in several long-established principles of company law. The various cuts have now been consolidated into the Companies Act 1985.

The two most important documents which need to be filed in order to effect the registration of a company are the Memorandum of Association and the Articles of Association (in practice, these usually take the form of one bound book-type document headed "Memorandum and Articles of Association," but this in fact contains a copy of each separate document, and it is important to understand the differences between them).

The Memorandum of Association is a deed which states and defines the constitution and the powers of the company; any acts beyond these powers are *ultra vires* the company and void, though the *ultra vires* doctrine has been substantially mofified by S. 9 of the European Communities Act 1972, which will be discussed later.

Under the Companies Act 1985 the memorandum now consists of six parts:

1. in the case of a company limited by shares or by guarantee the name of the company with 'limited' or 'Cyfyngedig' as the last word.
2. a statement as to whether the registered office is to be situated in England, Scotland or Wales.
3. a description of the objects.
4. a statement as to whether the liability of the members is limited.
5. details of the capital structure.
6. the association clause.

It must set forth the name, whether the registered office is in England or Scotland, the objects and capital of the company and, if limited contain the declaration to that effect.

The "objects" clause of the memorandum may be altered by special resolution of the company and confirmation by the Court is no longer necessary unless an objection is made to the alteration within 21 days by a requisite number of shareholders or debenture holders secured by a floating charge. This may be of importance to a bank when a company wishes to enlarge its objects, e.g. to permit it to give guarantees. The validity of the alteration cannot be challenged after 21 days from the date when the resolution was passed.

Under the Companies Act other changes in clauses in the memorandum can be permitted.

A company can change its name by special resolution and with the written approval of the Department of Trade but the registered office can be changed only within the country, England or Scotland, in which the company was registered. The actual country, being the domicile of the company, cannot be changed.

Under the Companies Act 1980 the memorandum of a public company will state "The Company is to be a public company" (see later).

It is essential when considering making an advance to a company for the banker to satisfy himself that the proposed advance is within the powers of the company and its directors in all aspects, and that any security given by the company similarly is properly authorised. Relevant case law is *Ashbury Railway Carriage & Iron Co. Ltd. v. Riche* (1875) and *Re Introductions Ltd.* (1969).

Section 9 of the European Communities Act 1972 contains provisions which may afford some protection to a bank which belatedly finds that it has lent money for an *ultra vires* purpose, but there is considerable doubt as to how much protection is in fact given, and from a practical point of view this section should be regarded only as a last resort, not replacing the need for care in considering whether acts are within the scope of the Memorandum. The Section provides that a person dealing with a company in good faith may treat any act the directors decide upon as *intra vires* the company and the directors, and good faith is presumed unless the contrary is proved. However, what is open to doubt is whether a person who has seen (and probably holds) a copy of the Memorandum could be regarded as acting in good faith in assisting the company in some venture which is beyond the scope of the document.

The *Articles of Association* contain the rules and regulations as to the persons by whom and the manner in which its business is to be conducted. The Articles supplement the memorandum, but do not enlarge the company's powers. The Memorandum is, as it were, the area beyond which the entire action of the company cannot go; inside that area the shareholders may make such regulations for their own government as they think fit.

The powers of the **Directors** who transact the Company's business are determined by the **Articles of Association**. The Articles cannot grant powers exceeding those given by the memorandum, but within these limits they may be altered at will by **special** resolution by the members.

Consequently, if the directors do act beyond their authority, but not *ultra vires* the company, then this act *ultra vires* the directors may be ratified by **ordinary** resolution of the members or the Articles may be altered by **special** resolution, with retrospective effect, to extend the directors' powers.

The memorandum and articles must be lodged with the Registrar of Companies and may be inspected by any person on payment of a fee not exceeding 5p. They are thus public documents and ignorance of their contents cannot be pleaded.

Any alteration of the memorandum or of the articles must be filed with the Registrar and copies issued subsequently must be amended.

The **Certificate of Incorporation** is issued by the Registrar of Companies after the necessary formalities have been complied with and states that the company has been registered. The authority to commence business is another certificate granted after allotment to public companies and without this authority they cannot contract or borrow. Private companies do not require this authority.

PRIVATE AND PUBLIC COMPANIES — CLASSIFICATION AND REGISTRATION

Under the Companies Act 1948 a private company was defined as a company which by its articles:

(a) Restricts the right to transfer its shares;
(b) Limits the number of members to fifty exclusive of employees and former employees;
(c) Prohibits an invitation to the public to subscribe for any shares or debentures of the company.

Some major changes in company law were made by the Companies Act 1980 and one of these was the distinction between public and private companies. A private company was one which restricted the right to transfer its shares, limited the number of members to fifty and prohibited public subscription for its shares; a public company was any other company. The last provision was repealed and with it disappears the restriction upon the right to transfer shares and the limitations upon the number of members for a private company. Under the 1980 Act a public company is identified by its name. The Memorandum of Association of a public company will now state: "The company is to be a public company". Secondly, such a public company must have a name which ends with the words "public limited company" or an abbreviation of this (usually "plc"). The nominal value of the company's allotted share capital is not to be less than £50,000.

Due to the removal of these restrictions of the 1948 Act, a private company has the prospect of growth and development which previously was open only to a public company. If the articles are amended to remove a board of directors' discretion whether or not to register a transfer, an increase in the value of the shares and the opportunity to enlarge the shareholder base would seem to follow. The holding of private company shares as security may thus become more acceptable as security. The opportunity for non-public share offers on a localised basis presents itself for the first time for the private company.

Under the 1980 Act, private companies wishing to remain private did not need to take any action. Private companies wishing to become public companies had to comply with a number of formalities, in addition to those related to the new definition of a public company, before they could change their status. This included their having to file a balance sheet with the Registrar of Companies made up to a date not more than seven months before the company's application. The balance sheet needed to bear the unqualified opinion of the company's auditors. Due to the criteria to be met by public companies, many existing companies (particularly wholly-owned subsidiaries) became private companies by passing a resolution to that effect. Companies which were already public companies had to register in a prescribed form.

SUMMARY OF CLASSIFICATION OF PUBLIC AND PRIVATE COMPANIES

Public companies

The main requirements for a public company — which alone may raise money from the public are:

1. Minimum authorised and allotted share capital of £50,000 (this figure may be altered by statutory instrument);
2. Memorandum to state that the company is public;
3. Memorandum to include as the last part of the company's name the words "public limited company" or "plc" (or optional Welsh descriptions for companies whose registered offices are in Wales);
4. Minimum number of members two (previously seven);
5. For a new company, issue of the Registrar's certificate enabling it to do business and exercise borrowing powers.

Private Companies

A private company is any company that is not public. A private company is not allowed to offer shares to the public but it is no longer necessary for the company to incorporate such restrictions in its articles. An offer or invitation to existing members of the company or under an employee's share scheme would not usually be regarded as an offer to the public.

Commencement of Business

The Companies Act 1980 states that a public company is not permitted to do business or exercise any borrowing powers until it has received a certificate from the Registrar allowing it to do so.

THE PROSPECTUS

When a company seeks to raise funds from the general public, it usually does so by issuing a document called a prospectus; the contents of a prospectus are laid down in the Companies Act 1985 and are elaborate and fairly onerous. The prospectus is the basis upon which the public is expected to apply for and receive allotment of shares in the company; and forms the basis of the contract upon which shares are allotted.

In *Derry v. Peek* (1889) the directors of a company issued a prospectus in which it was stated that the company was empowered to run steam trams in a town. This was not strictly true as the Board of Trade (then) had not granted the necessary authorisation, although the directors honestly believed that it was certain to be granted. In the event, the authorisation was declined, the company wound up and the plaintiff suffered loss, having bought shares on the faith of the prospectus. The plaintiff's action against the directors for fraud failed on the grounds that the directors **honestly** believed in the statement they had made. However, it should be noted that this was an action for fraud and the statutory provisions (which did not exist in 1899) are wide-ranging in that even an honest mistake can lead to liability if there are not reasonable grounds for it.

COMPANIES' BANKING ACCOUNTS

Before opening an account with a company the banker should obtain and retain a copy of the **Memorandum and Articles**; he should also see the **Certificate of Incorporation** and, in the case of a public company, the **Authority to Commence Business**. Even before this last is granted to the company the banker may open an account purely for the receipt of money subscribed under the initial offer of shares.

Firstly, the banker should notice in the memorandum what powers, if any, are given to borrow and give security, whether power is given to give guarantees, to invest or lend the company's money. The banker should also seek to satisfy himself that the company is trading in accordance with its objects.

In the Articles it should be noticed by whom the affairs of the company are to be conducted; the manner in which contracts, deeds and negotiable instruments must be executed and indorsed and the way in which the banking account is to be worked (though in fact these are hardly ever specified) whether all acts of directors must be done at a board meeting or not, and what, if any, power is given to the directors to delegate their authority. A resolution of directors to open the account should be obtained.

Bankers should be acquainted with the regulations relating to cheques and bills. If express provision is made in the Articles as to the persons to sign, then the directions must be complied with. Where no such provision is made, a resolution of the directors should define how cheques are to be drawn and indorsed, and should authorise some one or more persons to sign. This power is often given to any two directors or one director and the secretary. A copy of this resolution certified as true by the chairman and secretary should be sent to the banker together with specimen signatures of those so authorised. It is very necessary to see if power is given to make notes and draw and indorse and accept bills, and if so, in what form, for it is not every company that has power to do this.

The banker should satisfy himself that the Directors are duly appointed. In the case of a new company they may be named in the Articles or appointed by a separate authority signed by the signatories to the Memorandum. Otherwise, each case should be treated on its merits, but a search of the company's file kept by the Registrar of Companies will reveal the names of the Directors and of the Secretary as supplied by the company. Any changes must be advised within 14 days to the Registrar.

The banker will also require a certified copy of the Resolution appointing him as banker to the Company and naming the persons who are to operate on this account, whether it is in credit or overdrawn.

This mandate must be adhered to strictly — all cheques must bear the requisite number of signatures and any alteration must be initialled by all signatories. It is preferable that the alteration, if material, should be signed by all. The signature must be for the Company.

Where a company's cheques require the signature of two directors or one director and the secretary, a banker who pays one of the company's cheques on which an alteration has been initialled by one only of the signatories, does so at his peril.

To establish the liability of a company on a bill or note it must be shown:

1. That the company can contract by bill or note;
2. That the signature on behalf of the company was attached by someone having authority to do so.
3. That the signature is attached in such form as to bind it under the Act for a Promissory Note or Bill of Exchange is deemed to have been made, accepted or indorsed by or on behalf of a Joint Stock Company, if sealed with the corporate seal or if executed in the name of, or by, or on behalf of an account of the company by any person acting under its authority. Thus the name of the Company, if written by an authorised person, is quite sufficient but it is better to have the name of a person with a statement that he signs on behalf of the company and by its authority. A "per pro" signature is a very usual form. Of course, the correct name of the company must be used and if it be a limited company the word "limited" is normally a part of the name.

Finally, the banker should notice in the memorandum what powers, if any, are taken to borrow and give security, whether power is taken to give guarantees and what powers are given to invest or lend the company's money.

When checking that the company has power to give security and where the banker is looking for the company to give security in support of its guarantee, most bankers require the memorandum specifically to cover this situation.

COMPANY NAMES AND BUSINESS NAMES

Prior to the Companies Act 1981, the Registrar of Companies had been able to disallow a company name if it appears to him to be undesirable and due to this, the use of names which are too similar to those of existing companies were not allowed. Due to the large number of registered companies this task was becoming unmanageable and instead the Companies Act 1981 forbade the use of a name which is the same as that of an existing registered company. The Act prohibits names which are offensive or impute royal, state or other governmental connection.

The 1981 Act abolished the Register of Business Names and bankers are exonerated from the requirement to inspect a certificate under the Registration of Business Names Act 1916 where the trade name is not the corporate name of the company. Under the 1981 Act such businesses need to display the owners' names and addresses at the business premises and on all business stationery, and to supply this information on request to any customer or supplier. The business correspondence must also give an address at which service may be made and accepted.

The fact that a bank can no longer search to ascertain whether a customer has registered a business name makes the need for vigilance on the banker's part when collecting cheques payable to a business name even greater, to avoid claims for conversion.

LOANS TO A COMPANY

A trading company has implied power to borrow, even if no express power is given in the Memorandum or Articles, but a non-trading company cannot borrow unless expressly authorised to do so by its Memorandum. When it has power it may (subject to any restricitons in the memorandum) raise money in such manner as the directors think fit, as for example, by overdrawing its current account by legal or equitable mortgage, by bonds, by debenture, or by giving a floating charge on its property, for a power to borrow implies power to give security. As regards the purpose of the loan, the lender must not know that it is being mis-applied. In *Reintroductions Ltd.* (1969) a bank advanced large sums against debentures to a company whose sole activity was pig-breeding, which was *ultra vires* its Memorandum: The Court of Appeal held that as the bank knew the advances were for use in an *ultra vires* business, the debentures were void.

The borrowing powers of directors are sometimes limited by the Articles to a certain sum or it may be stated that the directors shall not exceed that sum without the sanction of the shareholders. If the borrowing powers thus defined are exceeded the company may not be liable for the excess.

Before making an advance or allowing an overdraft or accepting any charge or security on the company's property, the banker should refer to the Memorandum and Articles, whose contents he is deemed to know, to see that the transaction is regular in form and within the powers of the Company and of the directors and should obtain the authority of the directors to make the advance. The validity of the borrowing as affected by the amount and purpose should be regarded, though the banker need do no more than ascertain if authority to borrow is given for he has a right to infer that the conditions have been complied with. The debit balance, however, should never exceed the borrowing power of the company. The balance sheet (or preferably a series of balance sheets) should be keenly scrutinised. The Register of Charges kept by the Registrar of Companies should be searched because by S.95 of the 1948 Act (Section 395 of the 1985 Act) all mortgages and charges by a company (except charges on stocks and shares, life policies and products, and bills deposited as security) must be registered there within 21 days of their creation, otherwise they are void as against a liquidator or creditor of the company. In addition, the company must record in its own Register of mortgages all specific and floating charges. Failure to register in the company's register does not invalidate the charge. This register is open to all members and creditors and the public may see it on payment of a small fee.

TABLE A CLAUSE 69 1929 ACT

It should be noticed that if the borrowing powers are governed by Table A of the 1929 Act, then by Clause 69 the amount, for the time being remaining undischarged, of money borrowed or raised by the directors for the purposes of the company (otherwise than by the issue of share capital) shall not at any time exceed the **issued** (NOT the **nominal** nor the **paid-up**) share capital of the company without the sanction of the shareholders in general meeting. In such a case, the banker should ask for a certified copy of the resolution of the general meeting which authorises the borrowing if the amount he is asked to lend coupled with any existing borrowings of the Company is in excess of the issued share capital.

Clause 69 does NOT apply to a company whose articles

(a) expressly exclude the provisions of Table A, as a whole;
(b) expressly exclude the provisions of Clause 69; or
(c) expressly state **other** limits to the directors' borrowing powers.

A company's Articles may always be altered so as to exclude Clause 69 by a special resolution (retrospectively, if necessary).

TABLE A CLAUSE 79 1948 ACT

If the borrowing powers are governed by Table A of the 1948 Act, as will be the case unless Regulation 79 is excluded or modified by the Articles of a Company registered after 1st July, 1948, some important differences must be noted.

(a) Whilst the directors are still restricted in the extent to which they may **borrow** to the issued share capital (unless consent of a general meeting is obtained) a further restriction is imposed by the inclusion in the term "borrowing" of any **securities** given by the Company to cover its **liabilities** (which may not necessarily be debts) or to cover the **debts or liabilities of the third parties**.

This may be of considerable importance to a bank which is offered as cover for an advance, **made to an individual**, security by a company to which Regulation 79 applies. If the proposed advance is for £10,000, the issued capital of the company £15,000 and it is known that the company has already borrowed £10,000, then confirmation of the company in general meeting will be necessary for the issue of the security as the total "borrowing" will amount to £20,000.

(b) The limit to the directors' borrowing powers does not, however, apply to **temporary** loans **from the company's bankers** in the ordinary course of business.

As most banks' accommodation is ostensibly of a temporary nature it might be inferred that banks could ignore the Regulation. Unfortunately, "temporary" is not defined and in the absence of any ruling on the point care should be exercised unless the borrowing is in fact required for only a very short period.

(c) The Regulation provides that a lender **need not enquire** whether the limit is observed so that there is no **obligation** on the bank to question the directors as to the amount which the company has already borrowed. In practice this would be most unusual as prior to granting accommodation a banker normally looks into the company's existing commitments or calls for production of a Balance Sheet which would disclose them.

(d) If the lender is aware that the limit has been or will be exceeded, i.e. if he had **express notice**, he cannot close his eyes to the fact on the grounds that no enquiry need have been made. If enquiries have been made the results cannot be ignored.

ULTRA VIRES BORROWING

Ultra Vires means beyond their powers; a phrase applied especially to directors of companies exceeding their legal powers under the articles of association or the Acts of Parliament by which they are governed; though it is equally applicable to excess of authority of any kind. Except where the European Communities Act 1972 applies, any loan made to a company which exceeds the limit expressed in its Memorandum (or any loan made to a non-trading company whose Memorandum gives no authority to borrow) is void, nor has the banker any rights against security deposited by the company to cover the loan.

Where borrowing is *ultra vires* the company the banker's remedies are:

(a) Subrogation — by which he stands as a creditor of the company in the stead of such creditors as have been paid with the proceeds of the loan, unless the loan has been misapplied. He does not, however, get the benefit of any securities they may have held nor of any priority they may have enjoyed.

(b) to obtain an injunction preventing the company from parting with the loan or specific assets purchased with it;

(c) to sue the directors for breach of implied warranty of authority if he can show that, although aware of the authorised limit, he was not aware that the company had already borrowed to an extent which would make his loan *ultra vires*. It is wise to obtain from the directors a statement of the existing amount of borrowing when making the loan, and to lend by way of loan rather than overdraft.

Where the borrowing is *ultra vires* the directors, the banker's remedies are:

(d) to obtain ratification of the directors' act by the company in general meeting.

(e) for the company by special resolution to alter the Articles and extend the directors' powers with retrospective effect;

(f) if he was unaware through no fault of his own, that the directors had already borrowed up to their limit (i.e. if he relied on the ostensible authority of the directors) he may plead the

Rule in Turquand's Case

This is that:

"persons dealing with a Company are bound to read the registered documents and to see that the proposed dealing is not inconsistent therewith. But they are not bound to do any more; they need not inquire into the regularity of the internal proceedings" — *Royal British Bank v. Turquand* (1856).

Persons relying on this doctrine of ostensible authority must prove that

(i) they were aware at the time of the transaction of the delegated authority;
(ii) they relied on the knowledge; and
(iii) there was nothing in the transaction to put them on enquiry.

If they can do this the company will be bound by the directors' act. Note in this connection the provisions of Table A of the Companies Act 1948, where applicable.

(g) If still unsuccessful the banker must fall back on the remedies already set out in (a), (b) and (c).

LOANS TO DIRECTORS

The provision of the Companies Act 1948 relating to loans and guarantees for directors (Section 190) was repealed by the Companies Act 1980 and replaced by more extensive provisions, particularly in the case of public companies. In the latter respect, a public company is involved if the company in question is

(1) the subsidiary of a public company or (2) the subsidiary of a company which has another subsidiary which is a public company or (3) which has a subsidiary which is a public company. In such event, not only is there the general prohibition upon the company lending to or guaranteeing its own directors but lending is prohibited also to the directors of the parent company and persons connected with the directors. This latter category comprises a director's spouse, child and stepchild, a director's partner, and bodies corporate with which the director is associated. A director is associated with a company if he and the persons connected with him hold one fifth of the equity share capital or exercise or control one fifth of the voting power at a general meeting.

Furthermore, not only are ordinary loans and guarantees for directors involved with public companies prohibited but also transactions defined as "quasi-loans". These loans exist where the company agrees to pay or actually pays a sum for or on behalf of a director or, alternatively, reimburses expenditure incurred by a third party for or on behalf of the director, in each case in circumstances where the director is obliged or is liable to reimburse his company. It is difficult not to regard a company cheque paid for a director's expenses as being a potential quasi-loan, but whether or not it is such a loan depends on the existence of an obligation or liability to reimburse the company.

FINANCIAL ASSISTANCE FOR THE ACQUISITION OF SHARES

The Companies Act 1981 (Sections 42–44) amended the law concerning the giving of financial assistance by a company for the acquisition of its own shares.

Section 54 of the Companies Act 1948 made it unlawful for a company to give financial assistance for the acquisition of its own shares or those of its holding company. Contravention of the section was an offence rendering the company and defaulting officers liable to a fine of £100. There were exceptions for loans in the ordinary course of business and for the provision of money for the acquisition of shares for employees. The Section (which re-enacted a section of the 1945 Act) was introduced to curb a prevalent form of "asset stripping" — obtaining control of a company whose shares are undervalued by making an attractive offer to existing shareholders, then selling off assets and keeping the difference. It was considered that there was a risk to minority shareholders where asset strippers (using the company's own resources) gained control without buying all the shares and that the borrowing of money from the company offended the spirit of the law which prohibited a company trafficking in its own shares.

Banks were concerned with these restrictions in two ways:

1. A company may apply for an advance to enable it in turn to lend (a) to a director or (b) to any person for the purpose of acquiring its shares.

2. A director or prospective shareholder may apply for an advance offering as security a guarantee or charge by the company or stating that an advance will be repaid by means of a loan from the company.

A series of conflicting cases showed that bankers constantly had to be on guard against possible infringement of Section 54 even if such an infringement was not immediately apparent. Section 54 was criticised on the grounds that the provision by a company for the acquisition of its own shares only offended against the rationale of the rule that a limited company may not buy its own shares if it thereby reduced its capital. If the financial assistance was in the form of a loan which was fully repaid it did not. It was felt also that a penalty of £100 did not defer the unscrupulous asset-stripper who anyway could avoid the Section by a series of intermediary transactions. On the other hand, Section 54 prohibited a number of innocent transactions and was felt to be a strong disincentive to banks and other financial institutions who were conscious of the risk of being caught by the wide net cast by the Section extended by courts under the doctrine of constructive trust (*Belmont Finance Corporation v. Williams Furniture Ltd.* (1979)). Although Section 54 refers to a fine of £100 only for breach of the Section, this was of no comfort to bankers since if a transaction was challenged, the challenge would probably be based on a charge of conspiring to defraud minority shareholders and/or creditors, with a view to having the transaction and perhaps all following transactions set aside on the grounds of *ultra vires*.

The 1981 Act therefore sets out to retain and strengthen the aim of Section 54 of the earlier Act and thus provide an effective prevention of abuses which result in losses to minority shareholders and maybe creditors. Additionally, however, the amendments in the 1981 Act seek to exempt honest transactions by setting out conditions in which banks and other lending institutions can safely lend for the acquisition of shares, and also provide a means whereby managers of private companies can obtain assistance from the company in acquiring its shares, thus facilitating the transfer of control from existing shareholders. Under the previous legislation banks were reluctant to lend in this situation.

Sections 42 to 44 of the Companies Act 1981 give a complex set of provisions. The basic prohibition has been re-enacted and the exemptions from the prohibition for public companies have been slightly extended. For private companies, financial assistance is permitted provided that the prescribed procedures are observed. Financial assistance comprises assistance by way of gift, guarantee, security, indemnity, loan, novation or "any other financial assistance given by a company, the net assets of which are thereby reduced to a material extent or which has no net assets." Like Section 54 of the 1948 Act, the 1981 Act renders both the company and the officer in default potentially criminally liable for contravention of this section, the maximum penalty being two years' imprisonment and/or a fine or summary conviction. The civil remedies are not spelt out but presumably liability for negligence and liability under the doctrine of constructive trust will continue, although it is arguable that case law decided under Section 54 is not relevant to the new provisions, since Section 42 of the 1981 Act emphasises that Section 54 is repealed. Whether a breach of the Section renders the whole transaction void, and the money or security given by the company under it irrecoverable, remains to be seen but presumably it does as since the transaction is illegal it must therefore be *ultra vires* the company.

Although the provision of financial assistance by a company for the acquisition of its shares, directly or indirectly, remains unlawful, as does financial assistance to reduce or discharge a liability incurred for the purpose of the acquisition, there are exceptions to these general rules which both public limited companies and private companies can use. To take advantage of the exceptions the assistance by such companies in relation to their own or their parent company's shares must be in good faith and in their interests. If this motive exists, the assistance will not be prohibited if (1) the principal purpose in giving assistance is not the acquisition of the shares or (2) the giving of the assistance is "but an incidental part of some larger purpose of the company." These concepts are fraught with difficulties, however, and will probably be examined in future litigation.

Under Section 42(5), no longer will the payment of a lawful dividend to a shareholder who has recently acquired shares be suspected as being unlawful assistance for their acquisition. The 1981 Act re-enacts the three old exceptions to Section 54 with some modifications, but these exceptions only allow a **public** company to give such financial assistance if the net assets of the company are not thereby reduced (by reference to book values, not actual values) or the assistance is made out of distributable profits.

The exceptions are:

(1) The lending of money by a coany in the ordinary course of business where the lending of money is part of the ordinary course of business of the company;
(2) The provision of money for share acquisitions in respect of employee share schemes;
(3) The lending of money to employees other than directors, to enable them to acquire shares in the company or its holding company.

Section 43 relaxes substantially the basic prohibition for private companies provided that certain conditions are met and steps taken to validate the transactions.

CONDITIONS NECESSARY FOR PRIVATE COMPANIES TO GIVE FINANCIAL ASSISTANCE

1. No reduction in Net Assets. The financial assistance may only be given if the company's net assets are not thereby reduced, or if the financial assistance is provided out of distributable profits.
2. If more than one company is involved — e.g. a holding company or intermediate company — all the companies must be private companies.

3. Special Resolutions. The giving of financial assistance must be approved by a special resolution of the company in general meeting. If other companies are involved, they must similarly approve the transaction by special resolution.
4. Statutory Declarations by Directors.

The directors of the company (or companies) must make a statutory declaration in a prescribed form. This declaration has to contain the following:

(a) Details of the assistance to be given, particulars of the business of the company and the identity of the recipient of the assistance;
(b) a statement of the opinion of the directors concerning the ability of the company to pay its debts;
(c) an auditors' report to the directors confirming the opinion must be attached to the declaration.

These declarations have to be available for inspection by members at the meeting at which the resolution is passed, otherwise the resolution is not effective. There is also a strict timetable laid down whereby minority shareholders are enabled to apply to to the court for cancellation of the resolution. Under these provisions shareholders who hold not less than 10% of the share capital may apply to the court for cancellation of the special resolution. The court may cancel or confirm the resolution, make an order in terms as it sees fit, adjourn proceedings to give time for arrangements to be made for the purchase of the shares of the dissentient members, or provide for the purchase by the company of the shares of any of its members and for the reduction of the company's capital accordingly.

THE PRACTICAL EFFECT OF THE CHANGES ON LENDING BANKERS

Whereas under the previous legislation a lending banker needed to ensure that he did not lend to a company "in connection" with the acquisition of shares in itself at all, under the 1981 Act the bank must ensure that it lends only in the authorised circumstances. If this is not so, the bank could find that its lending is irrecoverable because the transaction was void, and further the bank could be liable under the doctrine of constructive trust if it knew the circumstances surrounding the transaction and was perhaps put on enquiry and did not investigate the facts. A bank could also lend money knowing that the directors had no grounds for giving the opinion required in their statutory declaration, and thus could conceivably be criminally liable for conspiracy to defraud the creditors and minority shareholders.

In practice, most lending for this purpose will be to private companies and the banker would be wise to insist that the Section 43 procedure of a statutory declaration of solvency by the directors followed by a special resolution of the company is carried out. This would avoid the need to rely on the difficult concepts mentioned earlier concerning principal purpose or larger purpose.

Where public companies are concerned (or where private companies insist on using the "primary purpose" exception) it will not be enough for the banker to accept that the primary purpose of the company is not to acquire its own shares merely because the directors say so. The banker must make reasonable entors followed by a special resolution of the company is carried out. This would avoid the need to rely on the difficult concepts mentioned earlier concerning principal purpose or laranker would have a good defence to any constructive trust based claim.

It is necessary to become familiar with the main changes brought about by the 1981 Companies Act and keep abreast of any legal decisions made in cases arising in this area of company law. This area of company law is now consolidated into the 1985 Act — Section 151 onwards.

WINDING UP OF COMPANIES

A Company has "perpetual" succession; its members may change but the company remains unchanged. Nor can it be made bankrupt, but when it becomes necessary to end its business and to realise and distribute its assets, it is "wound up" or goes into "liquidation". This may be

(A) Compulsory winding up by the court.

By Section 222 of the Companies Act 1948, a company may be wound up by the Court:

(a) If the company has by special resolution resolved that the company be wound up by the Court;
(b) If default is made in filing the statutory report of a public company or holding the statutory meeting;
(c) If the company does not commence its business within a year from its incorporation or suspends its business for a whole year;
(d) If the number of members is reduced, in the case of a private or public company below two;
(e) If the company is unable to pay its debts;
(f) If the court is of the opinion that it is just and equitable that the company should be wound up.

The ground most frequently invoked is (e) and Section 223 provides that inability to pay debts is deemed to occur in four ways; of these the most common is when a creditor to whom the company owes more £750 has left at the company's registered office a written demand for payment of the sum due and the company has for three weeks after that neglected to pay the sum or to secure it to the reasonable satisfaction of the creditor. Where the company genuinely disputes the debt, a winding up order will not be made.

A compulsory winding up commences at the date of the presentation of the petition. Between the presentation of the petition and its hearing (the Court may of course make a winding up order, dismiss the petition or hold it over until a future date) there are practical difficulties which arise as regards whether or not the banker should permit transactions on the company's account. It used to be thought that cheques presented by the company for cash (e.g. wages cheques could safely be paid, and bankers often permitted the account to continue provided transactions going through it were for purposes "in ordinary course of business" whether the account was in debit or credit. It used to be felt that this practice was a reasonably safe line to adopt on the grounds that a liquidator would hardly challenge subsequently the payment of cheques apparently drawn in the ordinary course of business. Furthermore, it seemed a reasonable bet that if he did, the Court would very likely uphold the payments under Section 227 of the Companies Act 1948. This view was encouraged by *Re Operator Control Cabs Ltd.* (1970). However, in *Re Gray's Inn Construction Company Ltd.* (1980), the Court of Appeal settled the principles which are to apply in deciding whether or not to validate dispositions and the conclusion from this case must be that no transaction on a bank account can be permitted after a petition unless and until an order from the court under Section 227 has been obtained.

In addition to the foregoing grounds for winding up, there is power to present a winding-up petition in the following circumstances:

(a) To the Department of Trade if, after an investigation by them, it appears expedient in the public duty;
(b) To the Bank of England, under Section 18 of the Banking Act 1979 should the bank or licensed institution end up valuing its assets less than its liabilities.

(B) Voluntary winding up.

This commences at the date of the passing of the resolution by the company and may be either of the following:

(1) a **members'** voluntary winding up, when a Statutory declaration under S.283 is made by the directors that the company will be able to pay its debts in full within twelve months. This type of winding-up is normally effected by the company passing a special resolution that it would be wound up voluntarily; though if articles provide for the duration of the company or mention any event on the occurrence of which the company is to be dissolved, then an ordinary resolution will suffice (S.278); or
(2) a **creditors'** voluntary winding up, when this declaration is not made and the creditors meet the company to co-operate in realising the assets. This is achieved by the company passing an extraordinary resolution to the effect that it cannot by reason of its liabilities continue its business (S.278).

(C) Winding up under Supervision.

This is a voluntary winding up which, by order of the Court, or on a petition by the creditors, is under the supervision of the Court.

By Section 317 of the Companies Act 1948, the respective rights of secured and unsecured creditors, provable debts and kindred matters are to prevail in the winding up of insolvent companies as in bankruptcy. The rights of Preferential creditors are similar.

If the company is **solvent** and is being wound-up for purposes of reconstruction or amalgamation, a banker will simply prove for his debt and retain his security until he receives payment, when he will give it up. If the company is insolvent the banker has four courses open to him:

(1) He may rely on his security and not prove at all;
(2) He may realise his security and prove for the balance;
(3) He may give up his security and prove for the whole debt;
(4) He may assess the value of the security and prove for the balance after deduction of the assessed value.

If the banker has taken adequate security he will be content to realise it but the realisation of the security may involve an action. But no action can be taken in the case of compulsory winding-up except by leave of the Court which in the case of a secured creditor is readily given. In the case of voluntary winding-up, actions may proceed freely but the liquidator has power to apply to the Court to stay the proceedings although action by a secured creditor to enforce his security is seldom stayed.

It was held in *Re T.W. Construction Ltd.* (1954) that after the commencement of the winding-up of a company the liquidator was not entitled to reclaim monies which had been paid into a bank in reduction of a debt, allowed pending the receipt of such monies; this was a bona fide transaction in the ordinary course of current trade, for the purpose of enabling the company to continue in business and the Court exercised the discretion vested in it by Section 227 of the Companies Act 1948.

However, as mentioned earlier, the position is now different as a result of the Gray's Inn Construction case and most banks would not permit any transactions on the company's account, whether the balance is in credit or overdrawn, without an order from the court. Whilst this can in practice cause difficulties, the problem can usually be overcome by way of the solicitors applying to the court for urgent consideration to be given to their request for court approval to permitting the transactions.

Advances for Payment of Wages and Salary

In the case of a company, but **not in bankruptcy proceedings**, where payment has been made for **wages or salary** out of money advanced by some person for that purpose, the person making the advance will have priority in winding-up to the extent to which those **preferential** claims have been satisfied from the advance.

This provision (Section 319) often enables a bank to nurse a company which is in low water. Preferential claims are limited to four months before the liquidation and to £800 per employee.

It is advisable, though not legally necessary, for an advance made in reliance on this preferential treatment to be debited to a separate "wages" account, otherwise in an ordinary, active account the earlier preferential debts may be wiped out by the operation of the Rule in Clayton's Case.

Preferential creditors rank before a floating charge and banks usually nowadays take a fixed charge over book dets when taking a debenture as security (This topic is discussed fully in Chapter 6.)

Fraudulent Preference

This can apply in winding-up just as it does in bankruptcy and may be impeached if within six months of the winding up (Section 320 Companies Act 1948).

PARTNERSHIP ACCOUNTS

Partnership is defined in the Partnership Act 1890, as the relation which subsists between persons carrying on a business in common with a view of profit. The relation between any members of any Company registered under the Companies Act or formed by Royal Charter, etc., is not a partnership within the meaning of the Partnership Act.

A partnership may consist of any number of persons, subject to the following limits imposed by the Companies Acts 1948 to 1967: Section 119 of the 1967 Act increases the maximum limit to 10 partners in a banking partnership under Section 429 of the 1948 Act to 20 where each of them is authorised by the Department of Trade for the purpose. Section 120 removes the maximum limit of 20 partners in a non-banking partnership imposed by Section 434 of the 1948 Act as regards firms of solicitors, accountants or stockbrokers, and gives the Department of Trade power to make regulations exempting other types of partnership from the limit (and these have been made in respect of some other professional partnerships). Section 121 does a similar removal in respect of limited partnerships.

A partnership is **not** a separate legal entity, as is a Company, distinct from the partners. The firm name is a convenient abbreviation of the names of the individual partners.

FORMATION OF PARTNERSHIP

Partnership is formed by agreement. The agreement may be oral, written (called Articles of Partnership), implied by conduct or be under seal (called Deed of Partnership).

A partnership may be at will, i.e. determinable by any one or more of the partners by notice to the other or others, or it may be a fixed period of time.

Except where the partners expressly agree to the contrary, the provisions of the Partnership Act apply.

Every partner must be a person having capacity to contract, but a minor may be a partner although not personally liable for the firm's debts and an alien may be a partner although the partnership would be dissolved if war broke out between the alien's country and our own. Mental disorder of a partner does not dissolve an existing partnership but may be grounds for dissolution by the Court.

A minor may repudiate the contract of partnership, but if he does not do so before, or within a reasonable time after, attaining his majority he will be held liable for debts **subsequently** incurred.

A limited company can be a partner but the liability of the members of the company is not thereby increased.

CLASSES OF PARTNERS

A *General* partner is one who is liable for all debts and obligations and who takes part in the management.

A *Sleeping* or *Dormant* partner is a partner who contributes capital, and shares in the profits and liabilities but not in the management; a partner taking part in the management is styled an *Active* partner.

A *Limited* partner is one whose liability is restricted to the amount of capital he actually provides; he is entitled to the return of this (but only on dissolution of the partnership) and to a share in the profits, and takes no part in the management, nor can he bind the firm. The death or bankruptcy of a limited partner does not dissolve the partnership.

An *Incoming* partner, i.e. a new partner, is not liable for debts incurred before he entered the firm save by special arrangement.

An *Outgoing* partner is not liable for debts created after his retirement, if notice of his retirement has been given. Notice should be given by circular to persons who have had dealings with the firm, in addition to the general notice. He must not permit the continuance of any apparent connection of his name with the firm, e.g. on billheads, advertisements, etc.

If any retiring partner consents to be held out to the world as connected with the firm, as, for instance, by allowing his name to remain written up over the shop, or used in the advertisements or invoices of the firm, he will continue liable. And even if he gives notice to one who deals with the firm that he (the retiring partner) has no interest in the partnership, but that he has allowed his name to be continued for a while, this is no disclaimer of liability, and he will continue liable to that person on any further dealing.

If a person who is **not** a partner so conducts himself or allows his name to be associated with a firm as to mislead business people into believing that he is a partner, and on the faith of such representation they give credit to the firm, then the law holds him liable to them as partner. This is called "HOLDING OUT" and he is said to be a "NOMINAL" or "QUASI" partner.

A "quasi" partner is not strictly a partner and does not share in the profits, but he is estopped by his conduct from denying that he is a partner; he is sometimes said to be a "partner by estoppel".

DISCLOSURE OF BUSINESS OWNERSHIP

The Registration of Business names Act 1916 has been repealed by the Companies Act 1981. The purpose of the 1916 Act was to compel businesses carried on in names other then those of their owners to register certain particulars of ownership at a central registry. That Registry is abolished and businesses are relieved of the obligation to register from 26th February 1982. In order, however, to enable those dealing with such businesses to know the identity of the owners, from that date businesses covered by the new Act will need to display their owners' names and addresses at business premises and on business stationery, and to supply this information on request to any customer or supplier. The bankers obviously will be exonerated from the requirement to inspect a certificate under the Registration of Business Names Act 1916 where the trade name is not the name of the proprietor or partners. (In *Smith & Baldwin v. Barclays Bank Ltd.* (1944) the production of such a certificate enabled the bank to retain its statutory protection when collecting for a personal account a cheque in favour of a firm because it had seen the certificate.) The business letters etc. must give an address at which service may be made and, in respect of the requirement to state on letters etc. the names of partners using the business name, if there are more than 20 partners the names may be omitted but an address must be given at which the names and addresses can be inspected.

RELATION OF PARTNERS TO ONE ANOTHER

In the absence of any contrary agreement all the partners are entitled to share equally in the capital and profit of the business and must contribute equally towards the losses of the firm.

Partners are joint-owners of all property brought into the firm, but on the death of any one of them his interest in the property passes to his personal representative.

EXTENT OF PARTNER'S AUTHORITY

Every general partner is an agent of the firm and of his other partners for the purpose of the business of the partnership, and the acts of any partner **within the usual course of the firm's business** bind the firm and his partners unless the person with whom he dealt knew that in fact the partner so acting had no authority or did not know or believe him to be a partner.

Notice the following **implied powers** of a general (or ordinary, as distinct from a **limited**) partner:

(a) To sell and buy goods for the purposes of the business.
(b) To give discharges for money received from debtors.
(c) To draw cheques, unless this is not the usual course of the firm's business.

In addition a partner in a **trading** partnership may bind the firm:

(a) By drawing, accepting or indorsing negotiable intruments in the name of the firm;
(b) By borrowing money on the credit of the firm;
(c) By pledging the partnership goods or securities for the purpose of its business.

But the implied authority of a partner does not extend to the execution of deeds, or, except where it is in the usual course of the firm's business, the giving of a guarantee, or the giving of authority to third parties to sign a firm's name or in agreeing to submit to arbitration.

The firm is not liable for the acts of a partner which are beyond the scope of his authority unless the partner had express authority or the act was subsequently ratified by the firm. A partner who exceeds his authority is personally liable. If the Articles or Deed of Partnership restrict the authority of one party, the firm will nevertheless be liable to third parties who have no actual knowledge of the restrictions provided the act is within the usual scope of a partner's authority for the "Articles" or "Deed" is a private document and does not affect third parties.

Additional powers may be given to any partner by express agreement, but a firm is always liablc for wrongful acts done by one of the partners in the course of partnership business. A partner's implied authority may be restricted by agreement between the partners, but any act within his **implied** authority will bind the firm as regards a third party who deals with him in ignorance of the restriction.

A firm of auctioneers is not a trading partnership so as to confer upon one partner the power to bind another partner by accepting a bill without authority in the firm's name in respect of an adventure outside the scope of the partnership's business.

A partner in a **non-trading** firm may bind a firm by drawing cheques, but he has not implied powers to draw and accept bills, or to overdraw the account, or to borrow money, or to pledge or mortgage the firm's property. Such powers may, however, be given to him by express agreement.

A **surviving partner** has power to deposit title deeds to secure a banking account in the name of the firm in so far as it is necessary for the purpose of winding up the partnership.

LIABILITY OF PARTNER FOR DEBTS OF THE FIRM

The Partnership Act 1980, provides that every partner in a firm is liable 3jointly with the other partners for all debts and obligations of the firm **incurred while he is a partner**, and after his death his estate is also severally liable for such debts, subject to prior payment of his separate debts; Section 9.

It must be noticed that the liablity is JOINT, but that it may be made JOINT AND SEVERAL by special agreement. Nevertheless, the Act makes each partner (or his separate estate after his death) fully liable for any deficiency after realisation of the firm's assets, subject to prior payment of his private creditors.

Thus in actions by or against a firm, the partners should sue or be sued by their firm name and not individually, for the liability of a firm is joint, not several, that is, a partner is liable jointly with all the others and not by himself. Although the liability is joint, yet all are liable, and if the property of the firm is not sufficient to pay the creditors, they may proceed against the private property of each partner, for every partner is liable to his last penny for the firm's debts, and if a partner dies the creditors can, as has been said, enforce their claim against his estate subject to prior payment of his separate debts.

It has been said that creditors should sue the firm and not the partners separately, but they have the option and may, if they wish, sue the partners separately. If they do sue each separately and obtain judgement against one of them, then the other partners are discharged.

An exception to this rule is that the liability for a wrongful act by a partner is joint and several; the firm may be sued or the partner who has committed the wrongful act may be sued separately. The normal partnership mandate used by most banks incorporates joint and several liability.

On a practical note, it should be remembered that when making an advance to a partnership, the partners will be personally liable for the borrowing and therefore the taking of guarantees from the partners would be superfluous.

LIMITED PARTNERSHIPS

Limited partnerships are constituted under the Limited Partnership Act 1907, and must be registered with the Registrar of Companies. In practice, however, little use has been made of the Act.

A limited partnership consists of not more than 20 persons some of whom are general partners and some limited partners. There must be at least one general partner. The limited partners contribute a certain sum and are not liable for the debts and obligations of the firm beyond that amount so contributed.

Limited partnerships, therefore, differ from limited companies, for though certain partners have limited liability, yet the firm has not. The limited partner is, therefore, very much in the position of a fully paid shareholder. He cannot withdraw his contribution any more than a shareholder can but in both cases it may be assigned. Like a shareholder, a limited partner takes no part in the management of the business. But a limited partner may inspect the books of the firm and examine the state and prospects of the business and advise thereon and in this respect differs from the shareholders of a company.

Dealings with limited partnerships are governed by the law of partnership. Each general partner can bind the firm and every general partner is liable for the debts of the firm. The whole firm may be declared bankrupt or any one of the partners may be declared bankrupt. The death or bankruptcy of a limited partner does not dissolve the partnership, but the death or bankruptcy of a general partner does dissolve the partnership. On the dissolution of a limited partnership its affairs are to be wound up by the general partners, unless the Court otherwise orders. Limited Partnerships are wound up in Bankruptcy and not under the Companies Act.

DISSOLUTION

A partnership is dissolved, without the intervention of the Court:

(a) If entered into for a fixed term, by the expiration of that term.
(b) If entered into for a single adventure or undertaking, by the termination of that adventure or undertaking.
(c) If entered into for an undefined time, by any partner giving notice to the other or others of his intention to dissolve the partnership, or by the mutual consent of all the partners.
(d) By the death or bankruptcy of any partner, unless the articles otherwise provide.
(e) By a partner suffering his share of the partnership property to be charged under the option of the other partners.
(f) If it becomes unlawful.

A Court has power to order a dissolution on the application of a partner:

(a) Where it appears necessary or expedient to a judge of the Court of Protection because of the mental disorder of a partner (Mental Health Act 1959).
(b) Where a partner becomes permanently incapable of acting as a partner.
(c) When a partner has been guilty of conduct prejudicial to the firm's business.
(d) When a partner persistently breaks the partnership agreement.
(e) When the business can only be carried on at a loss.
(f) When the Court considers it to be just and equitable.

After dissolution the authority of each partner to bind the firm continues so far as may be necessary to wind up the affairs of the partnership.

Losses, including losses of capital, are paid first out of profits, next out of capital, and then by the partners individually in the proportion in which they were entitled to share in the profits.

If, however, one of the partners is insolvent and unable to contribute anything, then his share of the deficiency must be contributed by the other partners in proportion to their capital and not in the proportions that ordinary losses are borne.

The assets of the firm, including the sums (if any) contributed by the partners to make up losses of capital, are then applied:

(a) In paying the debts and liabilities to third persons;
(b) In repaying advances made to the firm by any partner;
(c) In repaying capital put in by the partners;
(d) The residue (if any) is divided between the partners in the proportion in which the profits are divisable, i.e. equally unless the Articles or Deed of Partnership provide otherwise.

An incoming partner sometimes pays a "premium" on entering the firm. In such a case, if the partnership is dissolved before the expiration of the term fixed for its duration then the premium or a proportionate part of it may be recovered unless the dissolution is due to the misconduct of the partner who paid the premium or is effected by agreement of the parties without stipulation for return of the premium.

GUARANTEES COVERING PARTNERSHIP ACCOUNT

A continuing Guarantee or other third party security given to cover the firm's indebtedness must be regarded as determined upon any change in the constitution of the firm unless there is an agreement to the contrary.

OPENING A PARTNERSHIP ACCOUNT

The banker is under no obligation to obtain a copy of the Deed or Articles of Partnership, if any exist. If he does, however, he is deemed to have knowledge of its terms and must conduct the banking account accordingly. He should obtain instructions, **signed by all the partners**, as to how and by whom the account is to be conducted, and as to the withdrawal of securities lodged for safe custody. He will at the same time get their undertaking to be **jointly and severally liable**. This enables him

(a) to set-off the balances of private accounts of the partners against a debit balance on the partnership account;
(b) to rank level with private creditors instead of being subordinate to their claims on the private estates of the partners in the case of bankruptcy or the death of a partner.

If authority is to be delegated to outside partners the instructions of all the partners must similarly be obtained.

In *Alliance Bank Ltd. v. Kearsley* (1871) it was held that although any partner may open an account in the firm's name, a partner has no implied power to open an account for the firm in any other manner, e.g. in his own name, so as to make his co-partners liable for any debit balance.

The usual references should be taken up.

REVOCATION OF MANDATES

This can be effected by any one partner who accordingly can:

(a) Stop any cheque whether he signed it or not.
(b) Stop all withdrawals, whether all sign or not.

As death or bankruptcy of a partner results in dissolution of the firm, all mandates must thereupon be regarded as cancelled.

LOANS TO PARTNERSHIPS

Trading Firms

In spite of the fact that any partner has implied power to borrow, the bank will obtain an undertaking signed by all the partners to be liable for any overdraft — it will usually be incorporated in the mandate on opening the account. If the banker relies on the **implied** authority of the partner he must see that the transaction is within the ordinary business of the firm.

He will take into consideration the private estates of the partners when estimating the financial standing of the firm, remembering, however, that there may be private liabilities. This, of course, does not apply to **limited** partners, whose liability is limited to the contribution they have already made to the firm's capital.

Non-Trading Firms

The banker should obtain either an express request for a loan signed by all partners, or their express authority for one or more partners to overdraw the account since no partner has an implied authority to do this. Similarly, no partner has an **implied** authority to pledge security — express authority must be obtained.

Where securities have been deposited to cover future advances by a banker they extend only to advances made before any change in the firm.

A partner in a trading partnership can bind the firm by opening an account in the firm's name or by borrowing money for the purposes of its business.

If a partner pledges his separate property to secure future advances to his firm, an advance made after his death will not be chargeable against the property pledged.

A partner who is a minor will not be personally liable on an overdraft but he has power to bind the firm. Any action should be taken against the firm other than the minor. The partnership assets can be made available for the payment of the overdraft but there is no remedy against the separate estate of the minor partner.

DEATH OF A PARTNER

The partnership is dissolved and the surviving partners' duty is to wind up its affairs. They may continue the banking account for this purpose, but fresh mandates should be taken from **all** the surviving partners unless all sign.

The legal personal representatives of the deceased cannot claim to take part in the management of the firm.

An overdrawn account should be broken if it is necessary to prevent the operation of the rule in Clayton's Case for the estate of the deceased partner is liable only for debts incurred before his death. The surviving partners may operate a new account for winding up purposes and partnership property may be pledged to secure an overdraft incurred for this purpose — In *Re Bourne* (1906).

An equitable mortgage by the deposit of the title-deeds of certain real property belonging to the late partnership given by the surviving partners to the bank to secure an overdraft existing at the date of the equitable mortgage is entitled to priority over the lien of the executors of the dead partner.

If the surviving partners decide to take over the business and continue they constitute a fresh partnership and must give the banker new authorities, undertakings and security forms.

Some bankers, if there is no objection to it, continue to pay cheques signed by the deceased partner presented after his death; others insist on the confirmation of the surviving partners.

BANKRUPTCY OF A PARTNER

In the case of cheques drawn by a partner before his bankruptcy it is advisable to obtain the other partners' confirmation; in the case of cheques dated afterwards it is essential.

The account is dealt with as above; it is broken to prevent any reduction in the amount for which the banker may prove on the bankrupt's estate, assuming the partner to have undertaken to be jointly and **severally** liable.

MENTAL DISORDER OF A PARTNER

Although dissolution of the firm is not automatic, regard must be had to the Partnership Deed which may make mental disorder a ground for dissolution. An application may be made to the Court for dissolution, either by another partner or by a person acting for the mentally disordered partner. This is the most satisfactory course as it places matters on a legal footing.

If the account is in debit it is advisable to rule off whether or not an application is made for dissolution. If the account is in credit, fresh mandates should be obtained from the same partners.

RETIREMENT OF A PARTNER

Here again, if the remaining partners carry on, a new partnership is created and new forms must be signed. This is particularly essential if a new partner is introduced; unless the old debt is paid off, e.g. by the secured loan to the new firm, his agreement to the pledge of partnership assets to secure the old debt should be obtained.

BANKRUPTCY OF A PARTNERSHIP

This involves the bankruptcy of every partner in the firm and both its and their accounts must be stopped.

When the Court administers the estate of deceased partners and of bankrupt and insolvent partners, the partnership property is applied as joint estate in payment of the debts of the firm, and the separate property of each partner is applied as separate estate in payment of his separate debts. The surplus, if any, of the joint estate is applied in payment of the separate debts of the partners, or the surplus, if any, of the separate estates is applied in payment of the debts of the firm.

The whole firm may be made bankrupt or any one or more of the partners may be made bankrupt, but a Receiving Order against a firm operates as an order against each partner and adjudication is made against each partner by name and not against the firm.

Partners may not compete with the firm's creditors in an administration of the estate. For example, in the bankruptcy of a firm, the claim of the partner against the firm is postponed to the claims of the firm's creditors; and any claim of the firm against the partner is postponed to the claims of the partner's creditors.

If a partner has pledged his separate property to secure advances to his firm, the creditor may first prove on the joint estate and then realise the security on the separate estate, because to surrender the security would not augment the joint estate.

Bankruptcy of a partner dissolves the partnership and the bankrupt partner's estate is not liable for partnership debts contracted after the date of the bankruptcy and his authority to bind the firm ceases. He cannot, therefore operate the account of the firm, but the other partners may operate for partnership purposes. Hence, if one partner becomes bankrupt, the bank may continue to honour cheques of the firm, but if a cheque is presented drawn on the partnership account by the bankrupt partner, confirmation by the other partners should be required.

JOINT ACCOUNT CUSTOMERS

Joint accounts must be distinguished from partnership accounts since whereas a partner has certain implied powers to bind the firm, one party to a joint account has no implied power to bind the rest in any way.

At common law the liablity of joint-account holders is joint and therefore in the event of borrowing, either or both will be responsible for repayment but action against one party even if fruitless will preclude any action being taken against the other party.

OPENING THE ACCOUNT

The banker must obtain a mandate signed by **all** the parties stating how and by whom the account is to be worked, whether in debit or in credit. Express authority should be included to permit an overdraft at the request of the appointed signatory for unless such an authority is obtained **all** the parties will not even be jointly liable unless all sign cheques.

Joint and several liability should, however, be established if overdrafts are to be taken. Without this undertaking their liability is joint only and on the death of one party his estate ceases to be liable for any overdraft.

Similar considerations apply if authority is to be given to an outside party to sign on the account: all the parties to the account should join in the mandate. If, for instance, one party to the account was authorised by the original mandate to sign cheques, he would not thereby be authorised to delegate his authority to a third party.

Where there is an arrangement for either party to draw cheques on the account, a cheque drawn by one may be altered by another, and either can stop payment of a cheque whether signed by himself or the other.

DEATH OF ONE PARTY

Where the account is in credit the balance may be withdrawn by the survivors on the death of one party and the banker is not concerned with the claim of the deceased's representatives, who must be referred to the surviving parties. Similarly the banker is not concerned with determining the proportion of the joint balance which must be returned as part of the deceased's estate for duty purposes, although the Inland Revenue Authorities ask all bankers to remind the representatives of a deceased joint account party to mention the account in their returns.

On the death of one party, the banker will break the account, if it is in debit, to prevent the operation of the Rule in Clayton's Case, if he relies on the estate of the deceased for repayment and joint and several liability obtained. Even when the deceased has undertaken joint and several liability, his estate is liable only for debts contracted before his death.

Whether the account is in credit or overdrawn any cheques not signed by **all** the survivors would not be paid, but the general practice is to pay them if signed by the survivors, provided the account is in credit. If the account is overdrawn and the cheque is paid to the debit of a new account in the name of the survivors, they alone will be responsible for the overdraft thus created: the liability will be a **joint** liability of the signatories to the cheque until fresh mandates are obtained. If necessary they must deposit fresh security.

If the one who signed the cheques dies before they are presented, the cheques should be returned.

The balance of a joint deposit account can be set off against an overdraft on a joint current account of the same parties, but notice that a joint and several undertaking in the mandate gives the banker a right of set-off against private credit balances for an overdraft on the joint account. As all mandates are rescinded on the death of one party, fresh authorities must be taken from all the survivors if it is desired that less than all should act.

DEPOSIT OF JOINT ACCOUNT SECURITY

An authority for one party to pledge or charge securities on behalf of the joint parties does not permit him to give a charge **under seal. A delegation of authority to execute a document under seal must itself be under seal.**

SECURITIES HELD IN JOINT NAMES

In the event of the death of one party it is desirable to obtain a discharge from all survivors **and the legal personal representatives of the deceased** (unless the point has been specifically covered in the agreement). It will be seen that this differs from the procedure in paying over the balance of the account.

The reason is that the survivorship rule would not apply if the ownership of a sealed box, parcel or packet were "common" instead of joint: the bank would not be in a position to tell whether ownership were joint or "common".

BANKRUPTCY OF ONE PARTY

The mandate is cancelled, and the balance must be apportioned between the solvent party and the Trustee. The banker is not concerned in the apportionment but will require the discharge of the Trustee in Bankruptcy and of the solvent partners (note that this differs from the proceedings in dealing with Partnership Accounts). Even though in credit the account must be stopped.

If the account is overdrawn it should be stopped so that the banker may, if joint and several liability was undertaken, prove on the bankrupt's estate without prejudicing his rights against the other parties. If the liability is joint only, bankruptcy of one party will discharge his estate.

MENTAL DISORDER OF ONE PARTY

The account should be stopped pending instructions from the sane parties and the Receiver.

NOTICE OF DISPUTE BETWEEN PARTIES

Occasionally a banker will find himself in the position where the two (or sometimes more) parties to a joint account are in some sort of dispute. If both (or all if more than two) the parties to the account have to sign on the account, then the banker does not have the problem of deciding whether or not he needs to review the existing mandate, but where say the two parties to a joint account are clearly in dispute, then one of the parties (or maybe each of them separately) may try to draw out the full balance if either is authorised to sign alone. Since the majority of joint accounts are for husband and wife, such situations are often caused by family squabbles or more serious differences. The wise banker will ensure that he avoids being dragged into any arguments and, whenever faced with a situation where husband and wife (or other parties to joint accounts) are at loggerheads, he should advise them that he will no longer accept the instruction "either to sign" and that both must sign from that time on. Whilst not necessarily resolving the dispute between the parties themselves, this at best keeps the bank out of the arguments which could otherwise arise over access to the balance of the joint account, and the parties to the account will have to co-operate sufficiently with each other to sign jointly for any withdrawals from the account or accept that the funds in the account remain intact. Should any cheques be presented on one signature despite the bank having told the parties to the account that their previous "either to sign" instruction is now inoperative, the bank should (unless the party who has not signed will add his/her signature in confirmation) return the cheque unpaid. Care would need to be exercised as regards the answer on the cheque but "Cheque not drawn in accordance with mandate; further (or additional) signature required" would seem appropriate.

It will be appreciated that similar problems could arise between partners in a firm and, if in such a situation the bank's mandate is for any one partner to sign, the banker should in the bank's interest adopt the same line as with a joint account and insist on both (or all if more than two partners) signing in future. Clearly in the case of a partnership where there are several or a considerable number of parties, this may be impracticable and a sensible compromise would need to be reached but in practice the type of problem being discussed here is most likely to rear its head where two, or at the most a few, partners exist.

ACCOUNTS FOR MINORS

Any person under the age of 18 is an "infant" or "minor", the age of majority having been reduced from 21 to 18 by the Family Law Reform Act 1969. This statute used the term "minor" which perhaps sounds more appropriate when considering the operation of banking accounts for people who are not of full age.

There is no reason why a banker should not open and run an account for a minor and indeed banks are very keen to do this as a means of furthering their customer base, very much with an eye to the future. Basically, however, such accounts should remain in credit since under the Infants Relief Act 1874 "all contracts whether by specialty or by simple contract entered into by infants for the payment of money lent or to be lent . . . shall be absolutely void." Furthermore a minor cannot effectively give security.

In *Coutts & Co. v. Browne-Lecky and Others* (1947) it was held that the guarantor of a minor's overdraft cannot be made liable on the grounds that a guarantee presupposes that the debt to be secured can be legally enforced. This would apply also to other forms of security given by an adult third party for a minor's account, since the transaction would be treated as one of suretyship or guarantee and therefore of no use to the banker.

The forms of guarantee and other third party security documents used by banks recognise this legal point, and contain an "indemnity" clause whereby the guarantor or surety assumes primary liability which enables the bank to turn to them or resort to the security charged, should the minor default, notwithstanding the account-holder's own legal incapacity.

The case *R. Leslie Ltd. v. Sheill* (1914) confirms the danger to the banker where an advance is made to a minor as it was held that such money was not recoverable even where the minor had obtained the loan through fraudulently representing himself as being of full age.

Despite these factors, in practice a banker may well on occasions be perfectly happy to lend to a minor, perhaps for example where the banker knows the person to be trustworthy and reliable and capable of repaying the advance. In many instances, the banker will know the family of the minor customer which often will be of reassurance to the banker, although care still needs to be exercised since a situation could arise where an advance had been permitted to a minor, indirectly because of the family background, but where the parents turn out not to be in favour of the loan and therefore not prepared to assist in seeing the bank right. Indeed, the whole family relationship with the bank could possibly be soured by such circumstances. The banker could, if faced with a request for finance from a minor, consider having a discreet word with his parents if they are customers and/or well known to the banker and this often would provide a practical solution. Even so, caution is still required by the banker in view of his duty not to disclose — *Tournier v. National Provincial and Union Bank of England* (1924).

Despite his own limited legal capacity, a minor can act as an agent and, if so authorised can validly draw and sign cheques on the principal's account. If within the scope of his authority, the minor can overdraw his principal's account and the principal will be liable.

A minor may validly witness a signature although it needs to be remembered that the minor must be old enough to understand what he is doing if his testimony is to be reliable.

A minor can be appointed executor, but cannot act until he reaches full age; he cannot make a valid will (unless on active service) and cannot be appointed a trustee.

When operating a joint account, to which a minor is a party, the banker will need to remember that the minor will not be liable for any overdraft that may occur.

Whenever dealing with minors, the banker must bear in mind the minor's legal incapacity in several areas. Particularly, if operating a joint account or accepting instructions of any sort from a minor in the capacity of agent, the banker must ensure that his mandates and other documents are in order and clear cut, and even then should keep a close eye on transactions and what is going on generally.

THE CONSUMER CREDIT ACT 1974

The Consumer Credit Act of 1974 is based largely upon the recommendations of the Crowther Committee and replaces the older and somewhat fragmented legislation which previously governed the credit industry in this country. Whilst some provisions of the Act are already in operation, more regulations have yet to be introduced and as these emerge, the Act will have an increasing impact on banking procedures and operations.

The Act applies to England, Scotland, Wales and Northern Ireland, but not the Channel Islands or the Isle of Man.

The Act affects all businesses which grant credit facilities (principally up to £15,000) to individuals, sole traders, partnerships and other non-corporate borrowers.

The hire and rental of goods to individuals and non-corporate bodies can also be affected, and ancillary businesses such as credit and mortgage broking, debt collectors, debt counsellors and credit reference agencies will also be regulated by the Act.

The Act has no bearing upon the granting of credit facilities to limited companies and other corporate bodies. However, companies can be affected by the provisions of the Act in another way if they engage in any of the activities governed by the Act.

The main aim of the Act is to provide a system for controlling the whole range of consumer credit transactions by regulating the contractual rights and duties which exist between the respective parties — i.e. between lender and borrower.

This is to be achieved as follows:

(a) By requiring all businesses which provide credit, lend money, or hire out goods within the compass of the Act or engage in ancillary credit services to be licensed.
(b) By controlling the nature of advertising content for the provision of credit and by giving people the right to ask for quotations as to the true cost of credit, thus meaning they can "shop around" with some confidence.
(c) By prohibiting some forms of canvassing in order to curb some undesirable sales practices — e.g. often those associated with door-to-door salesmanship.
(d) By providing a deterrent against extortionate interest rates by affording means of redress through the courts.
(e) By prescribing the form and content of certain credit agreements and by stipulating that copy documents must be provided for the intending borrower. In some circumstances the Act also provides a "cooling-off" period before the borrower is bound by the agreement.

The following enlarges upon some of the areas involved:

THE LICENSING SYSTEM

Licenses are issued by the Office of Fair Trading. They are not issued automatically but only to those applicants who are able to meet the criteria set out in the Act. There is the standard licence (e.g. to a sole trader) and the group licence (e.g. to the Law Society).

A licence is normally valid for ten years and then has to be renewed. The Office of Fair Trading has the power to revoke, suspend or compulsorily vary a licence during its lifetime. Events may also occur which terminate a licence, e.g. the death, bankruptcy or mental illness of a person or the liquidation or receivership of a limited company.

It is a punishable offence for anyone to engage in the activities governed by the Act if not properly licensed. Obviously, a banker needs to bear this in mind if asked to lend to a customer engaged in business in the consumer hire and consumer credit industries and in such situations the banker should ask to see the covering licence.

The categories of licence are as follows:

Consumer Credit: those who provide individuals (i.e. any non-corporate entities) with credit for amounts up to £15,000 — e.g. by way of bank advance, credit cards, budget accounts, hire purchase, etc.

Consumer Hire: those who lease or rent goods for up to three months where payments do not exceed £15,000, e.g. renting TV sets.

Credit Brokerage: those who introduce individuals seeking credit or goods on hire to any of the following businesses:

(i) Businesses providing credit to individuals to £15,000.
(ii) Business providing goods on hire with payments amounting up to £15,000.
(iii) Businesses of other credit brokers.
(iv) A credit or hire business where agreements arising out of the introductions would be made under the law of a country outside the UK but would be governed by the Act if made in this country.
(v) Any business which provide individuals with credit (up to any amount) for the purchase of dwellings for their own occupation or the occupation of relatives.

Debt Adjusting and Counselling: this concerns those who give advice or negotiate for debtors whose debts fall within the £15,000 limit under the Act.

Debt Collecting: those who collect debts under £15,000.

Credit Reference Agencies: those who provide information about the financial standing of individuals (i.e. non-corporate entities).

CANVASSING

The Act makes it an offence to canvass business when not on trade premises. As far as banks are concerned the two categories of business affected by the canvassing prohibitions are:

(a) Certain of the ancillary services, e.g. credit brokerage, debt adjusting and debt counselling.
(b) Advances — i.e ordinary loans, personal loans and overdrafts of up to £15,000 and credit cards.

Bankers have given and continue to give considerable thought to these restrictions in order that they may continue to seek new business without infringing the Act and students should read up their own bank's guidelines on this topic.

The Act involves the regulation of agreements and will demand a clearly expressed contractual arrangement and in its provisions has regard to the manner in which the applicable terms shall be disclosed and documented. The banks have to ensure that their documentation falls into line with the requirements of the Act and the banks continue to work on this as further regulations are announced.

There are some agreements which are exempt and the two most important ones to a lending banker are certain advances for finance exports and certain advances where the total charge for credit does not exceed 13% or 1% over the Clearing Banks' average base rate whichever is the higher. Finance made available by building societies, local authorities, insurance companies, friendly societies and some other public bodies are also regarded as coming within the definition of an exempt agreement. This exemption, however, only applies where the monies are advanced for the purchase of dwellings or business premises, or alteration to these.

DEBTOR–CREDITOR–SUPPLIER

The Consumer Credit Act has introduced the possiblity of a lender having liability to a purchaser in the event of the purchased goods or services (for which the money was lent) being defective. From a banker's viewpoint, it must be noted that there must be an arrangement between the bank and a supplier (whether a customer or not) whereby the bank is prepared to consider providing finance to enable a prospective purchaser to buy goods and/or services from that supplier. The following conditions have to be met before an obligation of liability can arise:

(a) The cash price of item supplied must be more than £30 but not greater than £10,000.
(b) The advance must not exceed £15,000 and be to an individual, singly or jointly, a sole trader, partnership or other unincorporated body.
(c) The lender must be in the business of granting credit, e.g. a bank.
(d) The advance must be made under an arrangement between the bank (or other lender) and a supplier. This arrangement can be quite informal, e.g. bank advertising leaflets on the supplier's premises or the bank encouraging a supplier to send customers to its branches.

CHARGE FOR CREDIT

The Act has made some stringent requirements whereby the quoted total credit charge for a facility is all-embracing and whereby prospective borrowers have the right to be furnished with quotations from different lending bodies so that they can make comparisons and thus genuinely "shop around." Although many banks and other institutions involved in consumer finance, have had to set up systems to enable them to comply with the Act in respect of providing quotations (and the requirements laid down are complex and onerous) this aspect has not so far been in any real demand from consumers. Nevertheless, lenders have had to give themselves the capability of meeting the statutory requirements regarding quotations, and in practice this has meant increased use of computers due to the precision demanded by the requirements.

EXTORTIONATE CREDIT BARGAINS

Under the Act an individual, partner or other unincorporated body to whom a credit facility of any amount has been granted or who has provided security can apply to Court if the terms are considered to be extortionate. If the Court finds that the terms are extortionate it may reopen the transaction and relieve the borrower or provider of security to the extent to which the Court considers that they provided an excess of payment or security. These restrictions are not, of course, likely to be of any concern to the clearing banks.

REGULATIONS RELATING TO DOCUMENTATION

A considerable number of regulations were published in 1983 which came into operation in May 1985.

These regulations affect all lending of up to £15,000 except to corporate borrowers and compliance with these regulations will be very onerous to the banks. The requirements laid down in the regulations are mandatory and will entail the banks totally reorganising many advances, securities and debt recovery procedures. Additionally, banks will be required to produce automatically detailed financial information to borrowers.

The main requirements of the regulations involve the aspects given below:

1. The content and format of the following will be affected.
   (a) Loan agreements for credit facilities of up to £15,000 to individuals will need to be on standard forms. (These will be called "Regulated Agreements.")
   (b) Guarantees and Indemnities in relation to Regulated Agreements
   (c) Statements on what are referred to as "running accounts" (e.g. overdrafts, budget accounts)
   (d) Statements giving the amount required from the borrower to discharge his indebtedness
   (e) Credit Token Agreements (e.g. Barclaycard, Access, Automatic Telling Machine cards)
   (f) Notices which need to be served by a bank before taking action to terminate or enforce an agreement.

2. Provision of Copy Documents.
   It will be necessary to send to borrowers and sureties copy agreements and copies of security documents in accordance with stipulated timetables.

3. Cancellation or Withdrawal.
   Borrowers will in certain instances have rights either to withdraw before final agreement or to cancel soon after an agreement.

4. Information.
   Borrowers and Sureties will need to be sent specified financial information at certain times automatically, or within certain periods following a request.

5. Rebates when early settlement occurs.
   The regulations provide complex formulae for the calculation of minimum rebates on early repayment. Such rebates may apply even if an agreement is enforced by the court.

6. Upon the death of a borrower, the personal representatives will have similar rights to borrowers and provisions in agreements which seek to

make loans automatically repayable on the death of a borrower will be unenforceable.

7. Recovery Procedures.
   The regulations provide for special default or termination notices which must be sent before repayment can be enforced or an agreement ended.

8. In respect of joint accounts, what happens to one party must apply to the other, e.g. Statements must be individually addressed to each party to a joint account unless one party signs a formal notice dispensing with his when the credit is granted.

9. Penalties are introduced for non-compliance with the Act. These may involve criminal penalties for the lending institution and the individual concerned and revocation of a Consumer Credit licence where the Act has been wilfully disregarded. Additionally, an agreement and any security will be unenforceable except by the Court.

As a result of these new and complex regulations banks are having to reorganise their procedures fully to ensure that they will be able to meet the requirements. Furthermore, the need in several instances to provide detailed financial information is necessitating considerable changes to computer programmes.

The documentation procedures will be relative to the past very complicated, as will the procedures for taking security which will involve "consideration periods" and withdrawal rights. Quite clearly, the banks are faced with a difficult task in having to be able to meet these requirements as from May 1985 whilst at the same time trying to minimise the danger of the service they provide to customers being impaired.

ENFORCEMENT OF THE ACT

The Director General of Fair Trading is responsible for the working and enforcement of the provisions of the Consumer Credit Act with the assistance of prescribed enforcement authorities.

Chapter 4

Types of Accounts (cont.)

EXECUTORS AND ADMINISTRATORS

The personal representatives of a deceased person may be administrators or executors.

An *executor* is the person appointed in a will by the testator and to whom Probate is granted, whose duty it is to pay the testator's debts and distribute his assets according to the instructions in the will.

Probate is the official copy of a will with the certificate of it having been proved.

An *Administrator* is the person appointed by the court to administer the estate of the deceased when a person dies and leaves no will. On application he is granted "Letters of Administration", and distributes the estate in accordance with the law as to intestacy. Executors and Administrators are designated "legal personal representatives".

If the deceased person left a will but did not nominate an executor or if the persons nominated are dead or otherwise incapable of acting or decline to act, "Letters of Administration with the Will annexed" are granted and then the administrator must carry out the terms of the will just like an executor.

If Letters of Administration are taken out in the belief that no will exists, and a will is discovered after money or securities are withdrawn from the bank or property has been sold, the actions of the administrator are perfectly valid, for he has full powers until the Letters of Administration are revoked.

Where the will is held by a banker, he should only release it after evidence of death against the receipt or on the instructions of the executor(s) named therein, and if these are not known to him because the will is in a sealed envelope, he should open the envelope in the presence of the interested parties or their solicitor to ascertain who are the executor(s) whose receipt or instructions he may accept.

The title of an executor is not complete until he has proved the will; of an administrator until Letters of Administration are granted.

The banker is not safe, therefore, in permitting the personal representatives to deal with the assets of the deceased, until Probate (or Letters of Administration) has been produced, though a schedule of any securities he holds will be required to enable the application for Probate, etc. to be completed.

When asked to open an account for executors or administrators it is important that they are properly identified and introduced. Probate or letters of administration will not normally be available at that stage but obviously will need to be exhibited to the banker as soon as they have been obtained.

Executors and administrators have power to delegate their authority to one or more of their number but nevertheless in practice a banker should obtain a mandate signed by all the parties, setting out clear instructions for the operation of the account. The mandate will usually incorporate joint and several liability and the account will normally be designated on the following lines "X, Y and Z. Executors of A deceased."

When a deceased person was formerly conducting a business in his own name, practical difficulties may arise as until Probate is granted no one is legally qualified to act for the estate, and in any event personal representatives are primarily intended to wind up an estate not carry on a business. However, where a business needs to be carried on until it can be disposed of under the terms of the will, or otherwise if there was no will, the banker will need to adopt a common sense approach. Where executors or next of kin are known to the banker, he probably will permit them to operate an account for the business in their names until the position has been resolved. However, any borrowing granted would be taken in their own names and they have no power to bind the estate (except where perhaps authorised in the will).

An advance before Probate is often required by executors to enable them to pay Capital Transfer Tax. Executors have power to pledge specific assets of the estate before Probate but this pledge is only valid if probate is granted to them. Administrators on the other hand do not have any such power, the distinction being that executors derive their title from the will whilst administrators have no title until letters of administration are granted to them. As mentioned above, joint and several liability should be established and the executors should undertake to repay the advance out of the first monies received from the estate. The banker, when considering the request for the advance, should see a breakdown of the deceased's estate and will in particular be looking for sufficient assets of a liquid nature from which the advance can quickly be repaid once probate has been granted. The solicitor acting for the estate is usually asked to undertake to the bank to produce a grant of probate (or letters of administration) in favour of the parties involved.

Upon the death of an executor or administrator if another executor or administrator survives, then he will carry on, but when a sole or last surviving adminstrator dies, a new administrator is appointed. When a sole or last executor dies **his** executors carry on the duties of the executorship, but if such an executor dies intestate fresh letters of Administration are granted in respect of the original estate; as soon as intestacy supervenes the chain of succession is broken.

If the account is overdrawn, and reliance is placed on the joint and several covenant of the deceased personal representative the account should be broken to prevent the operation of the Rule in Clayton's Case.

If the account is in credit and the survivors wish to continue to delegate their power to less than their full number it is advisable to take fresh mandates.

An executor becomes a trustee when he completes the winding up of the estate and commences to deal with the income from the residue as directed by the will, and from this point he must conform with the rules governing Trusts.

Normally enquiries should be made when an executorship account has been continued for more than twelve months as to whether the executors are in fact acting in their capacity of trustees. The administration of an estate ought not to take longer than this period but there may be exceptional circumstances; e.g. difficulties in realising the estate.

TRUSTEES

When asked to open a trust account the banker should ask to see a copy of the instrument creating the trust (a will or a settlement) and from this he should note any details which affect the operation of the account.

Unless so authorised by the trust instrument or by Section 25 of the Trustee Act 1925, all trustees must sign cheques, receipts etc. Section 25 of the Act permits delegation but this section has been amended by Section 9 of the Powers of Attorney Act 1971 and a trustee can by power of attorney delegate for a period not exceeding twelve months the exercise of the powers and discretions vested in him. He cannot so delegate to his only co-trustee unless this is a trust corporation.

When asked to allow transactions based upon a delegation of authority, the banker must see the power and make a note of its terms.

If a banker makes an advance to trustees, the banker has no claim on the trust estate for unsecured loans — the liability is a personal one on the part of the trustees. He should, therefore, take a mandate by which the trustees undertake joint and several liability (otherwise they are jointly liable only) for any overdraft.

When trust securities are offered as cover for an advance on a joint trustee account the banker must satisfy himself that the borrowing and giving of the security are authorised by the terms of the trust. In this case, on the death of a trustee the account need not be broken unless there is a need to keep a lien on his estate. But, if the security is a Joint and Several Guarantee or similar personal security, the account must be broken at once if the banker wishes to preserve his lien on the deceased trustee's estate by avoiding the operation of the Rule in Clayton's Case to his detriment.

Secured advances should be made in conformity with the trust deed, but where no authority to borrow is expressed a trustee under a will may, if authorised to pay or apply capital money of the trust, raise the money by sale or mortgage of specific trust property, and the purchaser or mortgagee is not concerned to see that the money is wanted or that it is properly applied.

In the case of a private advance, if a charge is taken over trust property without actual or constructive notice that it is in fact trust property, and the bank obtains a **legal** title, that title will prevail over the equitable interests of the beneficiaries.

The bankruptcy of a trustee does not determine his right to act unless otherwise provided in the trust deed but an application may be made to the Court for the appointment of a new trustee.

In the event of the mental disorder of a trustee, further operations on the account should not be permitted by a trustee who is mentally incapacitated.

On the death of one of two or more trustees the survivors may continue to act, unless the Trust Deed requires the appointment of a new trustee. In this case the account must be stopped until the conditions of the Trust Deed have been fulfilled.

On the death of a sole trustee or a last surviving trustee his personal representatives may act as trustee pending the appointmcnt, either by these personal representatives or as directed in the Trust Deed, of a new trustee.

By S. 41 of the Trustee Act 1925, if it is found inexpedient, difficult or impracticable to appoint a new trustee or trustees without the assistance of the Court, then the Court has power to make such appointment, either in substitution for or in addition to any existing trustee(s) or where there is no existing trustee.

UNINCORPORATED BODIES

These comprise many different sorts of groups, but are associations of persons which exist to carry out a certain function, often relating to sporting, social or educational activities. They are neither companies nor firms but are merely groups organised and run by committees elected from their own memberships. Nevertheless, such organisations usually need a banking account and the account is in the name of the society and usually operated by the treasurer of the organisation together with one or more members of the committee. On opening an account of this nature, a banker should ask to see a copy of the rules which usually sets out the arrangements for the appointment, powers and duties of the organisation's officers. The mandate taken by the bank should be in accord with the rules.

Associations of this nature have no legal entity that is capable of being sued and therefore if borrowing is to be permitted the personal liability of one or more individuals should be obtained. If this is to be achieved by way of guarantee, then the guarantee document must contain an unambiguous *ultra vires* clause which makes it absolutely clear that the guarantors are to be responsible notwithstanding the legal desirability on the part of the association to contract. Otherwise the guarantors will not be liable on the grounds that the principal debtor has no legal power to borrow (*Coutts Bank v. Brown-Lecky* (1946)).

Friendly Societies are usually registered under the provisions of the Friendly Societies Acts 1896–1971. Where the Society is a registered one, the banker should obtain a Certificate of Registration. When asked to open an account a banker should obtain a copy of the rules and a mandate giving full particulars as to how and by whom the account is to be operated.

The Act permits Friendly Societies to borrow upon mortgage, executed by the Society's Trustees, of their real and leasehold estate, but power to mortgage must be contained in their rules. If, however, money has been borrowed and applied for the benefit of a Society, the debt cannot be repudiated for lack of formality in the security.

If asked to open and operate an account for an unregistered friendly society, the banker should treat this in the same way as the account of any other unincorporated club or society.

Trade Unions have statutory power to borrow upon mortgage of real or leasehold property but power to mortgage must be contained in the rules. The method of borrowing is by mortgage by the trustees. Every branch of a Trade Union is considered to be a distinct Union. It is advisable to take a certified copy resolution of the branch, and the rules should be a guide to any other procedure.

The Trade Unions and Labour Relations Act 1974 provides that a trade union is not a body corporate, but it is capable of making contracts and of suing and being sued in its own name.

INDUSTRIAL AND PROVIDENT SOCIETIES

These are bodies registered under the various Industrial and Provident Societies Acts and are corporate bodies whose members have limited liability. The best known class is that of Co-operative Societies.

They have statutory power to borrow but their rules must express the intention and state particulars of the security, amount of and method of borrowing. A mortgagee is not however bound to enquire after the authority for any mortgage by the society. A charge by such a society does not need to be registered under Section 95 of the Companies Act 1948 but debentures issued by a registered industrial and provident society must be registered as a Bill of Sale to be effective in respective of stock etc. This would not apply in the case of a floating charge over farming stock which would have to be registered under the Agricultural Credits Act 1928.

PAROCHIAL CHURCH COUNCILS

Accounts for these are frequently maintained at branch banks and under the Parochial Church Councils (Powers) Measure 1956 each Parochial Church Council is made a body corporate by the name of the parish for which it is appointed and has perpetual succession. The Measure does not apply to such portions of Wales as are subject to the Welsh Church Act 1914.

The activities of a Parochial Church Council include financial matters of the parish church and it is provided that the Council may appoint one or more of its members to act as treasurer(s) without remuneration; otherwise the church wardens, if members of the Council, should act jointly as treasurers. A bank opening an account for a Council should obtain a certified copy of the resolution of the Council appointing the treasurer(s) and stating how cheques will be signed. A Parochial Church Council can borrow for purposes within its province, but the Council's liability is limited to the extent of the funds placed at its disposal by the congregation. If security is offered, the written approval of the diocesan authorities should be obtained.

BUILDING SOCIETIES

Building societies are mostly incorporated and, if so, are governed by the Building Societies Act 1962 which replaced the earlier acts. There are a few unincorporated societies which are controlled by their own rules.

Incorporated societies have to submit their rules to the Registrar of Friendly Societies who will issue a certificate of incorporation. When opening an account, the banker should obtain a copy of the rules and inspect the certificate issued by the Registrar of Friendly Societies. A resolution of the directors of the society appointing the bank as bankers to the society should be obtained, incorporating a mandate covering the signing of cheques and delivery of securities etc. Specimen signatures will need to be provided.

Building societies may be permanent or terminating and borrowing powers vary as follows:

In the case of permanent societies the amount owing on loan or deposit must not exceed two thirds of amount for time being secured by mortgages from members excluding:

1. Mortgages on which payments are 12 months or more in arrears.
2. Mortgages in connection with which the Society has been in possession for 12 months.

Thus in calculating a society's borrowing capacity, deposits with the society need to be taken into account and these are likely to be a substantial amount in total.

With terminating societies the same rules apply or the society may borrow to a figure based on a year's subscription on its shares.

With unincorporated societies there is no statutory limitation or authority and powers to borrow and mortgage must be contained in the rules. It should be borne in mind that building societies by and large should not need to resort to bank borrowing due to the very nature of the organisations and therefore rarely will a banker be faced with a request for a facility from such a quarter. Nevertheless, the formalities for opening an account should be known and occasionally a smaller society may seek a facility sometime by way of a "standby" to cover a possible, temporary need say whilst awaiting maturity of one or more of its investments.

LOCAL AUTHORITIES

The Local Government Act 1972 which came into force in April 1974, made considerable changes in the pattern of local government and reorganised some 1300 old councils into 450 local authorities.

Banking accounts of local authorities must be in the name of the council (or in the name of the Treasurer with the added designation "Treasurer of ______ Council") and a resolution of the council must be obtained confirming that the Treasurer is authorised to maintain the account at the branch of the bank and giving details of how cheques will be signed.

The 1972 Act modifies the former law re borrowing and lending by reducing central control in view of the new situation. By S. 172 the powers of local authorities to borrow and lend money and with respect to their funds are set out in Part 1 of Schedule 13 to the Act, of which para. 1 provides:

(a) a principal council may borrow money for the purpose of lending money to another authority (including a police, river or harbour authority). N.B. a principal authority is defined in S. 270 as a council elected for a principal area, namely, a county, Greater London, a district or a London Borough;
(b) a local authority other than the Greater London Council may borrow money for any other purpose approved by the Secretary of State subject to any conditions given in the approval.

Para. 2(1) provides that where a local authority is authorised by or under this act or any other enactment to borrow money, they may raise the money by (a) mortgage; (b) issue of stock; (c) issue of debentures or annuity certificates under the Local Loans Act 1875; (d) bonds; (e) bills; (f) by an agreement entered into with the Public Works Loan Commissioners under S. 2 of the Public Works Loans Act 1965; or (g) by any other means approved by the Secretary of State, with the consent of the Treasury. Para. 2(2) allows the Secretary of State by regulations made with the consent of the Treasury to prescribe the form of the mortgage deed, regulate the issue of bonds etc.

However, loans for capital borrowing as set out above are usually taken up by the public rather than by a bank and it is really Para. 10(1) which is of interest to banks, as it provides:

A local authority may, without the approval of the Secretary of State under Para 1(b) (set out above), borrow by way of **temporary loan or overdraft from a bank** or otherwise any sums which they may temporarily require:

(a) for the purpose of defraying expenses (including the payment of sums due by them to meet the expenses of other authorities) pending the receipt of revenues receivable by them in respect of the period of account in which those expenses are chargeable;
(b) for the purpose of defraying, pending the raising of a loan which the authority have been authorised to raise, expenses intended to be defrayed by means of the loan.

Finally, Para. 20 provides: a person lending money to a local authority shall not be bound to inquire whether the borrowing or the money is legal or regular or whether the money raised was properly applied and shall not be prejudiced by any illegality or irregularity, or by the misapplication or non-application of any of that money. Nevertheless, a banker should exercise care since this protection does not apply should he become aware without enquiry of any irregularity: in such a case he must take notice, and cannot simply ignore it.

Para. 11 provides that all monies borrowed by a local authority whether before or after the coming into force of Schedule 13 shall be charged indifferently on all the revenues of the authority and all securities created by a local authority shall rank equally without any priority.

If security is felt to be necessary, this would usually take the form of a mortgage over the rates, but in practice most lending to local authorities, which is now mainly granted only on short term temporary bases, is unsecured.

SOLICITORS' ACCOUNTS

The accounts of solicitors are governed by the Solicitor's Act 1974 and the various Solicitors' Accounts Rules. These stipulate that a solicitor must place all monies he is holding on behalf of clients into current or deposit accounts in his name but with the designation "Clients a/c" added. A solicitor will usually need an office account or accounts for the day-to-day running of the practice.

A banker is not responsible for seeing that the rules imposed on the solicitor by statute are observed but he must not knowingly be a party to any breach of the rules. In practice, care is needed if a solicitor's office or other non-client's account is under pressure from the bank due to the overdraft level and a transfer in reduction is made from the client's account. In such a case, the banker should make enquiry in the hope of ensuring that no breach is taking place although the banker is very much in the hands of his customer and dependent upon his integrity.

A solicitor's clients account should not become overdrawn and if it does, particularly on a regular basis, the banker is almost certainly put on enquiry that irregularities are taking place.

A credit balance on a client's account cannot be set off against an overdrawn balance on office account, but a solicitor's private account credit balance may be set off against his office account.

Whilst bankers need to exercise care in the conduct of solicitors' accounts due to the stringent rules outlined above, bankers are increasingly having to give interest set-off or allowances of one sort or another in order to recognise the value of clients' accounts balances which are often relatively substantial. Connections with solicitors practices are regarded very highly by bankers, especially as a possible source of regular new business introductions which means that such banking connections are sought very competitively. However, whatever interest set-off allowances between the accounts may be agreed on commercial grounds, it is vital that a banker at all times takes care to ensure that he is not permitting a breach of the statutory requirements.

LIQUIDATORS AND RECEIVERS

A liquidator is appointed by the court (in a compulsory liquidation), or the creditors (in creditors' voluntary winding up), or by the members of the company (in a members' voluntary winding up). The duty and purpose of the liquidator is to collect in what is owed to the company, to realise assets of the company, and from the resultant proceeds, pay off the company's debts. Anything left after this would be distributed amongst the shareholders in proportion to their shareholdings.

When asked to open an account where it is a compulsory liquidation, the banker should ask to see the court order appointing the person liquidator, and also evidence of the sanction of the Department of Trade for him to conduct a banking account at a bank other than the Bank of England. In the other two types of liquidation, the liquidator can have an account at any bank he chooses. In the case of a creditors' voluntary winding up the banker should be furnished with a copy of the creditors' resolution and, in a members' voluntary winding up, a copy of the members' resolution.

The account should be designated with the name of the company, specifying whether the liquidation is compulsory or voluntary (and if voluntary, whether creditors' or members') and stating the name of the liquidator. In a compulsory liquidation, the liquidator must sign and cheques should be counter-signed by a member of the Committee of Inspection. In the absence of a Committee, the Official Receiver can countersign. If two liquidators are appointed both must sign. In a voluntary winding up the resolution may provide for one liquidator to sign alone.

In a compulsory liquidation, the liquidator may borrow against the assets of the company for the purposes of the liquidation, but for any other purpose the sanction of either the court or the Committee of Inspection is needed. The charge over the assets of the company given by a liquidator takes priority over all creditors, except those secured at the start of the winding up. In a voluntary winding up, the liquidator may borrow without seeking sanction, but a prudent banker may insist on the court's sanction (in a creditors' voluntary winding up) where substantial amounts are involved or where the liquidation seems likely to be complicated and protracted. Similarly, the approval of the company in general meeting should be sought in the case of a members' voluntary winding up. Note that a liquidator is not personally liable for sums borrowed unless he specifically agrees to this. In practice, liquidators do not usually have to borrow and therefore, bankers do not frequently find themselves confronted with requests for such lending.

A receiver of a company may be appointed in a number of ways, e.g. by the Court, by a mortgage if such power is contained in the mortgage deed, or, as is most common, by a debenture-holder. A receiver and manager is so called when his duties include the carrying-on of the business; where this is not so he is called a receiver. The appointment of a receiver has to be notified to the Registrar of Companies by the person making the appointment within seven days, and similarly notice needs to be given when a receiver ceases to act. The receiver will need a banking account to accommodate the receipts and payments arising out of the receivership, and in some cases the receiver may wish to borrow, particularly where acting as receiver and manager and continuing trading. On being asked to open an account for a receiver, the banker should ask to see a copy of the court order appointing the receiver (if so appointed) or a copy of the deed of appointment by the debenture holder. The receiver is the agent of the debenture holder who appoints him, unless the debenture provides that he is the agent of the company, which obviously makes the company responsible for his defaults, shortcomings and remuneration. When appointed by the court, the receiver is personally liable (since legally the court cannot be liable) but he is entitled to be indemnified out of the assets of the company in priority to the debenture holders and other mortgagees and creditors.

If appointed by the court, any borrowing by the receiver should be authorised by a court order. If appointed under a debenture, a receiver may borrow if the debenture included a power to carry on the business of the company. Section

473 of the Companies Act 1985 provides that a receiver and manager shall be personally liable on any contract entered into by him unless the contract provides otherwise, but he is entitled to be indemnified out of the assets. Sometimes, a receiver appointed by a bank under a debenture will ask for an indemnity from the bank which *inter alia* would indemnify him against personal liability for any bank borrowing he may undertake. Nowadays, however, most receivers do not seek such an indemnity, other than in those cases where for some reason there is nervousness about their appointment e.g. if the debenture was recently-taken or if, for some other reason, it was felt that the receiver was more vulnerable than usual to challenge.

Chapter 5

Cheques and Bills of Exchange: The Paying and Collecting Banker

INTRODUCTION

Whilst there are many facets of modern banking and the scope of activity of the clearing banks is nowadays very extensive, a fundamental and major function remains the payment and collection of cheques.

As paying banker, a banker pays cheques that are drawn upon him by his customers or by arrangement upon another branch by customers of that branch.

As collecting banker, he collects the proceeds of cheques drawn on other bankers and branches which have been paid in by customers for the credit of their accounts.

The paying banker is the banker who cancels the drawer's signature when the cheque is paid, either by the traditional method of initialling across the signature of the drawer or by doing whatever procedure the bank adopts which similarly represents the point of paying the cheque. In some cases, cheques are paid by stamping the cheques "Paid", usually with the date being included in the stamped crossing, or by perforating the payment date onto the cheque. Whatever, particular procedure is adopted, it is at that point that the active life of the cheque comes to an end.

As paying banker, the banker is under an obligation to his customer to honour the customer's cheque if it is legal and if presented by a holder in its original form within a reasonable time and before the banker has received an instruction to stop payment or received notice of the customer's death etc., and if sufficient funds stand to the credit of the customer and such a sum is at the disposal of the customer.

THE PAYING BANKER

The practical dangers that face the paying banker are that he pays a cheque:

1. That has been stopped or post dated;
2. That has been forged or has been altered fraudulently as regards amount or name of payee;
3. To a person who is not entitled to it, or for an unlawful purpose.

The following sections examine each of these dangers which face the paying banker.

COUNTERMAND OF PAYMENT

The drawer is the only person who can instruct a banker not to pay. However, if the payee gave notice to the banker that the cheque (which had been lost or stolen) had not been endorsed by him or had been endorsed specially and had subsequently been lost by him (not having reached the endorsee), the banker would not be paying in good faith for he would know that the cheque must bear a forged endorsement when presented. If possible he will obtain instructions from the drawer, but otherwise it may be thought best to return the cheque unpaid, marked with an answer which reflects the situation without placing the drawer's integrity in any doubt.

To be effective countermand of payment must actually come to the bank's notice and constructive countermand (e.g. that the bank is in a position to learn of it) is not enough: *Curtice v. London City and Midland Bank Ltd.* (1908).

It was held in *London Provincial and South Western Bank Ltd. v. Buszard* (1918) that for the purposes of countermand of payment, the branches of a bank are to be treated as separate parties, the "stop payment" being effective only at the branch to which it is sent so that notice of the "stop" given to one branch did not prevent another branch which was a holder for value of the cheque from recovering the amount of the cheque from the drawer. In *Burnett v. Westminster Bank Ltd.* (1965), a customer, who had accounts at two branches of the same bank, altered a cheque from one of the branch cheque books in ink to the name of the other branch and later instructed the latter branch to stop payment. As the computer could not read the ink alteration, the cheque was sent to the first branch where no action was taken on the alteration and the cheque was paid because they had received no countermand of payment instructions. It was held that, although there was a note inserted in the cover of the cheque book saying that the cheques in the book would be applied to the account for which they had been prepared, the cheque book cover was a document which the recipient could reasonably assume did not contain conditions varying existing contractual arrangements between themselves and the bank. The notice in the cheque books had been introduced by the bank when they became computerised whereas the customer had conducted an account at that bank long before then.

The decision in *Westminster Bank v. Hilton* (1926) shows that the drawer must furnish an **exact** description of the cheque, so that it can be easily identified.

A banker, in paying a "stopped" cheque, may be involved in a two-fold action:

1. For paying the stopped cheque.
2. For wrongful dishonour of other cheques which could have been paid had not the customer's balance been depleted by payment of the "stop".

The bank, having disobeyed his customer's mandate, will have to refund the amount for which the cheque was drawn to the customer and it was generally considered that the bank obtained no right of subrogation against the payee, but where the cheque had been issued in payment for goods the bank could minimise its loss by claiming those goods if they were identifiable. However the decision in *Barclays Bank Ltd. v. W.J. Simms Son & Cooke (Southern) Ltd.* (1979) improves the position of a bank in this situation. In this case the bank had paid a stopped cheque and the court held that moneys were recoverable where they had been paid under the influence of a mistake, provided there had been good consideration and that the payee had not changed his position in good faith as a result of the payment.

The customer's ability to stop payment of a cheque may be restricted by agreement with the bank; a good example of this being under the cheque guarantee card scheme, whereby the bank issuing the card undertakes that payment of the drawer's cheques will be made if certain conditions are observed and under this arrangement cheques so drawn cannot be stopped by the drawer. The conditions are (a) the cheque is signed in the presence of the payee, the signature corresponding with that on the card, (b) the payment is in respect of a single transaction within the UK or Northern Ireland not exceeding the limit (presently £50) (c) the cheque is drawn on one of the bank's cheque forms bearing the code number shown on the card and dated before the expiry date on the card and (d) the cheque has the card number written on the back by the payee.

If the banker suspects a cheque has not been issued and accepted in compliance with these cheque card rules, the cheque can be returned and in practice probably the banker would do this where the state of the drawer's account is such that the bank prefers not to see the cheque debited to it. Such a situation could arise where the cheque appears to have been sent in the post e.g. by being folded and the card number looks to have been written on it by the customer, or where more than one cheque made payable to the same payee are presented indicating that the total transaction exceeded the stipulated limited.

To avoid risk of losses through the payment of stopped cheques, banks should try to ensure that cheques are examined carefully against a record of stopped cheques before they are paid. When a customer instructs a bank to stop payment of a cheque, a careful search should be made to see that the cheque has not already been paid and then the details of the cheque can be entered on the stop lists. Most bank computer systems facilitate the stop payment instruction, based on the cheque number, being inputted so that if the cheque comes through it will be "flagged" by the computer. Care, however, is necessary on the bank counter to avoid the cheque being paid over the counter. Stop payment instructions may be given by telephone in the first instance, but written confirmation with a signature should follow this up. Should a cheque be presented before the confirmation arrives the answer should be "Confirmation of orders not to pay awaited". The answer on a stopped cheque should be "Order not to pay" or "Payment countermanded by order of drawer".

POST-DATED CHEQUES

Cheques are not invalid because they are post-dated but they may involve the paying banker in substantial loss. If a cheque is paid before the due date the risks are that:

1. The customer may countermand payment at any time before that date.
2. The customer may die or become bankrupt (or wound up if a company).
3. If a post-dated cheque is paid and the banker subsequently dishonours other cheques which could have been paid, he will be liable to the customer for damage to his credit.
4. There may be a garnishee order or summons made.

Although post-dated cheques are sometimes issued by perfectly creditworthy customers for practical reasons (e.g. to give them breathing space to ensure that goods supplied are satisfactory), the banker generally dislikes post-dated cheques. The practice of post-dating cheques is more often than not a sign of financial weakness as the drawer is usually buying time to provide the funds to meet the post-dated cheque. When a banker sees this practice being adopted he should be on guard and may well decide to inform the customer that the practice must stop if the customer wishes to continue banking with him.

FORGERY OF DRAWER'S SIGNATURE

The banker's authority to debit a customer's account is the customer's signature and without that the bank has no right to pay away the customer's money. However, in the case of a doubtful signature, if the banker refuses to pay and the signature is in fact genuine there may be a liability to the drawer for damages for breach of contract. In cases of doubt the banker does not have a duty to the presenter and payment may be delayed pending confirmation by the drawer. Care would be needed over the answer on the cheque which could suitably be "Confirmation of drawer's signature required".

Although a banker normally has no authority to debit his customer when the customer's signature has been forged, the customer may be estopped from denying the genuineness of the signature. In the case *Greenwood v. Martins Bank Ltd.* (1933) the House of Lords held that the plaintiff owed a duty of disclosure to the bank on his first discovering that his wife had forged cheques on his account and that as his conduct had, in the event, deprived the bank of their right of action against the forger (the wife having since died) he was estopped from asserting the forgery. A decision similarly favourable to the bank was reached in *Brown v. Westminster Bank Ltd.* (1964).

A banker is under a similar duty to the customer to report the non-payment of a cheque with a doubtful signature so that the customer may enquire into and protect himself against the circumstances of the forger. It may be that he has a dishonest employee and the mere fact that the cheque was returned to the presenter would not necessarily result in bringing the forger to the notice of the drawer.

As a precaution against forgery, the banker should take as many steps as practicable to prevent blank cheques falling into the wrong hands. Cheque books should not be issued to new customers until references have been obtained or until the bank's alternative procedures for opening new accounts have been carried out. Care should be exercised when handing out or sending cheque books to customers, the new cheque books being handed to the customer himself or to a known representative against a properly-signed order. Customers should be warned not to give out blank cheques and the bank should make a careful note of cheques which are reported lost or stolen. Any cheques which are in a different form to those supplied to the customer (e.g. cheques apparently borrowed from another party and amended, or in the form of the Stationers' Forms such as are supplied by clubs) should be treated with extra caution.

FACSIMILE SIGNATURES

Where the customer's signature is impressed on the cheque by some mechanical process it is obvious that the banker cannot know whether it was so placed under proper authority and therefore a suitable indemnity is required. The use of facsimile signature is generally only adopted by large corporate customers or local authorities etc. but the bank should always obtain an indemnity under resolution from the customer which clearly protects the bank against paying cheques "signed" by the facsimile machine and the customer should be made fully aware of the dangers inherent in issuing cheques on facsimile signatures.

FRAUDULENT ALTERATIONS

An alteration to the sum payable must be signed or initialled (preferably signed) by all the signatories who have signed the cheque. The fraudulent raising of the amount of a cheque is a material alteration (under Section 64 of the Bills of Exchange Act 1882) and the banker cannot normally debit the increase to the customer's account because there is no mandate. However, a decision in *Young v. Grote* (1827) was confirmed in *London Joint Stock Bank v. Macmillan and Arthur* (1918) which established the legal position as follows:

1. That the customer owes a duty to the banker to use reasonable care in drawing cheques so as not to facilitate addition or alteration.

2. If the customer does not use care and loss ensues, the customer and not the banker must stand the loss. The banker must not, however, be guilty of contributory negligence, e.g. if the alteration is obvious.
3. It does not matter whether it is by forgery or other crime that the loss occurs.
4. The banker is justified in declining to pay a cheque if there is reasonable ground for suspecting that it has been tampered with or if it is couched in an unusual or irregular form but his answer on the cheque should not be detrimental to the customer's credit.

Therefore the bank will bear the loss if the alteration is apparent or if it is non-apparent and the drawer used due care. The drawer will stand the loss if he fails to exercise proper care and the alteration is non-apparent.

In *Slingsby v. District Bank Ltd.* (1932) where further names were added after the payee's name, the court declined to rule that there was a duty on the drawer to leave no space after the payee's name as it was not a usual precaution to draw lines before or after the name of the payee.

PAYMENT TO THE WRONG PERSON

Money paid under a mistake of "fact" is a payment of money by one person to another under the mistaken impression either that a debt was due when actually no debt was due, or that the recipient was entitled to receive the money when this was not in truth the case. The mistake must be between the person paying and the person receiving and must relate to the actual transaction. Thus, if a banker pays a cheque and then immediately discovers that the drawer has insufficient finds to meet the cheque, the money is not recoverable for the mistake is between the bank and the customer rather than between the bank and the person receiving payment.

A person paying money by mistake may recover the money:

1. If the recipient did not act in good faith and was aware that he was not entitled to the money. It will be realised that the right against a person acting in bad faith is not of much practical value.
2. If the payer finds out the mistake before the position of the recipient may have been altered. But the money cannot be recovered:
   (a) Where payment is made on a negotiable instrument to an innocent person who has had the money in his possession for such a period that his financial position **might** be affected if he has to refund, e.g. by being deprived of the opportunity of giving notice of dishonour to prior parties, but it also includes the case where he might have spent it as his own money.
   (b) Where an agent has innocently received money and has paid it over to his principal or otherwise materially altered his position before he receives notice of the mistake.

Money remitted to a bank for credit of a customer must be refunded if it has been paid under mistake, unless the banker has altered the position as between his principal and himself, e.g., by paying cheques against the credit or advising the customer.

If a banker pays a forged or fraudulently raised cheque to an innocent holder, there is a mistake about the subject matter of the contract and the banker can recover the amount paid subject to the conditions mentioned above (i.e. before change of position, etc.). A banker will always be entitled to recover from a holder in "bad faith" but obviously whether he can do so in practice is an entirely different matter.

Even though a cheque may be drawn correctly in accordance with the mandate, the paying bank will be liable to its customer if it pays the cheque when it knows or ought to know that the cheque has been drawn for an unlawful purpose or that the party(ies) signing the cheque are misapplying the customer's funds. In *Selangor United Rubber Estates Ltd. v. Cradock (No 3)* (1968), a complex case involving the then relevant Section 54 of the Companies Act 1948, it was held that on the facts a reasonable paying banker should have realised that the payment out of the company's account was in respect of a share purchase transaction which was illegal under the Companies Act 1948 and so the bank was liable as constructive trustee to replace the money which had thus been misapplied. Additionally, the bank was liable to the company in contract for failure to exercise reasonable care and skill in paying the cheque in question without enquiring of the company's directions as to the purpose for which it was being applied.

A similar decision was made in *Karak Rubber Co. Ltd. v. Burden* (1972).

UNAUTHORISED AND FORGED ENDORSEMENTS

Under Section 59 of the Bills of Exchange Act 1882 a banker gets a good discharge if he pays a cheque "in due course". This means payment on or after maturity to the holder in good faith and without notice that his title is defective.

A person claiming under an unauthorised or forged payment is not the holder and the banker will not get a good discharge under Section 59 if he pays on a forged endorsement. He will be liable to the true owner for conversion.

Conversion is the wrongful interference with the goods of another for the purpose of taking them away from the person properly entitled to them. A person acting in good faith may still be guilty of conversion. In an action for conversion, the true owner, if successful, would be entitled in the case of a cheque or bill of exchange to its face value.

Bearing in mind that a banker has a duty to his customer to pay open cheques upon presentation and that the payee and thus the endorsement may well be unknown to the banker. Section 59 does not afford adequate protection but Section 60 recognises the difficulty.

Section 60 protects a paying banker should the endorsement on an order cheque be forged, as long as he pays it in good faith and in the ordinary course of business, and the endorsement purports to be in order.

It should be borne in mind that the case of forged endorsements the protection under Section 60:

- Extends only to **cheques** (unconditional: drawn on a banker, not applicable to bankers' drafts).
- Applies only to the banker on whom the cheque is drawn.
- Applies only to **paying** and not to collecting or exchanging cheques on other bankers.

In order to obtain the protection of Section 60 the banker must pay:

- In good faith (honestly).
- In the ordinary course of business.

A banker does not pay in the ordinary course of business if he pays before or after business hours. However, in *Baines v. National Provincial Bank Ltd.* (1927) it was held that a bank is entitled to a reasonable margin after its advertised closing time to deal with customers who are already on the premises. In addition to the protection of Section 60 being lost, there is always the possibility that the customer may countermand payment.

If a banker pays a crossed cheque contrary to the crossing he is again not paying in the ordinary course of business.

In relation to cheques paid under credit-opened arrangements, if the bank concerned is a branch of the account-holding bank, then the bank is protected by Section 60 since payment by a branch is payment by the bank rather than by the branch on which the cheque happens to be drawn. Where different banks are concerned, the bank at which the credit-open is arranged is not protected by Section 60 but would be a holder for value if the endorsement is valid. If the endorsement is forged and the paying bank has not been negligent, then the bank establishing the credit would be expected to indemnify against any loss sustained. In any event, a relationship of agency will exist and the principal will therefore be liable for the tort of the agent.

The banker–customer relationship does not impose a duty on a banker to pay his customer's acceptances and basically a customer has no automatic right to accept bills payable at his bankers. Section 60 does not apply to bills unless "drawn on a banker on demand" and since bills are not drawn on a banker, if the endorsement is forged the banker paying the domiciled bill gets no protection.

Section 80 protects a paying banker who pays a crossed cheque in good faith, without negligence and to a banker in accordance with the crossing. If he has met these conditions, the paying banker is placed in the same position as if payment had been made to the true owner.

Therefore both Section 60 and Section 80 afford protection to the paying banker, Section 60 applying to all cheques, whether opened or crossed. Since the conditions of protection are not exactly the same, it is possible that circumstances could arise where it would be better to seek protection under Section 80 but since actions for conversion are usually brought against the collecting rather than paying banker, it is not often that Section 80 rears its head.

The Cheques Act 1957 was passed largely to dispense with the need for the endorsing of cheques and generally to tidy up the statutory position regarding several aspects of the payment and collection of cheques. As regards the paying banker, the Act does not abolish endorsement but gives protection to bankers paying unendorsed cheques or irregularly endorsed cheques, so that the paying banker need not concern himself with endorsements (nor need the collecting banker, unless the cheque or analogous instrument (whether crossed or open) is negotiated, when endorsement will still be required).

As the Act introduced a completely new system relative to endorsement the Committee of London Clearing Bankers formulated certain practice rules for their own protection, which in effect have voluntarily cut down the widespread protection of the Act. Thus, banks continue to require the endorsement of cheques and analogous instruments cashed at the counter. Again, if the payee's name is mis-spelt or he is incorrectly designated, the cheque or analogous instrument may be accepted for collection without endorsement or discharge unless there are circumstances to suggest that the customer is not the person to whom payment is intended to be made.

1. Where a banker in good faith and in the ordinary course of business pays a cheque drawn on him which is not endorsed or is irregularly endorsed, he does not, in doing so, incur any liability by reason only of the absence of or irregularity in, endorsement and he is deemed to have paid it in due course. Where a banker in good faith and in the ordinary course of business pays any such instrument as the following, namely:
   (a) a document issued by a customer of his which, though not a bill of exchange, is intended to enable a person to obtain payment from him of the sum mentioned in the document;
   (b) a draft payable on demand drawn by him upon himself whether payable at the head office or some other office of his bank;

   he does not, in doing so, incur any liability by reason only of the absence of, or irregularity in, endorsement, and the payment discharges the instrument.
2. A banker who gives value for, or has a lien on, a cheque payable to order which the holder delivers to him for collection without endorsing it, has such (if any) rights as he would have had if, upon delivery, the holder had endorsed it in blank.
3. An unendorsed cheque which appears to have been paid by the banker on whom it is drawn is evidence of the receipt by the payee of the sum payable by the cheque.

Although the Cheques Act 1957 brought about fundamental changes in such of the practices followed by banks for many years, it did not take the opportunity of consolidating all the relevant law and therefore protection for the paying banker still has to be sought in Sections 60 and 80 of the Bills of Exchange Act in conjunction with the Cheques Act. In addition to this, Section 19 of the Stamp Act 1853 is still relevant in the case of endorsements on bankers' drafts.

THE COLLECTING BANKER

In collecting cheques for a customer, a banker may similarly be liable to a charge of conversion brought by the true owner. Although the collecting banker can claim to be indemnified by his customer, and can debit the customer's account with the amount the banker has had to pay to the true owner, as it is usually in practice the customer who is the fraudulent party this right to be indemnified may be of no practical use.

In the context of a collecting banker's protection, the Cheques Act 1957 repealed certain sections of some earlier statutes, replacing these by Sections 4 and 5 of the Cheques Act which provide as follows:

- 4.—(1) Where a banker, in good faith and without negligence:
  - (a) receives payment for a customer of an instrument to which this section applies; or
  - (b) having credited a customer's account with the amount of such an instrument, receives payment thereof for himself; and the customer has no title or a defective title, to the instrument, the banker does not incur any liability to the true owner of the instrument by reason only of having received payment thereof.

  (2) This section applies to the following instruments, namely;
  - (a) cheques;
  - (b) any document issued by a customer of a banker which, though not a bill of exchange, is intended to enable a person to obtain payment from that banker of the sum mentioned in the document;
  - (c) any document issued by a public officer which is intended to enable a person to obtain payment from the Paymaster General or the Queen's and Lord Treasurer's Remembrancer of the sum mentioned in the document but is not a bill of exchange;
  - (d) any draft payable on demand drawn by a banker upon himself whether payable at the head office or some other office of his bank.

  (3) A banker is not to be treated for the purposes of this section as having been negligent by reason only of his failure to concern himself with absence of, or irregularity in, indorsement of an instrument.
- 5.—The provisions of the Bills of Exchange Act 1882, relating to crossed cheques shall, so far as applicable, have effect in relation to

instruments (other than cheques) to which the last foregoing section applies as they have effect in relation to cheques.

Section 4 is of great importance to bankers and therefore needs further examination and explanation. It must be understood that the Section does not suggest that the bank is not guilty of conversion but that it shall not be so liable if the stated conditions have been met. In this way, Section 4 is therefore a defence open to the bank.

The "good faith" (which basically means the "honesty") of the bank is unlikely to be questioned and decisions that have gone against collecting bankers have been founded mainly on negligence.

Negligence is not defined by the Cheques Act but negligence means disregard of the duty to act with reasonable care in the interest of the true owner, and the customer is not always the true owner.

It has been laid down that "the test of negligence is whether the transaction of paying in a given cheque, coupled with the circumstances antecedent and present, were so out of the ordinary course that it ought to have aroused doubts in that banker's mind and caused him to make enquiry". In other words, having regard to all the circumstances has the collecting banker (on whom the onus of proving absence of negligence lies) fallen short of the standard of care required by the practice of bankers?

The enquiry must be made with such care as to elicit a satisfactory explanation. In *Motor Traders Guarantee Corporation Ltd. v. Midland Bank Ltd.* (1937) the explanation given satisfied the bank cashier, but nevertheless it was held that the bank had been negligent. The customer's account with the bank had been unsatisfactory for some time and because of this, and because of a Midland Bank regulation which required such matters to be referred to the manager, it was held that had this been done, the manager would not have been satisfied and therefore would have initiated further enquiry.

The following have been held to constitute negligence:

(a) Failure to take up references when opening an account: *Ladbroke v. Todd* (1914) or to ensure that they are genuine: *Guardians of St. John's Hampstead v. Barclays Bank Ltd.* (1923).
(b) Collecting a cheque crossed "Account Payee" for a person other than the specified payee — even if payable to a specified payee "or bearer": *House Property Company of London v. London County & Westminster Bank* (1915).
(c) Collecting, without enquiry, for the private account of an official of a company a cheque payable to the company and endorsed by that official. This was held to be negligence in the case of *Underwood v. Bank of Liverpool* (1924) even though the official was the **sole** director of a "one man company".
(d) Similarly, collecting a cheque payable to a firm for the private account of one partner without making enquiry.

(e) Collecting for his private account cheques payable to an official (e.g., Collector of Rates) in his official capacity, without special authority; similarly, collecting for the private account of an agent a warrant payable to him in his capacity of agent, viz. "D. McGraw for Marquess of Bute": *Bute v. Barclays Bank Ltd.* (1954).

(f) Collecting **without enquiry** cheques drawn by a company or firm in favour of **third parties** and paid in for the credit of an employee of the drawer or for credit of the wife of such an employee. (*Lloyds Bank Ltd. v. E.B. Savory & Co.* (1932)).
In the Savory Case, cheques payable to bearer drawn by a firm were collected without enquiry, some for an employee of the firm, some for an employee's wife. The cheques were paid in at one branch for credit of an account at another branch, which latter branch was ignorant of the connection between their customer and the drawer of the cheques. It was held that this was negligence and that knowledge of the customer's standing is knowledge by the **bank**, not by any particular branch.

(g) Collecting **without enquiry** a cheque for the personal account of an agent, the cheque being payable to such agent and drawn **by him** on behalf of his principal: *Midland Bank Ltd. v. Reckitt* (1933).

(h) Collecting **without enquiry** a cheque in favour of one company or partnership for the account of another: *London & Montrose Shipbuilding Company v. Barclays Bank Ltd.* (1926).

(i) Collecting **without enquiry** cheques payable to the **collecting bank** for the account of an employee of the drawer: *Lloyds Bank Ltd. v. Chartered Bank of India, Australia & China* (1929).

It is clear that the absence of enquiry has been a frequent reason why the collecting bankers have failed to demonstrate that they acted without negligence. Any unusual operations on an account may be coupled with other circumstances to the collecting banker's detriment. In other words the Court is quite likely to say that the circumstances in which the cheque was collected coupled with the knowledge that the bank had of the customer's affairs should have alerted the banker and caused him to make enquiry.

However, despite the Savory Case mentioned above, the court did recognise that it cannot be a bank's legal duty continually to update itself as to the identity of the employers of all its customers in *Orbit Mining and Trading Co. Ltd. v. Westminster Bank Ltd.* (1963). In this case W and E directors of the plaintiff company, were jointly authorised to sign cheques on its behalf, and W left some blank cheques signed by him with E who completed them to "Cash or order", countersigned them with his own illegible signature, similarly endorsed them and paid them into his private account with the defendant bank, which did not know of E's connection with the plaintiff company. The Court of Appeal took the view that as E's signature was illegible and indorsement was not needed, there was nothing to connect the one signature with the other which required scrutiny by the cashier, and so the claim failed.

In the following cases banks were held not liable, due to having made suitable enquiries and having obtained satisfactory replies:

Smith & Baldwin v. Barclays Bank Ltd. (1944). *Penmount Estates Ltd. v. National Provincial Bank Ltd.* (1945). *Slingsby v. Westminster Bank Ltd.* (1930).

In *Marfani & Co. Ltd. v. Midland Bank Ltd.* (1968), the plaintiff company's office manager, K, prepared a cheque for £3,000 payable to one, Eliaszade, had it duly signed and then opened an account with it at a branch of the defendant bank by posing as E and giving as a reference a man who knew him by that false name. In due course he withdrew the proceeds and left for Pakistan. The Court of Appeal decided that the bank had not been negligent and so was protected by S. 4 of the Cheques Act 1957, holding in particular that the facts did not amount to negligence:

(a) That the bank had acted on only the one reference.
(b) That the bank had not asked for identification by production of a document (e.g. a passport) or had not enquired as to K's employment in view of the reference concerning him.
(c) That the cheque had been cleared before the reference was received.

The Savory decision was criticised in the Marfani case where the judge stated "There were many other matters calculated to arouse suspicions in the social conditions of the 1920s. It was decided upon expert evidence, not of what is now current banking practice, but of what it was nearly 40 years ago. I find it no more than an illustration of the general principle that a banker must exercise reasonable care in all the circumstances of the case." The Marfani decision does not of course remove all the dangers that confront the careless banker, but at least it does recognise that negligence should, to some extent at least, be measured by present-day standards. Nevertheless, the judge did remark that the decision should not encourage any relaxation of the rules that banks had made as a result of earlier adverse decisions.

As stated earlier, Section 4 applies only when the banker receives payment for a customer or having credited the customer's account when the items were paid in, receives payment for himself. A "customer" is not defined by the Cheques Act but this topic was discussed in Chapter 1. It should be noted that the subterfuge of opening an account in the name of "Sundry Customers" for isolated or even a series of collections will not protect the collecting banker.

If the banker **buys** a cheque he collects it for himself, and has no statutory protection, although he becomes, of course, a holder in due course if there is no question of forgery or if there are no other circumstances impairing the negotiability of the cheque (e.g. notice of previous dishonour) and if the cheque is not crossed "not negotiable".

A holder in due course may sue in his own name and holds the cheque free from any defect of title of prior parties and may enforce payment against all parties liable on the cheque. To prove himself a holder in due course the banker must have taken the cheque, complete and regular on the face of it, in good faith, for value and without notice of any defect in the title.

A banker gives value (and so may claim to be a holder in due course):

(a) By paying cheques against uncleared items as a regular practice.
(b) By definite authority to his customer to draw against uncleared items.
(c) By actual purchase for cash of a cheque from a customer or any other holder, i.e. exchange in the accepted sense of the term.
(d) By taking a cheque in specific **reduction** of an overdraft (i.e. payment or part-payment of the debt due to him and not merely a credit in the ordinary course of business).
(e) Where the banker has a lien on the cheque he is a holder for value to the extent of the sum for which he has a lien.

Note that it may be advantageous to a bank to claim to be a "holder in due course" rather than to rely on S. 4 if there is any doubt as to whether the bank has been negligent. This point is illustrated by *Lloyds Bank Ltd. v. Hornby* (1933) where a new account was opened with a cheque for £250 against which the customer was allowed to draw before clearance. The drawer countermanded payment and the bank **as holder in due course** sued him in respect of the amount so advanced. The endorsement was not forged but the drawer endeavoured to bring in S. 82 (then in force) alleging that the bank was negligent in opening the account without a proper introduction. It was held that as the bank was a holder for value S. 82 had nothing to do with the case (to the extent that the bank had given value it was collecting for itself). Even had the bank acted negligently (although in fact it was found that there had been no negligence) the bank would still have succeeded provided the negligence was not tantamount to bad faith for it is not a condition of a holder in due course that he shall act without negligence.

It should be remembered that the payee of a cheque is not a holder in due course since the original delivery to the payee is not "negotiation" — *R.E. Jones Ltd. v. Waring & Gillow Ltd.* (1926).

When exchanging cheques, the banker collects for himself not for a customer and is therefore not protected by Section 4. Additionally, the bank obtains no protection if the cheque is tainted with forgery. Payment can however, be enforced against all parties if the bank is a holder in due course. If the cheque is crossed "Not Negotiable" the title of the bank will be defeated even if the endorsements are genuine. A bank, when exchanging a cheque, is not protected by Section 60 (because it is not the "paying banker") unless the cheque is paid under arrangement with the drawee branch of the bank.

Where a banker acts both as collecting and as paying banker in respect of a crossed cheque then to avoid liability he must be able successfully to claim the protection of both S. 60 (or 80) of the Act of 1882 or Section 1 of the Cheques Act 1957, and also S. 4 of the Act of 1957. This was the decision in *Carpenter's Company v. The British Mutual Banking Company* (1937), in which the banker was held to have been negligent in collecting (S. 82 was then in force), but nevertheless to have paid "in the ordinary course of business" within the meaning of S. 60.

As S. 4 also gives protection to a banker collecting open cheques, it would appear that a similar position now obtains as regards open cheques.

There is no statutory protection for a banker collecting or paying **bills** as distinct from cheques, but protection is extended to certain instruments analogous to cheques.

1. *Conditional Orders to Pay*
A conditional order is a document drawn on a banker by a customer ordering payment on demand of a sum of money to a third party subject to an attached receipt being signed and stamped by the payee (the condition must be addressed to the drawee and NOT to the payee). It is not a cheque or a bill and is not a negotiable instrument. The paying banker is not protected by Section 60 of the Bills of Exchange Act 1882, but in the case of crossed orders he is protected by Section 80 because Section 5 of the Cheques Act 1957 extends to these orders the "crossed cheques" Sections of the Act of 1882 so far as applicable. These orders also come within Section 4 of the Cheques Act 1957, so that the collecting banker has the same protection as in the case of cheques.

2. *Bankers' Drafts*
Drafts drawn by one bank on another are cheques and may be treated as such, but drafts drawn by one **office** or **branch** of a bank on another **branch** are not cheques, since they are not covered by the definition of a bill in Section 3 of the Act of 1882.

The banker paying an uncrossed draft has, therefore, no protection from Section 60 but he **is** protected by Section 19 of the Stamp Act 1853, which applies to "any draft or order drawn upon a banker payable to order on demand". This Section does not apply to Conditional orders, dealt with above, since they are not payable to order. He is also protected in the case of any drafts by Section 1 of the Cheques Act 1957 and in the case of crossed drafts by Section 80 of the Bills of Exchange Act 1882, because Section 5 of the Act 1957 extends to these drafts the "crossed cheques" Sections of the Act of 1882 so far as applicable. These drafts also come within Section 4 of the Cheques Act 1957, so that the collecting banker has the same protection as in the case of cheques.

If a banker refuses payment of a draft to a bona fide holder for value he becomes liable as **drawer** of a bill or possibly as maker of a promissory note (Bills of Exchange Act 1882, Section 5, ii). For this reason he cannot stop payment of a draft at the request of a person who has lost it, but if it were lost unendorsed he would not have any statutory protection if he paid knowing that the endorsement must be forged.

3. *Dividend Warrants*
A dividend warrant is an order by a company on its banker for payment of dividend due on stocks or shares of the company.

Section 95 of the Act of 1882, and also Section 5 of the Cheques Act 1957, extend the "crossed cheques" Sections of the Act of 1882 to dividend warrants although these are usually in the form of a cheque or a conditional order and may then be treated accordingly.

As regards dividend warrants which do not come within the category of cheques or conditional orders, the paying banker is protected by Section 19 of the Stamp Act 1853 and by Section 1 of the Cheques Act 1957, and in the case of crossed warrants by Section 80 of the Act of 1882. These warrants also come within Section 4 of the Cheques Act 1957, so that the collecting banker has the same protection as in the case of cheques.

It is somewhat doubtful as to whether or not **interest** warrants are covered by Section 95 — the case of *Slingsby v. Westminster Bank Ltd.* (1930) seems to indicate that they are. In any event, they now come within the provisions of the Cheques Act 1957, discussed above.

CROSSED CHEQUES

It has been seen that whether a cheque is crossed or not is of great importance to the paying banker and the following covers what is meant by a crossed cheque.

Crossing a cheque means writing across its face an addition of

(a) The words "and Company" or any abbreviation thereof between two parallel transverse lines, either with or without the words "Not Negotiable".
(b) Two parallel transverse lines simply, either with or without the words "Not Negotiable".
(c) The name of a banker, either with or without the words "Not Negotiable" (Section 76 of the Bills of Exchange Act 1882).

The first two are **general crossings**; the third is a **special crossing**.

Note by whom cheques may be crossed:

(a) The drawer may cross a cheque either generally or specially when he issues it.
(b) If uncrossed the holder may cross it generally or specially, or change a general into a special crossing.
(c) If uncrossed or crossed generally, a banker may cross it specially to himself.
(d) If crossed specially, the banker may cross it again specially to another banker for collection. (Section 77).

Crossings do not apply to bills other than cheques but under the Cheques Act 1957 they apply to certain analogous instruments (as mentioned earlier in the chapter).

Postal Orders and Money Orders may be crossed but this is governed by Post

Office regulations contained in statutory instruments and not by the Bills of Exchange Act.

The object of crossing a cheque is to prevent its being presented by a person for whom it is not intended. Though crossings do not absolutely prevent this they make it more difficult for a thief to cash cheques, for crossed cheques must be paid to a banker. Further, crossings provide protection to the paying banker, and to the drawer if the cheque has reached the payee. (S. 80 of the Bills of Exchange Act 1882).

Alterations and Additions to crossings may be made as follows:

Alterations
(a) A holder may change a general crossing into a special crossing.
(b) If crossed generally a banker may cross it specially to himself.

Additions
(a) A holder may add the words "Not Negotiable" to either a general or a special crossing;
(b) If crossed specially, a banker may cross it again specially to another banker for collection;
(c) It is not lawful for any person to obliterate or, except as authorised by the Act, to add to or alter the crossing.

It will be noticed that such additional words as "Account Payee" are not authorised by the Act.

"Not Negotiable" Crossings

It was decided in *Hibernian Bank v. Gysin and Hanson* (1938) that when these words appear on a **bill** other than a cheque they have not the special meaning given to them by S. 81, but restrict the **transferability** of the bill — they are words "prohibiting transfer or indicating an intention that the bill should not be transferable": S. 8(i).

These words **as part of the crossing of a cheque**, however, prevent the person who takes it from having or being able to give a better title to it than that of the person from whom he took it (S. 81).

It must be understood that the words do not prevent a transfer of the cheque. If the person who transfers it has a good title, the transferee will have a good title and the cheque may continue to change hands. If a crossed cheque marked "not negotiable" has passed from hand to hand and there is no defect of title, the holder can recover the amount of the cheque and, if the banker refuses to pay the cheque, the holder can sue the drawer.

If crossed "not negotiable" and there is a defect of title the real holder for value can claim the amount from the last holder who innocently receives payment of it through his bank. The last holder must recover from his immediate transferor.

In *Wilson & Meeson v. Pickering* (1946) it was held that a "not negotiable" crossing affected the title of a **payee**, although a cheque is **issued** and not negotiated to the payee. The words "not negotiable" printed on Postal Orders have no effect on the order. A postal order is not negotiable in its origin, and the words upon it merely point out a fact that already exists.

"Account Payee only" Crossings

These crossings are not mentioned in either the Bills of Exchange Act or the Cheques Act and thus have no statutory significance. They are not binding on the paying banker and do not affect the transferability or the negotiability of the cheque—*National Bank Ltd. v. Silke* (1891). Nevertheless, the use of "A/C Payee only" crossings is quite common and care is called for on the part of the collecting banker. In *Bevan v. National Bank Ltd.* (1906) it was said that to collect an "A/C Payee" cheque for a person other than the specified payee would be negligence (although on the facts of that particular case the bank was held not negligent). In the later case *House Property Company of London v. London County & Westminster Bank Ltd.* (1915) the bank was held liable. The Court of Appeal in *Importers Co. v. Westminster Bank Ltd.* (1927) held that it was not negligence for an English bank to collect "A/C Payee" cheques for a foreign bank which was its customer, where the "A/C Payee" crossings referred to the foreign bank's customers.

"A/C Payee only" was held to be the same as A/C Payee" in *Universal Guarantee Pty. Ltd. v. National Bank of Australasia Ltd.* (1965). However, it is argued that an "A/C Payee" cheque payable to one party to a joint account could safely be credited to the joint account, whereas a similar cheque but crossed "A/C Payee only" could not.

In practice bankers often collect cheques so crossed for their customers, although payable to persons other than their customers, where the customers are reputable and would be in a position to indemnify the collecting bank in an action for conversion.

BILL DISCOUNTING

Financing trade by way of bills of exchange has lost a lot of its former popularity except for overseas business where bills of exchange remain quite common. Nevertheless trade bills are still sometimes presented to branch bankers by customers with a request that they should be discounted.

When a banker discounts a bill, he does not make an advance but in effect buys the bill from the customer at an agreed price. The latter would normally be the face value less the discount (i.e. the equivalent of interest) calculated for the period up to maturity date.

The net amount of the bill will be credited to the customer's account immediately (i.e. face value less discount and (if any) commission) and the bank will have no right to retain any of the customer's current or other credit balances as cover for the contingent liability on the bill, except by special arrangement or in the event of the customer's bankruptcy.

The face amount of the bill should be debited to a Bills Discounted Account (this will represent an asset of the bank). Compared with an advance to a customer the granting of discount facilities has the advantages of a definite date for repayment and additionally safety by way of recourse to all parties to the bill as well as to the customer.

The following practical issues must be borne in mind when asked by a customer to discount bills:

1. Ensure that the bills covered are genuine trade bills resultant upon an actual transaction and not merely accommodation bills for the provision of temporary assistance or fixed capital.

   The relationship of the parties to the bill afford some guide.

   It is normal banking practice to discount only short-term bills, i.e. with not more than six months to run.

2. The financial position of the customer, of the drawer and of the acceptor and endorsees must be taken into consideration.

   In this respect, the customer who is asking for the bills to be discounted should be looked into from a credit risk point of view in the same way as the customer would if asking for an advance. At the end of the day the customer's account will be debited in the event of dishonour and the banker must therefore be satisfied that the customer's credit is good for the amount in question, e.g. a series of balance sheets should be seen and the question of security may need to be considered.

   Enquiries will be made of the acceptor's banker, and if necessary, concerning other parties to the bill. Have they other commitments to the bank?

   A record should have been made of the fate of other bills on the same acceptor and the amounts of any still outstanding will be noted.

3. Unless the acceptor's signature is known it may be advisable to send the bill to the bank where it is domiciled (i.e. where made payable) for confirmation that the acceptance is in order and that it has been signed under proper mandate.

4. The bill should be examined to ensure that it is technically in order — acceptance not qualified; endorsements purporting to be in order so that the bank may have no difficulty in establishing itself, if necessary, as a holder in due course.

   The bill should be endorsed by the customer for whom it is discounted, provided he is not the drawer, as he then becomes a party to the bill and is liable on it in the event of dishonour.

5. If the acceptor is a customer of the bank a note of the liability should be made on the ledger account.

6. Maturity dates of bills discounted should be carefully diarised and as an independent check it is usual to make an officer responsible for the examination of the actual bills each day: these are filed in order of maturity dates.

   The Clearing Bankers have agreed that "clean" bills (without documents attached) may be passed through the Clearing within seven days prior to the due date: the bank at which they are domiciled will hold until paid or dishonoured.

7. On the maturity of the bill the presenting banker will pass a corresponding credit to the Bills Discounted Account thereby cancelling the original debit made at the time of discount.

In the event of the bill being dishonoured, the customer's account should be debited immediately, his former contingent liability now having crystallised, and the bill returned to him. However, should the customer's account not be in a good enough state to allow the banker to debit it with the amount of the bill, the banker should debit a branch suspense account to preserve recourse against other parties to the bill and send immediate notice of dishonour to all the parties demanding payment of the amount.

A bill is said to be "retired" when it is withdrawn before maturity by way of payment being made to the banker who has discounted it (an adjustment would normally be needed in respect of unearned discount). Retirements may in some instances be a trade practice but unless the banker knows this to be so, he should exercise caution if asked to discount further bills accepted by the same party. It could possibly indicate an acceptance forged by the drawer who therefore needs to retire the bill to prevent it being presented to the (named) acceptor.

Chapter 6

Securities for Advances

INTRODUCTION

In order to form a good security the following characteristics should be present:

- Simplicity of Title
- Ease and Cheapness of Transfer
- Good saleability
- Stability of value
- Appropriate margin for loss
- Absence of onerous conditions or liability.

Security for bank lending may be either:

(a) *Direct Security:* this is security provided by the debtor to secure his own account; or

(b) *Third Party (or Indirect):* this is security deposited by a third party the secure the customer's debt.

(a) Direct Security: the following factors apply:

- It involves fewer complications; the terms and purpose of the deposit are beyond question, and all the necessary transactions connected therewith can be more expeditiously carried out.
- It will not be released by anything in the bank's method of dealing with the customer.
- It must be taken into account should the debtor go bankrupt — the banker is a "secured" creditor.

(b) Third Party Security:

- may be released by methods of dealing with the customer not covered by the guarantee or Memorandum of Deposit. For instance, there must be no misrepresentation as to dealings or as to the present state of the account; there must be no agreement made whereby payment of the debt is deferred;

and there must be no negligence in dealing promptly and properly with securities received from the customer. Of course, the banker protects himself as far as possible by the terms of the Memorandum of Deposit which is signed by the third party.

- involves more complications.
- has the advantage in the case of the principal debtor's bankruptcy that the banker may prove for the **full debt** and then come on to the security.
- may not always provide for **personal** liability of the chargor so that if the security depreciates in value no other right exists against the surety.
- invariably results in bad feeling when the banker is obliged to exercise his remedies.
- occasions difficulties for the principal debtor whose account if overdrawn must be stopped unless there are specific terms applying on the death of the surety.

LIEN, MORTGAGE AND PLEDGE

These are the three basic methods of acquiring security.

Lien was considered fully in Chapter 1.

A Pledge is the result of an express agreement, unlike a lien which arises out of implication. Whereas with lien the right to retain relates to possession already in existence, a pledge is a delivery of goods or documents of title to goods by a debtor to a creditor as security for a debt or some other obligation, on the understanding that the subject of the pledge will be returned to the pledgor when the debt has been repaid or the obligations fulfilled. A pledgee obtains a power of sale in the event of default but reasonable notice may have to be given to the pledgor. The essence of pledge is that there is a contract (which may be express or implied) together with delivery of possession.

A mortgage is the conveyance of the interest in property on condition that ownership shall revert to the debtor on repayment of the loan. A Mortgage may be legal or equitable. A legal mortgage gives the mortgagee a legal interest in the property; an equitable mortgage gives him an equitable interest in the property — in other words creates an equitable charge on the property but does not convey the legal title.

The mortgage passes the property in, but not usually the possession of, the goods mortgaged. The power of sale will normally depend on the terms laid down in the mortgage.

TYPES OF SECURITIES THAT THE BANKER MAY BE OFFERED

The following are the main types of security that a customer may offer to a banker:
Stock Exchange Securities
Debentures
Assignment of Book Debts
Title Deeds: Land and Buildings
Guarantees
Life Policies
Produce and Goods
Agricultural Charges
Hire Purchase Agreements.

The remainder of this chapter and the following three chapters are devoted to full consideration of these types of security.

STOCK EXCHANGE SECURITIES

Stocks and shares consist of a broad range or securities, basically coming within two divisions, these being (a) the public sector, i.e. national and local government borrowing and (b) the private sector, i.e. capital raised for non-government borrowing such as funds raised by companies and building societies. With both of these divisions, the body responsible for the indebtedness may be British or Foreign and the procedures for transferring the securities and charging them to secure bank advances can vary considerably.

REGISTERED STOCKS AND SHARES

Most securities are registered which means that the issuing body maintains a register of stockholders and shareholders whose ownership is evidenced by a certificate issued in the name of the owner. If the securities are transferable (some are not, such as National Savings Certificates) the legal title to them is transferred by a signed transfer, together with the certificate, being sent to the Registrar who makes the appropriate amendments to his register and issues a new certificate to the new owner.

When offered stocks or shares as security and they are registered securities, the banker has to decide whether to take an equitable title or a legal title.

AN EQUITABLE TITLE

Although a mere deposit of the securities gives the bank an equitable title (*Harrold v. Plenty* (1901)), a memorandum of deposit is normally taken which will be evidence of the intention to charge the security and will set out the terms of the contract. It will state that the security is to be a continuing security to prevent Clayton's Case operating against the bank and that the customer will, if required, do anything that is necessary to give the bank a legal title.

This, however, will not suffice to enable the bank to effect a sale, without going to Court, if the chargor refuses to complete a transfer. To surmount this difficulty it is normally possible to take, with the Memorandum of Deposit, a signed transfer.

Before the Stock Transfer Act 1963 the procedure depended upon whether the Articles of the Company stipulate for a transfer "by deed" or under hand, in that a blank transfer (one with the date and the name of the transferee missing) could be taken in the latter case but not in the former case. This is because a transfer form when it is worded as a deed must, to be valid as a deed, be complete at the time of execution — only by Power of Attorney or Court order can the blanks in a deed be validly filled in later. Disregard of this, in the usual case of Articles requiring a deed, meant that a bank got only an equitable title, which would be postponed to any prior equitable interests, but the position has been simplified by an alternative method provided by the Stock Transfer Act 1963.

This Act introduced a new and simplified document known as a stock transfer, applicable to fully paid-up registered securities issued by companies (limited by shares), bodies incorporated under a statute or Royal Charter, the UK Government or local authorities, and unit trusts. Exceptions from the Act include Building Society Securities, those on the Post Office Register (now known as the National Savings Stock Register) and National Savings Certificates. Any instrument executed under hand which complies with the contents of a stock transfer will be effective notwithstanding any provisions in the Articles to the contrary. Thus a deed is still effective where Articles require one, but so also is a stock transfer by virtue of the Act, and this makes the use of a deed an unnecessary complication where the Act applies.

In the case of a stock transfer the banker has **implied** authority to fill in the blanks, but in practice **express** authority will be given in the Memorandum of Deposit.

The only missing particular may be the date — the transferee may be stated as e.g., the bank's nominees. On the other hand the date **and** the name of the transferee may be omitted (a BLANK transfer), permitting the bank, when it becomes necessary to realise the security, to insert the name of a third party into whose name the shares may be transferred direct.

This is particularly useful if the shares are partly paid as the bank incurs no liability for calls, but such transfers should be retained with "bearer" securities when the name of the transferee is not inserted.

The reason for the omission of the date is to avoid the necessity of stamping the transfer. A transfer must be stamped within thirty days of its date, but it is not invalidated **as a written document** if the date is filled in only when the transferee decides to complete the transfer preparatory to registration with the company.

In this case, then it is necessary merely to obtain a signed blank transfer and hold without registration.

Though some banks do not take blank transfers and consider them an undesirable procedure, the deposit of certificates accompanied by a blank transfer has the following advantages. Stamp duty and registration fees are saved and the trouble of double registration is avoided. The bank escapes the liability for further calls if the shares are not fully paid. Sometimes the Articles of a company require its directors to hold at least a specified number of shares. If a director deposits only these qualification shares, then an equitable charge has to be taken, for a transfer of the shares to the bank or its nominee company would mean that the director would no longer hold the necessary qualification shares and ipso facto he would cease to be a director. The disadvantages are that the title is only an equitable one and may be set aside in favour of a legal title or of a prior equitable title. Of course, if the director concerned had no objection, an equitable charge could be taken over his qualification shares, and a legal charge over any other shares in the company which he might hold.

In many cases a bank will be prepared to take an equitable mortgage **without** requiring blank transfers to be held; in such a case (as has been mentioned above) there will be the additional disadvantage that realization of the security, should this become necessary, will require either the cooperation of the customer or an application to the court.

The banker who holds blank transfers may become registered or not, as he pleases. He will not obtain a legal title until the transfer has been registered and until this is done the security is imperfect. Of course if he learns of a defect — e.g. that the shares are held by his customer as a trustee — it will then be too late to perfect the security.

In all cases where the banker is content with an equitable title he should theoretically give notice of his lien to the company. The company may ignore the notice, may acknowledge it, or may reply stating that by Section 117 of the Companies Act 1948, they can take no notice of any trust, express, implied, or constructive (this, of course, is equally effective as an acknowledgement).

There are two reasons for giving such notice:

(a) A company sometimes states in its Articles of Association that it shall have a first and paramount or permanent lien on its shares for any money owing to it by the shareholder. A company may, therefore, have a lien on the shares of a person of whom it is a trade creditor, but although as a **registering** body it is bound not to register trust interests, it cannot as a **trading** concern ignore a banker's notice of lien and claim priority for any **subsequent** debts incurred to it by its shareholder. The company will, of course, have a prior claim for the debt due to it at the time of receipt of notice.

In the case of **fully paid** shares which are **officially quoted** on the Stock Exchange the company is not permitted to claim any lien on the shares and consequently notice of lien is not really necessary. On the other hand, a deposit of unquoted brewery shares by a publican would be an instance where notice of lien should be given.

(b) Notice of lien is a protection against the shareholder's obtaining by fraud a duplicate certificate and disposing of his holding.

On release of the security, the notice of lien should be cancelled.

The other way of protecting an equitable title, although little used in practice, is by means of a Stop Notice (which has replaced the former Notice in Lieu of Distringas). This procedure involves the bank applying to court for a notice which is served on the company and which states that the company must give the bank eight clear days' warning of any intention to pass a transfer of the shares in question. Such a step would only usually arise in practice in a recovery situation where the bank feared that a debtor may seek fraudulently to transfer a holding of shares.

A LEGAL TITLE

This is effected by taking a memorandum of deposit followed by having the shares transferred into the name of the bank or a nominee company by registration of a transfer executed by the chargor. A certificate in the name of the bank or its nominees will then be issued.

The bank will incur liability for calls if the shares are not fully paid or if they are shares with unlimited liability. For this reason banks are extremely careful before they effect registration in this manner of transfer of shares in respect of which a liability may arise.

Even if registration has been completed there is another danger, for the transfer may be a forgery and by sending it in for registration the banker warrants that it is genuine and undertakes to indemnify the company against any loss they may incur should it prove to be a forgery, for it was held in *Lord Mayor of Sheffield v. Barclay* (1905) that a banker who sends in for registration a forged transfer must indemnify the company which has acted on the assumption that the transfer was genuine. The banker would have no claim to the shares, the name of the original holder would have to be restored to the register and the banker would be liable for any dividends received.

If the shares have been sold to innocent third parties who have been registered and have had certificates issued to them by the company, then the company would still have to restore the name of the original holder and the banker would be liable to the company for the full amount of the shares at market price if they had to be purchased for the innocent third parties; the banker would also be liable for all bank dividends. Now, as the right of action on the indemnity only arises when the loss occurs, that is, when the company has to restore the original owners to the register, the bank might be held liable any number of years after the transaction had been apparently closed. To minimise the danger the company usually writes to the transferor, but the transferor is not bound to reply. By the Forged Transfer Acts 1891 and 1892, companies may create a fund for the compensation of losses arising under forged transfers.

EQUITABLE TITLES v. LEGAL TITLES

Generally speaking, legal titles prevail over equitable rights of which the legal mortgagee has no notice. Equitable rights as between themselves rank in date order.

Therefore if a banker takes a legal mortgage over stocks and shares before receiving notice of equitable interests (which would usually be those of beneficiaries under a trust) the bank will have priority. However, if only an equitable mortgage is held, then if the banker receives notice of a prior equitable interest, the banker cannot then convert his equitable title into a legal one. The relevant case on this is *Coleman v. London County & Westminster Bank Ltd* (1916).

The advantages and disadvantages of equitable and legal changes over registered securities can be summarised as follows:

Equitable Charge

Advantages

- it is simple and inexpensive (stamp duty and registration fees being payable only if the security has to be realised, although 50p stamp duty is payable if a dated transfer is held).
- the banker avoids personal liability on the shares.

Disadvantages

- The bank's title may be lost by forfeiture for non-payment of calls or by a prior equitable title being discovered.
- notice of lien to the company does not affect prior legal or equitable interests.
- Documents in connection with shareholding (e.g. relating to rights issues, bonus issues etc.) go direct to the customer. This may have the effect of substantially reducing the value of securities held by the Bank.

Legal Charge

Advantages

- The banker's legal title is prior to **all** equitable charges of which he had no notice when taking the charge.
- The banker as registered holder may sell on his own signature alone.

Disadvantages

- The banker may become liable for unpaid calls or should the transfer be a forgery.
- There is a cost to the bank by way of the clerical implications of the security being in the name of the bank's nominee company.

INSCRIBED STOCKS

This method of title to government stocks is now largely disused. Where it survives the holdings are not evidenced by the stock certificates but by **book entries**: the **Stock Receipt** is of no value and its deposit does not give the banker a charge over the Stock. This can be done safely only by having the holding transferred into the name of the bank or of its nominees; this is done by attendance of the customer **or his attorney** at the office where the register is kept.

Thus the bank would obtain a full legal title although a memorandum of deposit should also be taken so that the terms of the contract may not be misconstrued.

In rare cases, and where the borrower is of undoubted integrity, a loan may be granted against inscribed stock in the borrower's own name accompanied by an undertaking not to deal with it without the Bank's consent, and a Power of Attorney for use in case of need. This method gives the bank merely an equitable title without even the protection afforded by a share certificate. Another method sometimes available is to have the holding transferred into **Registered Stock** and charged as such.

Transfer of inscribed stocks in Commonwealth Securities and others domiciled at the Bank of England may be effected by a transfer in the common form instead of by Power of Attorney, but they should not merely for this reason be dealt with as registered securities.

Stocks on the National Savings Stock Register (formerly the Post Office Register) are sometimes referred to as "Inscribed" stocks but sale or transfer is effected by lodging the Certificate and a special form of sale or of transfer with the Controller of the National Savings Bank. Such stocks are occasionally taken as security by deposit of the Certificate with a signed transfer form in favour of the bank or its nominees, but the difficulty is that the Controller will not register any charges and the depositor may obtain a new certificate and sell the stock without the bank's knowledge. As, however, it is a simple matter to have the stock transferred to the Bank of England Register this is usually done and deposit of the certificate with blank transfer taken under Memorandum of Deposit.

BEARER SECURITIES

In the case of bearer bonds, shares or debentures, title passes by mere delivery and therefore the deposit of the bond, certificate or debenture (preferably with a memorandum of deposit) will give the bank a valid legal title provided the securities are taken for value, in good faith and without notice of any defect of title of the depositor.Thus such securities are fully negotiable meeting the requirements of Section 29 of the Bills of Exchange Act 1882.

The advantages of this type of security are that since title passes merely by delivery, no difficulties should arise upon realisation in respect of the completion of a valid transfer as with registered securities. Furthermore, there is no expense.

The banker may assume that the securities are the property of the depositor but **actual notice** of a trust or failure to satisfy himself as to anything of a suspicious nature may result in loss of his rights over the security on the grounds of lack of good faith.

Thus it is that when advances are made against bonds to bearer no steps beyond the deposit of the bonds are really necessary, for they pass by delivery and the holder gets a good title. The banker, however, should take a Memorandum of Deposit and should carefully examine the bonds, for the serial number on the bond and on each coupon should be undefaced, all the unpaid coupons should be attached and the date of payment should be on each coupon.

The Revenue stamp should be in order and no marking of any kind in ink should be present or made.

Bearer securities being fully negotiable, become security by way of pledge.

On the topic of bearer securities, the following two types of bearer items ought to be noted:

American and Canadian Share Certificates

These (particularly of American Railway and Industrial Companies) have a combined transfer form and power of attorney at the back and when this has been signed by the registered holder (usually a well-known London Stockbroker or trust company) the certificates pass as if they were bearer securities negotiable by delivery. The true owner must periodically claim the dividends from the registered holder. They may be taken as security by deposit with Memorandum of Deposit.

Scrip

Scrip is the **provisional certificate** of a person's shares in a joint stock company or Governmental loan. It is issued whilst instalments are being paid and is exchanged for the definitive share certificate when the instalments have been paid.

Often Scrip Certificates are not issued, the Letter of Allotment serving the same purpose. A Scrip Certificate is normally negotiable by delivery, but before title to shares represented by a Letter of Allotment can be passed, the letter of Renunciation on the back of the Letter of Allotment must be completed by the allottee. There is always a limited period for registration of renounced Letters of Allotment; subsequently the usual transfer must be executed.

An equitable charge may be taken, then, by mere deposit of a Scrip Certificate or by deposit of a renounced Letter of Allotment (with a blank transfer after a certain time).

NATIONAL SAVINGS SECURITIES

These consist of National Savings Certificates, Premium Bonds, National Development Bonds and British Savings Bonds. These items do not form good banking security in one sense due to the fact that the certificates or bond books are not documents of title, they are not transferable and charges over them cannot be protected by registration. However, they are stable in value and easily realisable but the weakness of them as security is that a dishonest holder can sell them or obtain a new bond book or certificate without the bank's knowledge.

With customers of undoubted integrity, these items can be accepted as security, the banker holding the bond book or certificate together with a signed repayment form authorising repayment to be made direct to the bank. A memorandum of deposit would set out the terms of the contract generally.

In *R. v. Chief Registrar of Friendly Societies, ex parte Mills* (1970) the bank sought to encash a holding of National Development Bonds which were held as security in the manner outlined above. The customer wrote to the Director of Savings countermanding the repayment instructions and the dispute was referred to the Chief Registrar of Friendly Societies. He ordered the bonds to be cashed and the proceeds paid to the bank and the court upheld his decision.

PARTLY PAID SHARES

These are not good banking security since they can involve a liability to a call. If a banker takes a legal mortgage, the bank, or its nominee company, will be liable for the call and, under Section 212 of the Companies' Act 1948, if the company goes into liquidation within one year of the bank having parted with the shares, the bank will be liable for the amount unpaid if the transferee cannot pay. Other disadvantages are that if calls are made the banker may have to finance his customer to enable the calls to be met, the alternative possibly being to forfeit the shares.

Such shares are usually less in demand than fully paid shares and may be more difficult to realise.

As stated at the beginning of this chapter, security involving liability should be avoided. With partly paid shares, calls may have to be paid and thus the advance may be increased rather than reduced. Shares of an unlimited company could become a very disturbing liability and definitely should not be regarded as acceptable banking security.

UNIT TRUST SECURITIES

If the sub-units are to bearer then they can be charged by mere deposit but a memorandum of deposit should be taken.

If the holdings are registered, the relative certificates may have a form of renunciation on the back which must be completed by the depositor and the certificate sent to the trustee of the trust. Alternatively the bank could become the registered holder by having the transfer effected by the usual transfer form, or some other form as prescribed by the trustee. The terms of the certificate should show whether transfer/sale is to be effected by stock transfer form, endorsement or some other method.

Generally speaking, these items are regarded as good security provided care is exercised when the security is being taken. Although production of the certificate is necessary before the security can be dealt with, duplicates can easily obtained and also the bank should ensure that the bank is not on notice that the securities are held in trust.

UNLISTED SHARES

Shares that are not quoted on either one of the major stock exchanges, including in this particular context the unlisted securities market, are not generally speaking attractive items of security due to difficulty in valuation and realisation. It must not be overlooked, however, that such shares, which in practice are often shares in private companies, can be extremely valuable as is amply evidenced quite frequently when shares are released on to the market through an issuing house and the holders realise handsome profits. In the absence of a market quotation, however, shares are in practice problematical as security for advances as the only way of valuing them may be to seek a valuation from the directors of the company or try to assess a break-up value from a recent balance sheet.

A private company is not permitted to offer its shares to the public but it is no longer necessary for a private company to incorporate these restrictions in its Articles.

DEBENTURES

A debenture is a document given by a company or corporation, usually under seal, as evidence of a loan and any charge securing it.

"Naked" or unsecured debentures are of little interest from a banker's point of view.

Debentures which create a charge on the property of the company are called Mortgage Debentures but the Stock Exchange objects to an instrument being called a Mortgage debenture unless it is secured by a trust deed, i.e. the series is secured by a deed which vests the assets in trustees for the debenture holders.

The advantages to the holders on the appointment of trustees are:

1. The legal estate is vested in the trustees and this prevents a subsequent mortgage from getting priority;
2. The trustees may be given power to sell and thus to realise the security without the aid of the Court;
3. The trustees are able to take prompt action if the company defaults instead of leaving it to the initiative of some debenture holder;
4. The company may be made to insure, repair, etc. by covenants in the trust deed.

The amount secured may be made payable to the **registered holder** or payable to **the bearer**. In the former case debentures can only be transferred by duly stamped instruments: in the latter case they pass by delivery and are negotiable instruments.

A **First Mortgage Debenture** is one which gives a first charge on the property of the company.

Debentures can be useful to the more substantial companies, mainly those with a Stock Exchange quotation, because they can sometimes raise money more readily by debentures than by creating a mortgage; they have choice as to the security they offer and can reduce the indebtedness by subsequently redeeming the debentures or even by purchasing them in the open market.

They are useful to lenders because the security is more easily transferable and marketable than mortgages and the debenture holders have various remedies if the security is in jeopardy.

Debentures may be issued at a discount. Those with no fixed date for payment are called perpetual debentures; if payable on a fixed date they are determinable debentures.

A clause in the prospectus that "the debentures are redeemable within so many years by half-yearly drawings" means that a certain number of the debentures will be paid off every half-year until the whole are paid off within the time stated. The debentures to be redeemed each year are decided by drawing as in a lottery.

If debentures are registered, the issuing company may have a lien on them for calls on shares in the name of the registered owner of the debentures made prior to notice of any equitable mortgage of the debentures. This applies to public companies when a public issue of debentures is made.

DEBENTURES AS SECURITY FOR A BANK OVERDRAFT

"Non-Bank" Debentures

Debentures payable to bearer may be made a valid security by deposit of the debentures and it is usual, and advisable, to take in addition a memorandum of deposit.

Debentures payable to a registered holder may be made a valid security by deposit of the debentures with a blank transfer and a memorandum of deposit. But the better plan is to have them transferred and registered in the names of nominees of the bank.

It may be either a "fixed sum" debenture or an "all monies" debenture.

A "fixed sum" debenture provides for the payment of a specified sum at a fixed date and payment of interest until the principal is repaid and is usually one of a series each securing a like sum and all being expressed to rank *pari passu* in point of charge. A fixed sum or "limited" debenture has the advantage of being marketable, but there is the danger that if a bank took such a Debenture direct from the Company it might be argued that it was held as an investment, not as security for the Company's account in its books, and while the bank would nevertheless possess the rights and remedies given to it by the document (e.g. the right to appoint a Receiver in certain circumstances) it might be unable to sue the Company on a Banking Account as such. To avoid this a separate Memorandum of Deposit or agreement (sometimes known as a "*Buckley*" Agreement) must be taken which clearly states that the debenture is held to secure a loan granted by the bank thereby connecting the debenture with the bank borrowing, and most banks have a printed "bridge form" for this purpose. The parties are usually the Company, the bank, and the bank's nominees (in whose name it is customary for the debenture to be registered) and the agreement provides *inter alia:*

(a) That the Company will execute a debenture to the Nominees as trustees for the bank to secure repayment of any money from time to time owing by the Company to the bank;
(b) That the nominees will hold the debenture in trust for the bank;
(c) That the payment of interest; and charges in respect of the Company's banking account for any period shall be deemed to satisfy payment of interest on the debentures for the same period.
(d) That the bank are entitled to sue the Company for the monies secured by the debenture.

Debentures may be redeemed (even by the company's purchasing them on the open market) and by the Companies Act 1948 (Section 90) redeemed debentures may be **re-issued to rank** *pari passu* with the original issue unless

(a) the articles provide otherwise; or
(b) the company is under a contract not to re-issue the debentures; or
(c) the company has done some act showing an intention to cancel the debentures.

No transfer to a nominee is necessary in order to keep the redeemed debentures alive.

On re-issue debentures must be re-stamped (where applicable) and the amount of redeemed debentures available for re-issue must always be shown in the company's Balance Sheet.

Debentures deposited to cover advances from time to time on current account are not to be considered to have been redeemed because the account has ceased to be in debit whilst the debentures remained so deposited and consequently they may be taken as a continuing security.

The position may not be the same if the debentures are deposited to cover an advance by way of loan. Upon repayment it would be wise to regard the debentures as redeemed and not available without re-issue as cover for future advances.

Before making an advance to a Company, a banker should therefore ascertain whether the company has power to re-issue any debentures which have been redeemed and if so ensure that they are cancelled or that the company's Articles are amended to restrict the power to re-issue by the company with priority over his own charge.

Debentures Executed in Favour of Lending Banks

An "all monies" debenture secures all monies at any time owing and this is the usual form taken by a bank in the shape of a fixed and floating charge. It is a single document — most banks have their own printed form — which contains all the usual restrictive clauses to provide for its being a continuing security, to prevent *Clayton's Rule* from operating against the bank, to prevent other charges, etc., etc. Further, to prevent specific mortgages being created by the Company in priority to the debenture, banks often insist on holding all their title deeds. The advantage of these unlimited debentures is that any amount of borrowing is covered, whereas if a "fixed sum" debenture were held, it would be necessary to take another debenture if the borrowing exceeded that sum.

In August 1971 *ad valorem* stamp duty on legal and equitable charges and on the type of debenture taken by banks was abolished.

(The full practical steps involved in taking a debenture as security are set out on the appropriate checklist in Chapter 10.)

Debentures Offered by Newly Incorporated Company

The case of In *re Simms* (1930) is an indication that some degree of care is necessary when a debenture is offered as security by a company incorporated within the previous three months. If the cover for the debenture consisted of assets which were transferred by way of sale to the company and subsequently that transfer is set aside as a fraudulent conveyance the bank may lose its security entirely.

The charge created by a debenture may be either "**fixed**" or "**floating**" or a combination of the two.

A FIXED CHARGE is given on freehold property or other permanent assets with the object of preventing the company from disposing of such property. **A FLOATING CHARGE is a charge given on the assets of a company but it is in such a form that the company may deal with any of its assets in the ordinary course of business.**

Until fairly recently most bankers when offered a debenture as security would take a fixed charge over the land and buildings and get possession of the title deeds, and a floating charge over the remainder of the assets. Nowadays, many banks automatically take a fixed charge also on book debts and their standard printed form of debenture incorporates this. This is to give the bank priority as regards its charge on debtors over the claims of any preferential creditors who do, of course, rank before a lender secured by floating charge.

Characteristics of a floating charge as explained in *Re Yorkshire Woolcomber's Association* (1903) are:

1. It is a charge on both present and future assets;
2. The assets change continually in the ordinary course of business;
3. The company carries on business until the debenture holders intervene;
4. It becomes "fixed" or "crystallized" if the loan becomes repayable and the lender takes steps to enforce his charge.
5. It gives priority over unsecured creditors.

So paramount is this freedom of a Company to use assets subject to a floating charge that the sale by a company of its whole undertaking and business to a new company, notwithstanding that the assets were subject to a floating charge, was held to be valid: *Foster v. Borax Co.* (1901).

Invalidity of Floating Charges

A floating charge created within twelve months of the commencement of winding-up shall, unless it is proved that the company was solvent at the time of the creation of the charge be invalid except to the amount of cash paid at the time or subsequent to the creation of the charge, with interest at 5 per cent, or such other rate as may be prescribed by the Treasury, Section 322 of the Companies Act 1948 (now Section 617 Companies Act 1985). In other words, it does not cover the previous advances.

The charge is valid

1. If the solvency of the company at the time of the charge can be proved (which in practical terms is extremely problematical if not impossible).
2. If it is given in respect of fresh advances.

Occasionally a bank which has lent money to a company endeavours to strengthen an unsatisfactory position by obtaining a floating charge covering book debts, stocks, and whatever free assets are available. The company is obviously in an insolvent position and in such circumstances, as far as the **existing** advance is concerned, a period of twelve months must elapse before the charge becomes effective.

Any subterfuge such as by creating a fresh advance on a new account to enable clearance of the old debt will not be countenanced by the Courts. If, however, the account is continued in the normal way, and is reasonably active, the credits paid in will, in accordance with the *Rule in Clayton's Case* be appropriated in repayment of the debt existing at the time of the charge, whilst subsequent drawings would be in the nature of fresh accommodation and therefore covered by the floating charge. This principle was recognised in *Re Thomas Mortimer Ltd.* (1925), and was approved by the Court of Appeal in *Re Yeovil Glove Co. Ltd.* (1965).

If then the turnover on an overdrawn account is reasonable in comparison with the amount of the advance, the charge will gradually become effective from its inception and may become fully effective long before the twelve months hardening period has elapsed, even though there has been no increase in the actual amount of the advance.

When lending on the security of a floating charge it is essential that the banker should call for the company's **Balance Sheet** regularly. In addition to this in many cases the banker may require to be provided with a regular return of assets/liabilities so that the banker can regularly monitor the asset cover under the debenture.

It will be noted that the disadvantages do not apply to a specific legal charge which affords good cover for an existing advance even though the company is insolvent unless indeed the charge can be impeached as a fraudulent preference.

Some potential dangers were highlighted in *Re G. T. Whyte & Co. Ltd.* (1982) where the judge upheld the liquidator's claim that a floating charge issued to replace the mortgages formerly held by the company's bankers within 12 months was invalid. The judge drew attention to the fact that money lent at the time the charge was created was not "cash paid" to the company, but merely a continuation of an earlier loan, and that the purpose of the floating charge was to substitute a better security.

Preferential Creditors and Floating Charges

A further defect in a floating charge is that whether the company goes into liquidation or whether a receiver is appointed under the terms of the charge, preferential creditors must first be paid: Section 319 Companies Act 1948 (now Section 614 of the 1985 Act).

In respect of assets covered by a fixed charge preferential creditors will have no priority over the proceeds of such assets.

Priorities

One of the disadvantages of a floating charge, which leaves the company perfectly free to deal with assets covered by the charge in the ordinary way of business, is that the company is free to make specific mortgages of its property which will have priority over the floating charge evidenced by debentures. Hence a clause is frequently inserted in debentures that the company shall not be able to create mortgages or charges in priority to or *pari passu* with the debentures of that issue.

In spite of this clause a lender who subsequently takes a specific charge will take priority over the debentures if he takes his security for value and **without notice of the prohibition in the debenture**. The company must register the floating charge but inspection of the register of charges kept by the Registrar of Companies would not necessarily reveal the existence of the restrictive clause, and so fix the second lender with notice.

In effecting registration of a floating charge which contains such a prohibition it is advisable for the bank to ensure that particulars of the restriction are also registered so that subsequent lenders are on notice. Registration of a floating charge might be effective when the property charged consists of **land and buildings** for under the Law of Property Act 1925, it is quite possible that such registration may amount to notice to all for the Act provides that such registration of a charge against a company's property which appears in the Registrar of Companies' register operates as a land charge exactly in the same way as if it had been registered as a land charge under the Land Charges Act. It is a point still to be decided and, if a company applies for an advance against title deeds, the precaution should be taken of finding out if Debentures have been issued, and if so, whether they preclude the company from making specific mortgages and charges.

Disadvantages of Floating Charge

1. It is only an equitable charge;
2. It does not prevent the company from making specific charges unless otherwise agreed;
3. The holder of a floating charge may lose his priority if specific mortgages are made without notice of such agreement;
4. It does not cover previous advances if the company is wound up within twelve months of the creation of the charge unless it is proved that the company was solvent at the time of creating the charge;
5. The charge "remains dormant" or "floats" whilst the company is a going concern or until the person in whose favour the charge is created intervenes;
6. Preferential creditors take priority;
7. Execution creditors may be able to seize assets before the bank has taken steps to protect its position;
8. the most realisable assets have usually already been realised to stave off pressing creditors by the time the banker crystallises his charge;
9. Certain "assets" may be subject to reservation of title and thus not be available to the debenture holder (see later).

FIXED CHARGE ON BOOK DEBTS

As mentioned earlier many banks now incorporate in their standard form of debenture a fixed, rather than floating charge over book debts. This raises the question of the effectiveness of such a charge over future book debts since basically under the fixed charge, as debts are paid the fixed charge is gradually reduced and will eventually cease. A floating charge would cover debtors as they are at any time and from time to time. This problem was considered in *Siebe Gorman & Co. Ltd. v. Barclays Bank Ltd.* (1978) where the bank's charge contained a first fixed charge on all book debts and other debts now and from time to time owing to the company. The charge further provided that during the continuance of the security the company shall pay into its account with the bank all monies which it may receive in respect of book debts so charged and shall not without the prior consent of the bank in writing purport to charge or assign the same. It was held that it was possible in law for a mortgagor, by way of continuing security for further advances to grant to a mortgagee a charge on future book debts in a form which created in equity a specific charge on the proceeds of debts as soon as they were received and consequently prevented the mortgagor from disposing of an unencumbered title to the subject matter of the charge without the mortgagee's consent, even before the mortgagee had taken steps to enforce the security. Thus the debenture conferred on the bank a specific charge in equity on all future debts to the company.

RESERVATION OF TITLE

The sale of goods on the basis that title passes only when the goods are paid for is not in itself a new concept, but it is over the past seven or eight years a matter which has exercised the minds of lending bankers. This occurred as a result of the "Romalpa" case (*Aluminium Industrie Vaassen B.V. v. Romalpa Aluminium Ltd.* 1976) which involved the application of reservation of title clauses by suppliers (in this instance aluminium supplied by a Dutch firm, AIV, to a foil manufacturer, Romalpa) to a company which subsequently appointed a receiver. The effects of the clauses are:

1. That the goods being supplied remain the property of the supplier until he is paid; and
2. If these goods are sold before payment is made then the sale proceeds are seen as being held in trust for the supplier.

The implication of this case was that banks could no longer be certain that a floating charge could be applied to goods and raw materials held by a manufacturer (or other company) which went into receivership. The case caused concern on several fronts and lending bankers were concerned even if lending unsecured on the basis that arguably the true position of the company was concealed causing bankers and others dealing with the company to be misled. Furthermore, there was the matter of tracing materials and goods supplied where a company was turning raw materials into finished products or assembling products from a variety of parts. Other relevant cases, and ones which to some extent limited the impact of the Romalpa case were *Re Bond Worth Ltd.* (1979) and *Burden (UK) Ltd. v. Scottish Timber Products Ltd.* (1979).

Claims by unsecured creditors under reservation of title clauses relating to goods they have supplied, are nowadays a common feature in company receiverships and liquidations. Whilst many of these are settled by agreement and compromise between the receiver or liquidator and the creditors concerned, cases do arise from time to time.

In *Re Peachdart Ltd.* (1983) the company was in receivership and an attempt was made by the supplier to recover leather in stock, the proceeds of sale of manufactured goods and part-manufactured goods and the proceeds of sales made prior to and outstanding at the date of the receiver's appointment. It was held that the supplier had the right to recover goods in stock but the right to the proceeds of sales prior to the receiver's appointment was lost due to the debenture holder's fixed charge on book debts. As regards the attempt to retain title over part-manufactured goods, it was decided that once the process of manufacture had started the property in the goods would vest in the vendor only as security for any outstanding balance.

In other words the vendor had no more than a charge over the partly-completed stock which was void for non-registration.

In *Sugar Distributors Ltd. v. Monaghan Cash & Carry Ltd.* (1982), the supplier sought to recover sugar in the possession of the receiver and also the proceeds of sub-sales. The first issue was clear cut but the second was more complex as the conditions of sale did not specifically refer to tracing. However, it was held that the buyer was in a fiduciary position and thus must hold any proceeds of sale on behalf of the unpaid supplier.

To some extent the initial alarm caused to bankers by the Romalpa case has lessened on the practical front, although most banks have now built into their procedures and "checklists" a note to ascertain from company customer borrowers (or certainly from those where the bank is looking to current assets, in particular stock and work-in-progress, for security cover) to what extent, if any, the customer is purchasing materials and goods subject to retention of title. It would be wrong to say that prudent bankers have become complacent about Reservation of Title; it is however true that bankers have had to learn to live with this as an added risk in many lending situations.

SECTION 95 COMPANIES ACT 1948 (NOW SECTION 395 COMPANIES ACT 1985) — REGISTRATION OF CHARGES

The following **mortgages and charges** created by a joint stock company are required by the above section to be registered with the Registrar of Companies: Any charge

(a) For the purpose of securing any issue of debentures;
(b) On uncalled share capital

(c) Created or evidenced by an instrument which in the case of an individual would require registration as a bill of sale;
(d) On any land or any interest therein (even if the mortgagee holds the deeds); a rent charge common to some parts of the country, is not included in the category of "land" for purpose of the section (prior to the 1948 Act there was some doubt about this);
(e) On any book debt; an assignment of debts due or accruing due under a contract, which in reality is a charge though purporting to be an absolute assignment, requires registration. *Re Kent v. Sussex Sawmills Ltd.* (1946);
(f) Which are floating charges on the property of the company;
(g) On calls made but not paid;
(h) On a ship or any share of a ship;
(i) On goodwill, on a patent or licence under a patent, on a trademark, on a copyright or licence under a copyright.

Failure to register within 21 days of the creation of the charge renders it void as against the liquidator and creditors of the company, but the debt holds good and becomes immediately repayable. The lender becomes an **unsecured creditor**.

It is of considerable importance to note that the charge must be registered within the prescribed period of the date of **creation**, i.e. the date on which it was actually executed whether or not it was dated subsequently and irrespective of the time when the advance is made. However, on two occasions, *Charnley's Case* (1924) and *Re C. L .Nye Ltd.* (1970) the Court of Appeal has held that a document dated subsequently to its creation and registered within 21 days of the date it bore was valid, because the Registrar's certificate of registration of the mortgage or charge shall be conclusive evidence that the requirements of the Act as to registration have been complied with.

Registration of a charge involves publicity and as companies sometimes feel that registration may have an adverse effect on trade credit various expedients are adopted to avoid such a course. None of these is satisfactory from the banker's point of view.

(a) An equitable mortgage of property by deposit of deeds without the completion of a form of charge requires registration for the Act envisages circumstances in which such a charge will be taken.
(b) If deeds are deposited and a charge executed but at the company's request registration is not effected and the charge becomes void.
(c) A written undertaking may be given not to charge the property without the bank's consent. This affords no security.
(d) Similarly a written undertaking to give a charge if the bank calls for it is of no use as security.

The company is primarily responsible to see that a charge is registered, but any interested person may register and recover the fees from the company.

A Certificate of Registration is issued by the Registrar and a copy of such certificate must be endorsed on every debenture and registrable charge.

Cancellation of registration is effected by filing with the Registrar of Companies a memorandum of satisfaction in whole or in part, or of the fact that part of the property or undertaking has been released from the charge or has ceased to form part of the company's property or undertaking, as the case may be. This document must be executed under the Common Seal of the company and be verified by a statutory declaration by a director and the secretary.

In addition to the Registrar of Companies register the company must keep its own Register of Mortgages, and this must contain **all** mortgages and charges affecting the property of the company. Consequently it contains items not registered with the Registrar of Companies, e.g. a charge on stocks and shares, bills deposited to secure an advance, mortgages of a life policy, or a charge on produce. Omission from this Register does not invalidate the charge.

THE REMEDIES OPEN TO A DEBENTURE HOLDER

On default by the company any floating charge crystallizes and

1. the debenture holders (or any one of them on behalf of all) may sue to obtain payment or to enforce the security by sale;
2. a receiver may be appointed (if the debenture authorises this) or the debenture holders may apply to the Court to appoint one;
3. an application may be made to the Court for foreclosure;
4. a winding-up petition may be presented;
5. where trustees have been appointed under a trust deed (and this is usual in the case of a series of debentures) they may realise the security without the aid of the Court, provided a power of sale is given in the trust deed.

RECEIVERS

In the normal way the debenture itself makes provision with regard to the powers and duties of a receiver.

A receiver appointed by the Court, however, is **personally** liable (since the Court cannot be) but is entitled to be indemnified out of the assets of the company in priority to the debenture holders.

Where a bank is lending on the security of a debenture and discovers that its position is in jeopardy, prompt steps have to be taken to appoint a receiver in order that the receiver can intervene to safeguard the company's remaining assets and realise as much as possible out of the bank's security.

The appointment of a receiver is not a step which a banker takes lightly and indeed it is nowadays quite common for bankers to insist on an accountant carrying out an investigation of the troubled company's affairs in the hope that a solution for saving the business can be found without the bank having to undertake greater risk. However, if it is decided to appoint a receiver, the bank will make formal demand for repayment of the indebtedness including interest to date. The terms of the debenture will set out the grounds upon which the floating charge crystallises and in practice this almost always is when formal demand is made and the company defaults. A bank will seek to apoint as receiver, an accountant who is experienced in insolvency work and on whom they can rely to act promptly and efficiently.

A form of appointment is drawn up by the bank as debenture holder and executed on behalf of the bank and handed to the receiver. The form of appointment can vary considerably from bank to bank but it will set out that as the amount secured by the debenture has become due and payable, the stated party is thereby appointed to be receiver of all the property (the word is used in its wider sense here) charged by the debenture.

The appointment of the receiver requires to be registered within 7 days with the Registrar of Companies. Additionally, where a receiver or manager has been appointed, every invoice, letter etc. on which the company's name appears has to contain a statement that a receiver or manager has been appointed.

The express powers of the receiver will usually be stated in the debenture itself. These usually include a power to carry on the business of a company, sell assets and virtually do anything incidental to achieving their objective. Usually under the terms of the debenture, the receiver is appointed an agent of the company in order that the company not the bank will be responsible for his acts and remuneration. Nevertheless the accountant will normally request an indemnity from the bank.

Under the wide powers granted in bank debentures, the receiver normally takes control of all the assets of the company and continues the business for so long as he considers necessary to collect the maximum amount towards repayment of the bank debt. On some occasions the receiver may run the company for some time and sometimes the business is put back on its feet thus enabling the receiver to be withdrawn. On other occasions the company may be put into liquidation shortly after the receiver's appointment.

When a receiver is appointed the company has to prepare within 14 days a statement of affairs in a form set out in the Companies Act.

The following particulars have to be given:

1. The company's assets and liabilities.
2. The names, addresses and occupations of the company's creditors.
3. Any security held by creditors.
4. And any other information as may be set down.

The receiver has to file this statement of affairs with his comments with the Registrar of Companies within a period of two months. Twelve months after his appointment and subsequently at twelve monthly intervals (where appropriate) the receiver has to file with the Registrar an abstract of receipts and payments during the period in question.

As regards the application of the proceeds of realisations, the receiver has to have regard to any rights of creditors or other parties having prior claims.

Statutory preferential creditors have to be paid in priority to the bank in respect of monies realised from assets which were subject to the floating charge.

Basically where the bank's debenture comprised a fixed and floating charge, the following would apply:

Proceeds of assets under fixed charge would go to the bank (after satisfying any prior mortgages).

The floating charge proceeds would be applied in the following order:

1. The costs of the realisation of the assets.
2. The costs and remuneration of the receiver.
3. the amounts due to preferential creditors
4. The bank's debt.

When the receiver has realised the assets and paid off the preferential creditors, the remaining amount he holds will, less his costs and remuneration, be paid over to the bank in reduction of the debt. Notice of the receiver ceasing to act has to be given to the Registrar of Companies and the receiver has to produce a set of final accounts.

INTERESTED DIRECTORS

Occasions may arise when, in respect of a proposed transaction, the personal interest of a director is in conflict with that of the company.

Directors are to some extent trustees for the company and cannot make contracts with the company, otherwise there would be a conflict between their own private interest and their duty to the company.

Express power to enter into such contracts may, however, be given by the Articles, but in those circumstances there is usually a proviso that the director may not vote on the matter. He must in any case disclose the nature of his interest.

A somewhat similar situation arises when directors have given their personal guarantee or security as cover for a bank advance **to the company**, and it is subsequently proposed that a debenture or other security should be issued by the company in substitution for, or in support of, that given by the directors. Clearly in such a case the directors will thereby be released from or relieved of liability.

Unless, therefore, the directors are authorised to vote on contracts in which they are interested, the resolution authorising the issue of the security should be passed by an **independent** quorum of directors, or failing this (e.g. if all the directors are sureties) confirmation of the **company** in general meeting should be obtained. Failure in this respect may result in the security being invalidated: *Victors Ltd. v. Lingard* (1927).

Careful perusal of the Articles is, therefore, essential in all such circumstances.

In the case of companies incorporated after 1st July, 1948, **provided Regulation 84 of Table A of the 1948 Act is applicable**, a director may in limited instances vote in respect of contracts in which he is interested. This applies to "any arrangement for the giving by the company of any security to a third party in respect of a debt or obligation of the company to which the director himself has assumed responsibility in whole or in part under a guarantee or indemnity or by the deposit of security". The confirmation of an independent quorum of directors or by the company is not now necessary.

ASSIGNMENT OF BOOK DEBTS

This item of security is not one which arises very often in practice nor is it one viewed with much enthusiasm by bankers. Nevertheless it is necessary to be aware of the issues which are relevant to this type of security since occasionally a banker may wish to take such an assignment. This would usually in practice be over one fairly sizeable debt and could well be in circumstances where the customer is engaged in contract work. It would not be usual for such assignments to be taken over a number of debts due to the complicated steps required in each case, and, when lending to a company where debtors are to be relied upon for security cover, the banker would normally effect his security by means of a debenture incorporating a fixed charge on book debts (as explained earlier in this chapter).

The following practical points ought to be noted:

1. If it is an assignment of contract monies, the banker should carefully peruse the actual contract to see that the monies can in fact be assigned and whether there are any terms which would enable the debtor to repudiate the contract and also to ensure that the customer himself is capable of fulfilling its terms.
2. The assignment must be specific and not general for a general assignment of existing and future book debts is void against the trustee in bankruptcy as regards debts not paid at the commencement of the bankruptcy unless registered as a Bill of Sale, but registration is not necessary if a trader assigns (a) existing debts from specified debtors; (b) debts growing due on specified contracts; (c) debts included in a transfer of a business made bona fide and for value; (d) debts included in an assignment for the benefit of creditors generally. A part of a debt and future debts (such as monies to become due as and when work is done under a contract) can only be assigned equitably.
3. Although a future debt cannot be brought within the terms of Section 136, Law of Property act 1925, so that no legal assignment can be taken, such equitable assignments, made for valuable consideration, are equivalent to contracts to assign and will be enforced by the courts.
4. A legal assignment is more direct but to comply with the law of Property Act it has to be:

(a) In writing, signed by the assignor.
(b) Absolute, and not by way of charge only.
(c) Followed by express notice in writing to the debtor.

It is considered that 'signed' means, in the case of a company, executed under its Common Seal. A legal assignment must be absolute and never partial so that the debtor will not be inconvenienced by having to seek out two creditors. It is absolute although it is by way of mortgage or by way of trust. As a practical step, the debtor's acknowledgement of the notice is obtained, because notice determines priorities.

When the legal assignment is complete the banker can sue in his own name and give a good discharge without the concurrence of the assignor. The debtor must in no circumstances "pay the debt to the assignor", but even with a legal assignment the debtor, if subsequently given notice by the assignor not to pay may pay the money into Court or call upon the parties to interplead, that is, commence an action to decide who is to receive the money.

PRACTICAL PROCEDURE

Having obtained a legal assignment the banker must nevertheless bear in mind the following points:

1. Assignment of book debts is subject to equities. The debtor has the same rights to set off and counter-claim against the assignee as he had against the assignor at the time of notice of the assignment.

   Hence, in giving notice of the assignment the banker should ascertain from the debtor

   (a) the present amount of the debt.
   (b) Whether there are any counter claims by way of set-off.

2. As notice determines priorities, the banker should ascertain from the debtor whether there are any prior charges.
3. If the assignment is given by a company to secure advances it must be registered under the Companies Act as a charge on book debts: *Re Kent and Sussex Sawmills Ltd.* (1946). The same applies where a company deposits hire purchase agreements as security.

   On the other hand, it was held in *Paul and Frank Ltd. v. Discount Bank (Overseas) Ltd.* (1966) that the standard letter of authority whereby the benefits of an E.C.G.D. bad-debt policy were assigned to the bank was not registrable under Section 95 for the "debt" was purely hypothetical unless and until a valid claim arose under the policy.

Chapter 7

Securities for Advances (cont.)

LAND AND BUILDINGS: TITLE DEEDS AND LAND CERTIFICATES

The term "land" includes not only the land itself but also any permanent buildings on it, certain fixtures attached to the buildings, all growing crops, timber etc. and anything under the land (except precious metals, coal and oil which automatically belong to the crown).

There are two legal estates in land, these being freehold and leasehold.

Freehold: this is legally defined as an estate in "fee simple absolute in possession." A freehold interest is the highest interest a person can have in land. It is usually evidenced by a land certificate or conveyance. A freeholder can grant leases out of the freehold estate.

Leasehold: this is where a freeholder grants a legal interest in the land to another person for a specified period of time. The person creating the lease is called the "lessor" and the party in whose favour the lease is given is the "lessee."

If permitted by the terms of the lease, the lessee can create a sub-lease out of the lease. During the period of the lease, the freeholder retains the deeds to the freehold and at the expiry of the lease, the land reverts to the freeholder. A sub-lease is sometimes called an "underlease."

The document which evidences title to a leasehold interest is a land certificate, a lease or an assignment thereof. The document creating a subsidiary lease of all or part of a leasehold interest is called an "underlease" or "sub-lease."

All land is either registered or unregistered, the significance of this in the context of a transfer or mortgage of the land being as follows:

UNREGISTERED LAND

Title to unregistered land is evidenced by deeds and documents representing the chain of title. Each time the property is sold, a conveyance or an assignment is executed and all the deeds and documents are passed on to the purchaser.

The following main types of deeds and documents may be found relating to title to unregistered land:

1. Conveyance (if freehold estate).
2. Lease or sub-lease (if leasehold estate).
3. Assignment (if leasehold estate).
4. Counterpart lease if freeholder or lessee has granted a leasehold interest.
5. Abstract of Title — compiled by a solicitor, usually at the time the title changed hands. This recites the chain of title in some detail and often indicates that comparison has been made with documents elsewhere.
6. Local Authority Searches
7. Land Charges Department Searches.

REGISTERED LAND

Title to registered land is evidenced by a land certificate issued by the Land Registry. This is a more efficient method of passing on title to land than that for unregistered land, as the title to the land is evidenced by one document only, i.e. the land certificate. When title to the property changes the Land Registry amend the name of the owner (called the proprietor) of the land, and the land certificate is re-issued to the purchaser.

Of the pre-registration deeds which may accompany the land certificate, a lease is usually the most important, and will have great significance in the title to the property.

The Land Certificate is divided into three sections:

Section A — The Property Register: This states the title number, a short description of the property, and says whether it is freehold or leasehold.

Section B — The Proprietorship Register: this gives the type of title, the name and address of the owner (proprietor) of the property, the date of registration.

Section C — The Charges Register: This gives brief details of charges, leases, covenants, etc.

On registration one of the following four types of title to the property will be granted by the land Registry and this will be noted in the Proprietorship Register.

1. Absolute Title. This is always granted on freehold property, and gives the owner a state-guaranteed title. The land certificate is the one essential document of title. Absolute Title on leasehold land can only be granted on first registration where proof exists of the freehold title from which the lease was created.

2. *Good Leasehold Title.* Where a leaseholder cannot produce evidence of the freeholders title to grant the lease (as is usually the case), a Good Leasehold Title is granted on first registration. It may be converted to Absolute Title after 10 years, provided there is proof that the owner or successive owners have been in possession for that period.

3. *Possessory Title.* By granting this little used title to a property, the registrar guarantees dealings after registration, but does not guarantee against any defects in the title prior to registration. Possessory Title on freehold land may be converted to Absolute Title after fifteen years, and a leasehold land may be converted to Good Leasehold Title after 10 years.

The Registrar may grant Absolute or Good Leasehold Title even though the application may have applied for Possessory Title.

4. *Qualified Title.* This is extremely uncommon and is granted where Absolute or Good Leasehold Title is applied for but the Registrar is unable to grant such title. Qualified Title is subject to any rights or interests arising before a specified date, or as specifically described in the register.

LEASEHOLD PROPERTY AS SECURITY

The value of leasehold property as security depends on:

(a) The length of the lease;
(b) The terms of the lease;
(c) The nature, condition and situation of the property.

Advances on short leases are not advisable. At the end of the lease the property reverts to the lessor and often heavy claims are made on account of dilapidations. There may, however, be valuable options to renew.

Short leases are not normally very saleable and, if a purchaser can be found, the price offered is generally a very poor one. Long leases are more suitable as security but there are many disadvantages.

1. The property continually decreases in value as each year lessens the length of the lease.
2. A ground rent has to be paid annually and failure to pay usually entails a forfeiture of the lease.
3. the lease contains covenants which are sometimes onerous and restrictive and non-performance of the covenants may entail forfeiture of the lease and consequent loss of the security.
4. Underleasing may not always be allowed.
5. The condition and situation of the property is important.

Property conveniently situated, readily accessible, easily let, marketable, and in good repair is naturally a better security than poor property.

Certain interests in or charges on land, e.g. rights of way and legal mortgages are recognised as being legal estates because they are either estates in fee simple or for a term of years absolute.

MORTGAGES OF LAND: LEGAL OR EQUITABLE

A legal mortgage is a transfer by deed by the mortgagor of a legal estate in the land to the mortgagee as security for a loan to the mortgagor.

A legal mortgage may or may not be accompanied by the title deeds or land certificate, and if it is not so accompanied it is called a "puisne mortgage". Puisne mortgages are legal and not equitable mortgages.

Legal Mortgages of Freeholds

These can be created:

1. By a lease of the land for a term of years, subject to a proviso for cesser of the term on redemption, that is, on repayment of the loan the lease will be extinguished. (A term of 3,000 years is suggested by the Law of Property Act 1925);
2. By a charge by deed expressed to be by way of legal mortgage. The effect of this is to give the mortgagee the same protection and remedies as if a lease (as in 1) for 3,000 years had been created in his favour.

The freehold remains vested in the mortgagor.

Legal Mortgages of Leaseholds

These can be either

1. By a sub-lease for a term less by one or more (usually ten) days than the unexpired period of the lease; or
2. By a charge by deed expressed to be by way of legal mortgage which will have the same effect as a sub-lease for a term ten days less than the unexpired period of the lease.

The idea of the ten days is that should a second mortgage be executed the second mortgage will be given a sub-lease for a period a day longer than the first mortgagee's term and so on.

The advantage of a charge "by way of legal mortgage" is that the same form of charge can be used both for freeholds and leaseholds.

Minors and Land

A minor cannot hold legal estate in land nor may he be a legal mortgagee.

Equitable Mortgage

An equitable mortgage is an agreement to execute a legal mortgage if and when necessary. An equitable mortgage can be created, for both freehold and leasehold land:

1. By a mere deposit of the title deeds, etc. with intent to create a charge.
2. By deposit of deeds accompanied by memorandum of deposit or charge by deed.
3. By giving a charge on the land either by deed or by writing under hand without deposit of the deeds. Such a charge is termed a "General Equitable Charge".

FORMS OF CHARGE USED BY BANKS

Legal Mortgage

A legal mortgage must be effected by deed. It should contain an undertaking to pay the advance with interest and to continue paying interest as long as the principal is not repaid; a power to sell or to appoint a Receiver in case of default normally within a much shorter period than that prescribed by the Law of Property Act; covenants to insure premises and fixtures and to apply the proceeds in case of fire to repairing and replacing the damaged property. It should be declared to be a continuing security; if a lease is taken as a legal mortgage it must be by way of underlease, and not an assignment for the full term. Thus the mortgagee does not become liable for the due fulfilment of the covenants of the lease. Of course, the non-performance of the convenants by the mortgagor may entail forfeiture of the lease and the consequent loss of the security. The mortgagee will be given power to consolidate and the mortgagor will contract out of his statutory powers to grant leases and accept surrender thereof.

Equitable Mortgage

The Memorandum in these cases is usually under hand but if it contains a clause which gives the Mortgagee a Power of Attorney, or of Sale, or of appointing a receiver, it must be by deed. A mere oral agreement to deposit does not constitute an equitable mortgage. All the title deeds need not be deposited, but real and material portions of them should be deposited. A mere deposit of deeds is only a security for the one advance, in the absence of agreement to the contrary, but to put the matter beyond doubt, banks usually take a Memorandum drawn to cover future advances; besides a Memorandum removes all ground for question and litigation.

An equitable mortgage by deposit of deeds will extend to any interest the mortgagor may acquire, and will include fixtures, both existing and any that may be subsequently annexed. If the property is let the tenants' trade fixtures do not pass under the mortgage. An equitable mortgage by deposit of a lease does not compel the mortgagee to take a legal assignment of the suit of the lessor, not does it make him liable for the due fulfilment of the convenants of the lease.

There will be the usual covenant to insure and the bank will have power to consolidate. As in the case of a legal mortgage the mortgagor will contract out of his right to grant leases, etc.

PRIORITIES OF MORTGAGES AND LAND CHARGES

This depends upon:

1. Holding the deeds or land certificate.
2. Notice of prior rights.
3. Registration of charge where necessary.

The procedures vary as to whether or not the land is unregistered or registered.

H.M. Land Registry has two departments; the Land Registry, and the Land Charges Department.

The Land Registry

This is where all details of *registered* land are filed under a register of, properties recorded by title numbers. The Land Registry has representative offices covering all areas.

The Land Charges Department

This department holds various registers where interests in *unregistered* land can be noted. The Land Charges Act 1925 set up this system of registration to protect purchasers and to preserve the rights of those having equitable interests. These rights are known as "land charges" and the principle is that registration is notice to the whole world, while an unregistered charge is void against a purchaser for value. The charges registrable are briefly as follows: (i) Petitions in bankruptcy; (ii) receiving orders in bankruptcy; (iii) puisne mortgages, i.e. legal mortgages not protected by a deposit of deeds; (iv) limited owners' charges; (v) general equitable charges which include equitable mortgages not protected by a deposit of deeds; (vi) estate contracts, which arise when there is an agreement to sell or lease land; (vii) restrictive covenants; (viii) equitable easements; (ix) death duty charges; (x) any charge affecting any land by virtue of the Matrimonial Homes Act 1967. A mortgage of unregistered land, whether legal or equitable, does not require registration if backed by deposit of title deeds. Where title deeds are not deposited, the priority of all mortgages of unregistered land, whether legal or equitable, will depend upon the date order of their registration. The charges are divided into various classes, the main ones being:

Class C (i) — puisne mortgages
Class C (iii) — general equitable charges
Class D (ii) — restrictive covenants
Class F — charges under the Matrimonial Homes Act 1967.

Searches

Therefore when a banker is proposing to take a mortgage of land, searches should be made in accordance with the following:

1. Unregistered Land.
   (i) Land Charges Register at the Land Registry, containing the charges registrable under the Land Charges Act 1925 enumerated in the preceding paragraph.
   (ii) Local Land Charges Registers, kept at the office of the Local Authority for Local Land Charges and also at the office of the County Council concerned.
   (iii) Register of Charges kept by the Registrar of Companies (at Companies House) if the land is owned by a joint stock company.
2. Registered Land.
   (i) Land Registry. A search will be permitted only on written authority of the proprietor or upon production of the Land Certificate in which event it will be written up-to-date with all charges standing against the land on the register. The date upon which the Certificate was last compared with the register will be noted on the certificate.
   (ii) Local Land Charges Register } as for unregistered land.
   (iii) Companies' Register } as for unregistered land.

The Local Land Charges Registers record charges acquired by local authorities under various Acts of Parliament, in the main relating to issues arising out of road improvement plans, town planning schemes and repairs to properties under the Public Health Acts.

PROCEDURE FOR TAKING UNREGISTERED LAND AS SECURITY

When title deeds are offered as security, the intending mortgagor must deposit the deeds and accompanying documents with the bank. The next thing is for the bank to establish a clear chain of title and initially the bank should check the deeds and documents against the schedule that accompanies them to ensure that they are complete.

The "root of title" is a document which will form the starting point for checking the title and deals with the whole legal and equitable interest in the land, describing the property adequately and containing nothing to throw any doubt on the title. For freehold land the root is the latest conveyance or legal mortgage more than fifteen years old. In other words, the banker should find who was the legal owner fifteen years ago, and the root is the deed which vested the property in that person. The title of the owner at that time will be regarded as a good one because it would have been checked at that time, and all the subsequent transactions should be examined by scrutinising the relative deeds and documents right up to the time of the present owner.

In view of the importance of establishing a proper title and the legal knowledge and experience this may call for, the banker will normally send the deeds to a solicitor who will examine the deeds and confirm to the bank that after the bank has taken its mortgage the bank will have a "good and marketable title" to the land. In practice most banks allow a solicitor's report on title to be dispensed with in certain instances such as where the bank is to lend not more than a certain figure against the security (the figure obviously being a matter purely for that bank to decide), or where the land and property itself is not worth more than a certain figure. In making such rules as this, a bank is merely taking a practical view of the possible risks it may run, balancing on the one hand the possible losses it may incur by in some cases not obtaining a good title against, on the other hand, the savings made due to not obtaining a solicitor's report on title in all instances.

In the case of leasehold land, it is not possible to investigate the title to the freehold, so the root may be more recent than fifteen years. The first document will be the "head" lease which is the first grant of a lease by the freeholder and the leasehold chain only goes back to that time, the right of the freeholder to grant the lease being assumed.

Once a good root has been established (by the banker himself or by a solicitor where one is employed) the legal title will be checked in chronological order in the various hands through which it has passed. There will usually be deaths, marriages, and sometimes bankruptcies, which will be recited in the appropriate deeds and in the abstract of title which accompanies the deeds. Abstracts are documents which schedule the chain of title from the root of title to the present day and where a solicitor is being used, the abstract should be marked as having been compared by the solicitor with the actual documents. (Abstracts come about by virtue of being prepared by a vendor's solicitor on a sale, when the solicitor has to show a good root of title at least fifteen years old and a clear title from then up to the time of sale.)

Once a satisfactory title has been established, the banker must decide what form of mortgage he is going to take. In most instances the banker will seek a legal rather than equitable mortgage due to the superior remedies this affords. The usual method of taking a legal mortgage is to have the customer execute a charge by way of legal mortgage (see earlier in this chapter for the ways in which a legal mortgage can be created) and the standard legal charge form of a bank will usually be drawn up this way.

(There are some very important factors which need taking into account by the banker, irrespective of whether a legal or equitable mortgage is to be taken, when deciding whether an "own account" or "third party" charge form is appropriate. Additionally, the question of independent legal advice arises in certain circumstances and, where residential property is to be given as security, there can be further complications. These aspects are discussed separately later in this chapter and covered also in the relative checklists in Chapter 10.)

When the bank's form of charge has been executed, the banker (or their solicitor where he is involved) will search against the customer's name on the Land Charges Register by submitting the official search form (Form K15) to the Land Charges Department which is based at Plymouth. A fee of 50p is payable for each name searched against and a certificate of search is issued on Form K17 (where the reply is "No subsisting entries") or on Form K18 (where details of any entries are given). The object of searching is to check that the bank's position is protected as far as the past is concerned. In respect of the future, the bank will safeguard its position by keeping possession of the title deeds as this act gives notice to any possible subsequent lenders against the deeds that there is already a loan outstanding. However, although the banker has received the deeds from the customer, which indicates there is unlikely to be any borrowing outstanding against them (as a prior lender would presumably have taken the deeds and retained them) it is necessary to make sure, as an earlier lender who has not retained the deeds would have to protect his interest by registering it at the Land Charges Department. Thus the search by the banker (or his solicitor) is to ascertain if any such entry exists.

Once the search reveals a clear title, the banker must retain the deeds at all times and as he has possession of the deeds he does not need to give notice to the world of his interest by registration at the Land Charges Department. If a need arises for the mortgagor (or someone else on his behalf) to inspect the deeds, this should be done at the bank. Alternatively the deeds could be released to a solicitor, provided the bank was satisfied as to the reliability of the solicitor, against an undertaking from the solicitor to return the deeds or pay over the proceeds of sale where the mortgaged land and/or property is being sold.

Further searches necessary are those relating to the registers maintained by local authorities which could reveal important changes possibly affecting the value of the property, e.g. preservation orders, new road or motorway plans, slum clearance plans, demolition orders etc. A search should therefore be made and as the results of a local authority search can be rather involved, it is best to employ the services of a solicitor who will search on the appropriate official form and in due course will let the bank have the results of the search by way of the "local search certificate" which is the duplicate of the search form used, and which will in most cases allow the bank to note the result of the search in its security records as "No subsisting entries". The solicitor would have been asked to comment on any plans or incumberances which may materially affect the value of the security.

Having progressed the bank's security to this stage, it is important to ensure that adequate fire insurance exists covering any property on the land that has been charged. The relative fire insurance policy should be obtained from the customer and sent to the company (the banker should be satisfied as to the standing of the insurance company) in order to have the bank's interest endorsed on it or alternatively, the banker may hold on to the policy from this stage and give notice of the bank's interest to the company and obtain an acknowledgement. Some companies are content with acknowledging the bank's interest, others require to endorse the bank's interest on the policy itself. The individual banks have arrangements whereby they are covered by contingency policies which enable them to dispense with the need for giving notice to the insurance companies in relation to policies for private dwellings where the cover does not exceed a certain figure (this is revised from time to time). However, the bank nevertheless needs to check that a valid policy is in force at the date of the charge and that the amount of the policy (relating to buildings only) is adequate at the date of the bank's charge. The premiums on the policy must be kept up to date and preferably should be paid by standing order.

In the case of a limited company customer, a search would be necessary on the companies register at Companies House. A charge on land would require registration within 21 days under Section 95 of the Companies Act 1948 (Section 395 of the 1985 Act) and the certificate of registration should be kept with the deeds.

When the security has been completed, the banker will enter details of this in his security records in accordance with the security procedures laid down by the bank. Any fees or commissions involved will be debited to the customer's account.

TAKING REGISTERED LAND AS SECURITY

There are two methods of taking a charge over registered land and these correspond to a legal and equitable mortgage respectively.

A legal mortgage of registered land is effected by means of a special form of charge which is sent in duplicate, together with the land certificate, to the Registrar. In exchange, a certificate of charge on which will be listed particulars of any prior charges, is issued and with which is bound up the original charge. The land certificate is retained by the Registrar together with the duplicate charge. Only legal estates can be registered. Therefore registration is not possible unless a charge is made by deed or by creating a lease, or a charge by deed by way of legal mortgage.

In practice, most banks use their own standard form of legal charge (which is a form approved by the Registrar) which contains all the usual provisions as to continuing security, etc. To perfect their legal Mortgage, the legal charge and a duplicate will be sent to the Registrar together with the appropriate registration form (Form A4) and the land certificate. A certificate of charge will be sent to the banker and the bank's charge is now registered as a legal mortgage.

In practice many banks do not automatically register legal charges but take a legal charge from the customer and lodge a notice of deposit which will enable them to register their legal mortgage at any time.

An equitable mortgage of registered land may be created by deposit of the Land Certificate with or without a Memorandum of Deposit. **Notice of Deposit of a Land Certificate** is sent, on a special form in duplicate, to the Registrar, who acknowledges receipt by returning the duplicate. The Notice will operate as a caution and the Registrar is then required to give notice to the mortgagee of any proposed dealing with the property, and this enables the equitable mortgagee to take steps to protect his interests.

As equitable mortgages cannot be registered **in practice**, a banker usually takes a Land Certificate together with a legal mortgage over the land, but instead of registering his charge immediately he lodges a **Notice of Deposit** of a **Land Certificate**. He may then, having taken a charge under seal, register his legal mortgage at any time; he must do so within fourteen days of receiving notice from the registrar of a subsequent charge if he wishes to retain his priority: to the relief of banks, in *Barclays Bank Ltd. v. Taylor* (1973) the Court of Appeal reversed the decision at first instance and upheld the validity of this procedure.

The Administration of Justice Act 1977 *inter alia* amended Section 106 of the Land Registration Act 1925 and removed the proviso that caused the difficulty in this case.

Where the customer cannot produce the Land Certificate because either the title is in the process of first registration or the transfer to him has not yet been registered, the banker can safeguard his position by getting his customer to sign a Notice of Intended Deposit of a Land Certificate and lodging it at the Land Registry. This Notice will operate as a caution in the same way as a Notice of Deposit and the Land Certificate, when ready, will be issued to the banker, who can then take his usual form of charge. There is no need to give Notice of Deposit because the original notice of intended deposit will hold good.

When investigating the title for registered land the banker should establish the type of title granted to the registered owner and should investigate any encumbrances on the title that may be recorded in the Proprietorship Register of the land certificate. The banker should ensure that any title documents which should accompany the land certificate are present. If the title is a possessory or qualified title, all available deeds must be held and the title prior to registration will have to be examined as though the land were unregistered. For leasehold property, the actual lease or underlease must be held.

If taking a registered charge, the customer will sign the bank's form of legal mortgage and deposit the land certificate as outlined earlier. The banker will make a search on the Register using the official Land Registry form and the search may only be made with the authority of the proprietor (owner) or his solicitor, who therefore will need to sign a suitable form, this being an Authority to Inspect the Register. The duplicate of the search form will be returned with the result of the search and is known as the "official certificate of search". If the search shows a clear title, the banker has twenty days from the date of the result of the official search within which to register his charge unless the protection period is extended by a further search.

The procedure for registering the charge is that the bank sends to the Land Registry the form of legal charge (ensuring that it has been completed and dated correctly), a copy of the legal charge, the appropriate registration fee (based on the sliding scale of charges published by the Land Registry), the result of the Search Certificate and an appropriate certificate signed by the bank which, under the Land Registration Fee Order 1976, confirms in a prescribed form either the value of the land and property (or the equity if appropriate), the maximum advance to be secured (if less than the value) or that the mortgage is to secure only contingent liabilities. After registration has been effected a charge certificate will be sent to the branch with the legal charge sewn into the certificate. The banker should check that the bank's charge is correctly registered and the branch address recorded. The certificate must have been compared to the register *after* the date of the bank's charge (the stamp on the cover of the charge certificate will confirm this or otherwise) and it should be checked that there are no other unknown charges registered on the certificate.

SECOND MORTGAGES (AND THEIR DEFECTS)

Second mortgages may be legal or equitable. In general they used not to be regarded as good banking securities but the continual increase in the value of real property has made them more respectable — i.e. there are now often cases with a good margin between the existing mortgage and the current valuation, so that a second mortgage is worth taking. The first mortgagee usually holds the title deeds and, therefore, the second mortgage whether it be a legal mortgage (i.e. a puisne (younger) mortgage) or an equitable mortgage (i.e. a general equitable charge) must be registered as a land charge in order to obtain priority over subsequent mortgages. In practice, second mortgages are almost invariably legal rather than equitable. The first mortgagee is entitled to be paid before the second mortgagee. The first mortgagee may basically sell the property without considering the interest of the second mortgagee. Even if the second mortgagee pays off the first mortgagee the sale of the property may not yield enough to pay both charges. If notice of the second mortgage is not given to the first mortgagee there is the danger of "tacking".

When a second mortgage is proposed, enquiries are made of the first mortgagee so that full details will be known, and once the mortgage has been executed the second mortgagee will give notice of execution to the first mortgagee.

A second mortgage of registered land is effected by sending a special form of Registered Second Charge in duplicate to the Registrar, who will issue in exchange a Certificate of Second Charge, with details of all prior charges. Before registering the second charge the Registrar will give notice to the first mortgagee.

When a first mortgagee makes additional advances he may "**Tack**" these to his earlier advances and claim priority for the total advance over a second mortgagee, **but only**:

(a) If an arrangement to that effect has been made with the subsequent mortgagees.

or (b) If he has no notice of the subsequent mortgage at the time of making the further advance.

or (c) If the terms of the mortgage bind him to make further advances. In this case he can tack whether or not he has notice of the subsequent mortgages.

Note that the obligation to make further advances must be a term of the **mortgage**. The mere fact that the mortgage provides that it be security for further advances does not constitute an obligation to make further advances. Thus the usual method of arranging an overdraft limit would not give the bank the right to tack after receipt of notice of a second charge.

Therefore the bank on receiving notice of a second charge should, if lending on current account, break the account, to prevent the operation of the Rule in *Clayton's Case* to the detriment of the bank. Failure to do this would mean that any payment to credit would reduce the amount secured by the mortgage and any payment out would be a fresh advance which would rank **after** the second mortgagee's claim: the bank lost its security in this way in *Deeley v. Lloyds Bank Ltd.* (1912).

In the context of mortgages, "consolidation" occurs when several mortgages are made by the same person to the same mortgagee. It is the name given to the option of the mortgagee to refuse redemptiom of any one mortgage until all the mortgages are redeemed together, but it is exercisable only when it is expressly reserved in the mortgage deeds. This is usually the case in bank mortgage forms and consequently the bank may refuse to release one set of deeds until repayment of the whole of the debt due. The form reserves the right to consolidate by excluding Section 93 of the Law of Property Act 1925.

The object, of course, is to prevent a mortgagor from redeeming a valuable property, and leaving the bank with another which may be quite unsatisfactory as security.

The difference between tacking and consolidation is that:

In the case of tacking land is mortgaged by the same person to **different** mortgagees.

In the case of consolidation, several mortgages are made by the same person to the **same** mortgagee (not necessarily the first).

Tacking by a person other than a prior mortgagee is forbidden. Thus a third mortgagee will not be able to tack his mortgage on to the first mortgage by taking a transfer of the first mortgage in order to obtain priority over the second mortgagee.

SUB-MORTGAGES

A sub-mortgage is a mortgage of a mortgage, i.e. a mortgagee (Y) can give as security to a third party (Z) a charge over the mortgage given in his favour by the mortgagor (X). Thus Y will be the sub-mortgagor, Z will be the sub-mortgagee and the original mortgage given by X becomes the head mortgage.

A sub-mortgage may be legal or equitable except that where the head-mortgage is equitable, any sub-mortgage must necessarily be equitable. Effectively, the benefit of the mortgage is itself being given as security, and the sub-mortgagee is thus protected by the liability of the original mortgagor

and the sub-mortgagor. The value of the sub-mortgage is the amount outstanding at any time on the original mortgage, although it should be checked that the value of the property is adequate security for this sum.

A legal sub-mortgage recites the head mortgage and assigns the mortgage debt, and where the head mortgage is by demise, the property will be demised to the sub-mortgagee for a term less by at least one day than the term held by the mortgagee; where the head mortgage is a charge by way of legal mortgage the sub-mortgage is effected by a transfer of the benefit of the head mortgage. The legal sub-mortgagee can exercise both the power of sale in the original mortgage and that in the sub-mortgage, subject to the two equities of redemption. An equitable sub-mortgage is effected by depositing the original (or "head") mortgage, probably with a memorandum of deposit, or by completing a general equitable charge. A sub-mortgage of unregistered land cannot be protected by registration, but a sub-mortgage of registered land may be protected (if legal) by registration of a sub-mortgage caution, or (if equitable) by Notice of Deposit of charge certificate or a sub-mortgage caution (if under seal) or a caution (if under hand).

Notice of sub-mortgage should be given to the original mortgagor, so that he will make his payments direct to the bank; note that each such payment received represents a reduction in the value of the sub-mortgage as the bank's security.

RIGHTS OF MORTGAGEES

Legal Mortgage

The following rights are given to a legal mortgagee by the Law of Property Act 1925: they are, however, subject to any contrary intention expressed in the mortgage deed. The terms of the charge must always be consulted before exercising remedies against the security.

1. Sue on the Personal Covenant to Repay

By writ and judgement.

The right to sue on the personal covenant is a personal remedy only, that is, the mortgagee may bring an action for the repayment of the loan and interest due to him. The legal mortgagee has 12 years in which to sue, dating from the date of the advance or the date of part payment of principal or interest or by written acknowledgement of the debt whichever is the latest.

This remedy may be used to advantage when the borrower possesses other means and the mortgagee does not wish to take action against the security. Some modern bank forms do not contain this covenant.

2. Sell the Property

This may be by aution or private treaty provided the price is reasonable. The proceeds must be applied to (i) discharge of prior encumbrances to which the sale is not made subject; (ii) costs of the sale; (iii) repayment of mortgage and interest; (iv) the residue to the person entitled thereto.

The power to sell may not be exercised until:

(a) Demand for repayment and default for three months, or
(b) Interest in arrears for two months, or
(c) Breach of some other covenant in the mortgage deed.

Bank mortgages usually provide for much shorter notice than that given by the Act.

3. Appoint a Receiver

This would be done where the premises are let, or it is desired to wait before selling but to keep the interest on foot in the meantime. The income must be applied (i) to discharge outgoings (rates, taxes, repairs, etc.); (ii) in payment of interest; (iii) any surplus to reduce principal.

The object of appointing a receiver to manage the property and collect the rents is to obtain all the advantages but none of the risks of taking possession.

A similar restriction is placed on power to appoint a receiver as in power to sell: i.e. a default for three months, etc.

It must be noticed that where mortgages are created after 1925 and the power to sell or to appoint a receiver arises only because the mortgagor has committed an act of bankruptcy or has become bankrupt these powers can only be exercised with leave of the Court.

4. Foreclosure

The consent of the Court is always required once again.

The Court will usually make an order nisi. which becomes absolute if outstanding for six months, and then vests the property in the mortgagee who can sell and retain the **whole** of the proceeds. This remedy is not normally exercised by a banker.

To obtain an order for foreclosure an action must be brought against the mortgagor and the object of the action is to deprive the mortgagor of his legal estate and make the mortgagee the absolute owner. The Court generally orders a sale.

5. Enter into Possession

This is not often done owing to the onerous obligations involved, for the mortgagee must collect all rents at his own expense and undertake many other duties and liabilities.

If a mortgagee enters into possession and remains in possession for 12 years without acknowledging the title of the mortgagor, he may by deed enlarge his mortgage term into a fee simple, that is, become the freeholder.

A mortgagee in possession has the power to grant leases or, if a receiver has been appointed, the mortgagee can delegate the power of leasing to the receiver.

The remedies and powers of a mortgagee of leaseholds are practically the same as those of a mortgagee of freeholds, except that the original lease may contain restrictive covenants and that the mortgagee's rights apply to the mortgagor's terms and not to the freehold.

Equitable Mortgagee

The rights of an equitable mortgagee are generally set out in full in the Memorandum of Deposit, but apart from this he has power:

1. To sue for payment.
2. To bring an action to compel the mortgagor to execute a legal mortgage if he has so undertaken or where deeds have been deposited. The remedies of a legal mortgagee are then available as above.
3. To bring an action for foreclosure.
4. To bring an action for sale.
5. To apply to the Court for the appointment of a receiver.

An equitable mortgagee (having no legal estate) is not entitled to take possession unless such power has been expressly reserved by the charge.

If an equitable mortgage is **under seal** the mortgagee has similar powers to a legal mortgagee **to sell or to appoint a receiver**. He cannot, however, without an order of the Court convey a legal title to a purchaser unless the Memorandum of Deposit under seal contained an irrevocable clause appointing the mortgagee attorney for the sale of the land or to execute a legal mortgage, or a declaration by the mortgagor that he holds the land in trust for the mortgagee with power given to the mortgagee to remove him and appoint new trustees.

MATRIMONIAL HOMES AND RESIDENTIAL PROPERTIES

The Matrimonial Homes Act 1967 re-introduced the deserted wife's equity (i.e. her right to remain in the matrimonial home) which was rejected by the House of Lords in *National Provincial Bank Ltd. v. Ainsworth* (1965). Section 1 of this Act gives a statutory right of occupation to the spouse other than the one entitled by virtue of any estate or interest to occupy the matrimonial home. Thus if the house is held by the husband in his sole name, his wife cannot be evicted or excluded by him except with the leave of the Court, nor can a husband where the house is held by his wife. During the continuance of the marriage this statutory right of occupation is stated to be an equitable charge on the estate or interest of the other spouse, and any order made will also take effect against persons deriving title under the other spouse (e.g. purchasers and mortgagees) who are affected by the charge. This will be so where prior to the purchase or mortgage the charge has been registered, in the case of unregistered land as a land charge in an additional category designated Class F and in the case of registered land by lodging a notice or caution. If such a charge is registered, a mortgagee will doubtless insist on its withdrawal or postponement and therefore a bank as prospective mortgagee is not affected greatly by the Act since the bank would require such withdrawal or postponement in relation to the bank's charge before granting any advance and if it is not registered, the bank will not be bound by it. The Act provides that a spouse's right of occupation shall not be an overriding interest within the meaning of the Land Registration Act 1925. Overriding interests are certain rights which are always binding on any person who acquires any interest in registered land, even though there is no reference whatever to them in any part of the register. These interests can be ascertained by enquiry of the occupier. The necessity for a purchaser or mortgagee to enquire as to rights of occupation was shown in *Hodgson v. Marks* (1971) where the Court of Appeal held that even where a vendor was or appeared to be in occupation, another person might in certain circumstances be in "actual occupation" within the meaning of S. 70 of the Land Registration Act 1925 and thus have an overriding interest. A new type of equity was created in *Williams & Glyn's Bank Ltd. v. Boland* (1979) where a husband and wife bought a house with joint earnings, but the house was put into the name of the husband only and he charged it to the bank without telling his wife. When seeking possession, the bank made no enquiry as to whether the wife had an interest in the property and the Court of Appeal rescinded the order for possession on the ground that since the wife was physically present and living in the house she was in actual possession of it and therefore her equitable rights were an overriding interest. The House of Lords subsequently upheld the Court of Appeal decision.

It should be noted that the term "overriding interest" relates only to registered land but from a practical point of view the impact of the Boland case is the same where unregistered land is concerned as the court saw no reason why this new equity should not exist in unregistered as well as registered land.

As a result of this, banks now ensure as far as possible that when taking as security a residential property they have the charge executed by not only the registered owners but by any other adult persons who occupy the house, thus in the case of the latter suitably obtaining a charge over whatever interest it might be held they had. Therefore, when residential property is to be charged as security, enquiries always should be made to ascertain whether there are any adult persons living in the property as well as the party or parties in whose name the legal estate is vested.

The practice adopted by the different banks varies somewhat and indeed this whole area of law relating to land remains problematical and has been the subject of a report by the Law Commission (see later). However, the following is a reasonable way of approaching the problem in practice:

1. Where the legal estate owner, then both spouses must join in the charge.

2. Any other adult person(s) other than the legal estate owner living in the property should be asked to join in the charge.
3. If the legal estate owner marries or in the case of the banker learning that another person is also occupying the property, all parties should execute a fresh charge form in place of the original charge. Alternatively, the new spouse or occupier should sign a separate charge form.

In respect of the three instances as stated above, the form of charge taken should be worded so that the interests of the party are embraced in addition to the schedule describing the property itself. The following sort of description could be used to charge the interests of the mortgagors:

> "... the mortgagor charges by way of legal mortgage the premises described in the schedule hereto to the full extent of such interest as the mortgagor has in the said premises or in the proceeds of sale thereof and howsoever arising."

If a situation arises whereby a person resident at the property, after enquiry by the bank claims to have no interest in the property, then written confirmation of this should be obtained by means of a formal disclaimer which should always be executed with the benefit of independent legal advice (the question of independent legal advice generally is explained later in this chapter). The form of disclaimer could be on the following lines:

> "In consideration of the bank granting or continuing banking facilities .... upon the security of a mortgage or legal charge dated .... in your favour over the dwellinghouse situate and known as .... I .... hereby irrevocably confirm and warrant that I have no interest whether legal equitable or otherwise in the said dwellinghouse and I hereby declare that I will not at any time in the future claim as against you any such interest in the said dwellinghouse or in any proceeds of sale thereof howsoever arising.
> Dated this .... day of .... 198. .
> Signed sealed and delivered by the said ....
> In the presence of:
> Witness ....
> Address ....
> ....
> Occupation ....
> (A legal advice clause — see later — should always be added to this type of disclaimer)."

It would be unwise to use the above type of disclaimer in the case of a spouse, only a banker would be well-advised to accept residential property as security only where the spouse will execute the legal charge.

Sometimes banks find that a mortgage they have obtained has been executed in their favour by one of the parties in whom the land is vested and as a result the bank holds no mortgage over the legal estate. In such instances it was thought that the mortgage from one of several joint owners would at least constitute an effective charge over the equitable interest of the mortgagor in the proceeds of sale, but in *Cedar Holdings Ltd. v. Green and Green* (1979) it was held that such a mortgage does not achieve this consequence and thus is totally ineffective. However, in *First National Securities Ltd. v. Hegarty and another* (1982) it was held in similar circumstances that such a document, whilst abortive as a legal charge, created a valid equitable charge over the one party's beneficial interest in the joint home.

In *Midland Bank Ltd. v. Farmpride Hatcheries Ltd. and Willey* (1981) the Court of Appeal refused an injunction to Mr. and Mrs. Willey to restrain the bank from recovering possession of the property of a company in which they resided. They claimed that when the bank took its mortgage over the company's house, they were in occupation of the house under the terms of a service agreement which had allowed them the use of the house for twenty years. In this case Mr. Willey was estopped from setting up any facts which would show he had an overriding interest which would have priority over the bank's interest and thus to some extent a limit was put on the application of the "Boland" case mentioned earlier.

The two cases *Re Holliday (a bankrupt)* (1981) and *Re Lowrie (a bankrupt)* (1981) also involved the court exercising discretion in the matter of the forced sale of matrimonial homes.

The Matrimonial Homes and Property Act 1981 came largely into force in early 1983 and effectively extended the Matrimonial Homes Act 1967 to trust property. The Act introduced the right for any spouse to register "matrimonial rights" by a caution at the Land Registry (if registered land) or a Class F charge at the Land Charges Registry (if unregistered land). In September 1982 an Act came into force in Scotland giving a spouse the right to retain or (if not already in residence) gain occupation of the family home even when the property is not vested solely or jointly in that spouse's name. Thus in Scotland a mortgagee's security will be at risk if the spouse refuses to sign or consent or is unavailable to do so, or if the mortgagor denies that he or she has a spouse, or forges the consent. The Law Commission has reported on the position in England and Wales and recommended registration as the fairest way to give spouses (and other interested parties) protected rights of occupation without making the position of purchasers and mortgagees unacceptably risky (as is the case under the Scottish legislation above). Whether or not this will be implemented in the foreseeable future is open to some doubt due to the very onerous burden it would in practice place on the Land Registry. As an alternative, an act something on the lines of the Scottish one, could be introduced but it is difficult to see that this would significantly eliminate the uncertainties and problems.

INDEPENDENT LEGAL ADVICE

Over the past few years, security taken by banks has tended to be attacked increasingly by mortgagors and guarantors who have sought to escape liability, often by claiming that they were not aware of what they were entering into when they executed the security documents. Until fairly recently banks have been additionally sensitive to the risk of female sureties trying to upset security on the ground of *non est factum* but the Sex Discrimination Act 1975 has resulted in the banks ceasing to differentiate on grounds of sex.

In *Carlisle and Cumberland Banking Co. v. Bragg* (1911) the guarantee document was entrusted to the person who had most to gain by it being signed (i.e. the principal debtor) and subsequently the guarantor was held not to be bound by his signature on the guarantee by successfully pleading *non est factum*. However, the whole doctrine of *non est factum* was fully reviewed in the House of Lords in *Saunders v. Anglia Building Society* (1970) and it was held that the doctrine could be invoked only for the benefit of those unable to read due to blindness or illiteracy or those suffering from illness, defective education or innate capacity.Even then, a reasonable amount of care must have been exercised before a defence of *non est factum* could be submitted.

In *Lloyds Bank Ltd. v. Bundy* (1974), which involved a guarantee, the security was set aside on the grounds that the bank had failed in its duty to its customer (who was the guarantor) by not ensuring that he understood the nature of the liability he was undertaking and the consequences which would follow if the bank had to have recourse to its security.

Nowadays most banks try to ensure that all guarantors and other parties giving third party security receive independent legal advice regarding the documents they are signing and their implications. Whereas up to now, the practice of most banks has been to identify instances where it is particularly important that the person giving the security is independently advised, the trend is now towards making it a basic rule that legal advice must be obtained whenever third-party security is being given, with any exceptions to this rule being permitted only where a conscious decision to this effect has been made for what is felt to be a good reason.

This independent legal advice should be insisted upon when a person:

- gives a charge (or guarantee) which secures any liabilities other than his or her own, or
- joins in a charge because of an overriding interest, as outlined earlier in this chapter.

Independent legal advice must be evidenced by some form of "legal advice clause" added to the security document and signed by the solicitor. A standard wording could be as follows:

> "I hereby confirm that prior to the execution of this document I explained the contents and effect thereof to .... who informed me that he/she understood the same.
> Signature .... Solicitor.
> Address ....
> ....

DISCHARGE OF MORTGAGE

Unregistered Land

When the borrowing has been repaid the deeds can be handed back to the mortgagor and if an equitable charge had been held, the charge form would be placed on a suitable bank file for "lapsed security papers." In the case of a legal mortgage, the property needs to be re-conveyed and this would usually be effected by the bank executing under seal the form of receipt and release usually printed on the back of the bank's form of legal mortgage. The released charge forms part of the chain of title to the land and therefore needs to be placed with the deeds. Sometimes a more formal discharge is requested by the mortgagor and this could take the form of a deed of re-conveyance being executed by the parties. This may also be required where more than one property has been charged on the form and not all the properties are being redeemed.

Where the mortgagor has repaid the advance it is not necessary to search for subsequent mortgages, but a search must be made on the Land Charges Register before the deeds and any surplus proceeds are handed back where the customer has failed to repay and the bank has sold the property under its power of sale.

Registered Land

If the bank has a legal charge this could be discharged by the usual form of receipt in the nature of a reconveyance but the usual, and most practical, method is to send to the registry the charge certificate accompanied by the special form of discharge (Form 53). Provided that there are no other outstanding entries, the Registrar will cancel the charge certificate and remove the bank's form of charge, entering the certificate up to date and returning it to the registered proprietor. Where the land is being discharged as a result of the sale of part of the land, Form 53 is used but the following form of words would be added "As to the land shown and edged with red on the accompanying plan, signed by me, being part of the land comprised in the said charge."

If the charge had been created by notice of deposit, this notice can be withdrawn by the bank by completion of the appropriate form (Form 85) and sending this together with the land certificate to the registry. The land certificate will be updated by the Registrar and returned to the registered proprietor. The bank's form of legal mortgage could be filed away on the bank's file for "lapsed security papers."

In the case of the bank wanting to realise its security and where the bank holds the land certificate protected by a notice of deposit, the bank will have to take out a charge certificate to obtain a legal title. The co-operation of the customer will not be necessary as the bank will hold a completed legal charge signed by the customer, which until now has not needed to play a part. When the bank has the legal title it can effect a sale by means of a Land Registry Transfer form. After realisation of the security there is no reason why any surplus should not be handed over to the mortgagor without the need to search the register, since if there had been any subsequent charge notice of it would have been given by the Registrar.

CONCLUSION

The procedures for taking land and buildings as security are inevitably rather complicated due to the several factors which have to be borne in mind whenever a banker has agreed to lend against this type of security. Suggested checklists for first and second legal charges over both registered and unregistered land are given in Chapter 10.

Chapter 8

Securities for Advances (cont.)

GUARANTEES

A guarantee has been defined as an engagement to be collaterally answerable for the debt, default or miscarriage of another person. It has to be differentiated from an indemnity which is a promise to be *primarily* liable.

The standard illustration of the difference between subsidiary and sole liability is that arising out of *Birkmyr v. Darnell* (1704): when two persons go to a shop and one buys, and the other says to the shopkeeper "let him have the goods and if he does not pay you, I will", this is a guarantee. If, however, he says instead "let him have the goods and I will pay you for them" he is undertaking to pay directly on his own behalf, not merely if the other party fails to pay. This would be an indemnity.

A guarantee must be evidenced by signed writing (Statute of Frauds 1677, S.4); an indemnity need not be in writing.

Note, however, that under the terms of Section 105 of the Consumer Credit Act 1974, even indemnities must be in writing in respect of agreements coming within the scope of the Act, and if they are not, they will only be enforceable if the court so orders. Neither a guarantee nor an indemnity need be under seal, but if it is **not** under seal (as is usually the case) consideration is essential.

It is not always easy to determine whether an undertaking is a guarantee or an indemnity and it is important to distinguish between the two, because whereas a guarantee requires signed evidence in writing an indemnity does not. On a practical note, however, a banker is not likely to accept even an indemnity unless in writing. In the unlikely event of a bank having accepted an oral arrangement say involving the provision of outside security, it would at a later stage be open to the party to argue that the circumstances were tantamount to a guarantee and thus the arrangement is unenforceable under the Statute of Frauds 1677.

The mere use of the words "guarantee" or "indemnity" in documents is not conclusive as the document and underlying transaction would be looked at as a whole. The question of guarantees and indemnities has been considered by the courts over recent years in connection with hire-purchase documents, in particular the "recourse agreement" whereby a motor dealer backs in favour of a hire-purchase company the agreement made between the finance company and the hirer. Different decisions have been made in different cases depending on the circumstances and documentation applying to each case. In *Goulston Discount Co. Ltd. v. Clark* (1966) the finance company (plaintiff) could only sue the hirer for the arrears of the instalments and, as they were not successful in recovering these from him, they pursued the dealer (defendant) under his recourse agreement. The issue was that if the recourse agreement was a guarantee, the defendant's liability could be no more than that of the hirer, i.e. to pay the arrears. If, however, it was an indemnity, the defendant would be liable for the whole of the hire-purchase price. It was held in that case by the Court of Appeal that the particular document was an indemnity.

In *Edward Owen Engineering Ltd. v. Barclays Bank International Ltd.* (1978) the Court of Appeal considered what they said was a new business transaction by way of a performance guarantee or performance bond. They found that such an arrangement had many similarities to a confirmed letter of credit and the bank was required to honour the guarantee according to its terms and was not concerned with whether either party to the contract which underlay the guarantee was in default.

CONSIDERATION

A guarantee must be signed by the guarantor and must be supported by a consideration (unless under seal), but a **statement** of the consideration is unnecessary (Mercantile Law Amendment Act 1856). Bank guarantees usually express it as "affording banking accommodation" or "continuing the account" or "giving time" for repayment.

If the **consideration** is expressed in a Bank guarantee, it should not be stated as the lending of a **definite sum**, for unless the condition is exactly as fulfilled, the guarantee will be of no avail: *Burton v. Gray* (1873). It is better to make the consideration the continuing of the debtor's account, or in some other form.

One of the five requisites of consideration is, that it must **not** be a **past** benefit. Services rendered in the past, however valuable, are not regarded as sufficient consideration to support a promise. In *Roscorla v. Thomas* (1842) a warranty in respect of a horse was given after the sale of the horse had been concluded. It was held that the warranty was not binding as the monetary consideration was past, and thus would not support the defendant's promise.

Therefore, if a bank takes a guarantee in respect of a dormant debit account, either the guarantee should be under seal, or else in the case of a guarantee under hand there must be an express or implied promise to forbear as consideration. To create this the bank may make a written demand for repayment on the customer and then, after receipt of a letter from the intending guarantor offering a guarantee if the bank will grant time to the customer, it will agree to do so against delivery of the completed guarantee.

When stating the consideration in forms of guarantee, banks need to ensure that future advances on any accounts or by other methods available to a customer are embraced. The dangers in not having a sufficiently wide form of wording were demonstrated in *National Bank of Nigeria Ltd. v. Oba M. S. Awolesi*(1964) and difficulties should be avoided by ensuring that the wording requires the guarantor to assume liability for any debt on the existing account or on any other account which may be subsequently opened, or for any liability otherwise contracted, such as discounts, bills, promissory notes, negotiations, etc.

SOME PRACTICAL POINTS ON GUARANTEES AS SECURITY

It could be said that there are several disadvantages attaching to a guarantee, these boiling down to the form of the guarantee itself, the rights of the guarantor and the question of the solvency of the guarantor coupled with the guarantor's likely co-operation or otherwise if called upon to substantiate his liability.

The technical drawbacks which, if not specifically catered for could be a problem, are by and large removed by the standard form of guarantee used by most banks which has evolved over a period of many years and which reflects past problems that occurred. These are explained later in this chapter when the features of a standard-type bank guarantee document are discussed.

As regards its effectiveness as security, a guarantee depends upon the continued solvency of the guarantor and obviously a guarantee, unless backed by tangible security charged by the guarantor in support of his liability under the guarantee, entails some risk of instability since the financial standing of the guarantor may change from time to time during the period for which the bank is relying upon the guarantee as security. Looking very practically at the matter, a banker should always have in mind that a guarantee (despite the fact that the bank holds a formal, printed document which is entered in its security records along with other items of security) is basically only a promise to pay if called upon so to do. Should the occasion arise where the banker has to call upon a guarantor to substantiate his liability then, unless the guarantee was supported by tangible security, this is analogous to the banker demanding repayment of an unsecured debt owing by the guarantor. Should the guarantor fail to substantiate his liability, then the only practical remedies open to the banker are those afforded by the bank instituting legal proceedings against the guarantor. This is quite different from the case of the bank holding tangible security when steps can be taken by the bank to realise that security.

A banker holding a guarantee as security can and should make status enquiries on the guarantor and indeed in the case of an unsupported guarantee this is the only way the guarantor's ability to pay can be assessed (unless the guarantor happens to bank at the same bank and branch where his financial standing will be known).

Status enquiries and the range of answers that can be given by bankers, was a topic discussed in Chapter 1. Thus an unsupported guarantee could vary, as far as the standing of the guarantor is concerned, from "Undoubted" to "Unable to speak for your figures (but we do not think that our customer would enter into any obligation which he could not see his way clear to fulfil)". Enquiries on guarantors should be made every six months. A guarantee that is fully supported by tangible security provided and charged by the guarantor, is as good as the supporting security itself, although it is sound practice even with fully-supported guarantees to put through regular enquiries for the information of the guarantor's banker. Another possible advantage gained from doing this is that if the guarantor should die, the lending banker could expect to be informed of this by the guarantor's bank if they knew of the existence of the guarantee.

DISCLOSURE

A guarantee is not a Contract *Uberrimae Fidei* (of the utmost good faith), i.e. it cannot be set aside on the grounds of failure to disclose a material fact. Nevertheless, as the contract is closely construed in favour of the surety, the banker must avoid any risk of a charge of **misrepresentation** which might render the contract voidable.

As regards disclosure to a prospective guarantor, a banker can assume that the guarantor has made himself acquainted with the financial position of the customer he intends to guarantee. The banker is not therefore bound voluntarily to make any disclosure regarding the customer's indebtedness to the bank.

No disclosure need voluntarily be made as to how the debtor's account has been conducted, whether the debtor has been in the habit of overdrawing or whether he has been punctual and honourable in his dealings: *Hamilton v. Watson* (1845). It has similarly been held that no disclosure need be made when the husband of a woman whose account is guaranteed is an undischarged bankrupt having authority to draw on her account: *Cooper v. National Provincial Bank Ltd.* (1945).

But if there is an **exceptional** relationship or contract between banker and customer, then disclosure must be made. In the last mentioned case it was suggested that there might be a duty to disclose voluntarily in the case of an undischarged bankrupt cloaking his trading activities by operating a banking account in his wife's name, **the account in effect being his own and not his wife's**.

Although the banker need not **volunteer** any information, if any information is given then the disclosure must be a full and fair one. Moreover, if the guarantor asks questions the banker must make straightforward replies which are not capable of being misunderstood.

If the guarantor is under any misapprehension regarding the debtor, however, it is the Banker's duty to correct it: *Royal Bank of Scotland v. Greenshields* (1914) and *Westminster Bank Ltd. v. Cond* (1940). As to the banker's right to disclose, having regard to the rule of secrecy, if asked for information by a proposed guarantor, the bank should arrange for a joint meeting of all parties to discuss the matter, or obtain the authority in writing of the customer to be guaranteed.

The bank should not suggest the name of a prospective guarantor to the borrower for subsequently the guarantor might contend that thereby the bank had made the principal debtor its agent; any misrepresentation by him might then suffice to avoid the guarantee. Again, the form of Guarantee should never be handed to the principal debtor to enable him to obtain the signature of the guarantor, for if he deceives the guarantor as to the nature of the guarantee the guarantor may escape liability on the plea of *non est factum* (not his deed, i.e. mistake as to nature of contract) but this is much less likely since *Carlisle & Cumberland Banking Co. v. Bragg* (1911), was overruled by the House of Lords in *Saunders v. Anglia Building Society* (1970). Their Lordships laid down that the plea of *non est factum* can only rarely be established by a person of full capacity and although it is not confined to the blind and the illiterate any extension of its scope would be kept within narrow limits; in particular, it is unlikely that the plea would be available to a person who signed a document without informing himself of its meaning: the burden of establishing the plea falls on the party seeking to disown the document and that party must show that in signing the document (which must be radically different from the type of document it was believed to be) he acted with reasonable care. Even apart from this aspect, however, there is the possibility of forgery of the guarantor's signature if the form is not signed under supervision, and the normal practice is to send the form to the guarantor's bank, where he can attend to sign it.

As far as disclosure after the guarantee has been given is concerned, the guarantor is entitled to be furnished with particulars of his liability at any time. He is not entitled to be given details of, or to inspect the principal debtor's account.

The limit of the liability alone should be disclosed, e.g. if the guarantee is for £10,000 and the overdraft is £12,500, the excess should not be disclosed without the approval of the principal debtor. In other words, if the indebtedness on the guaranteed account is less than the amount of the guarantee, the balance on the account will be advised to the guarantor as the amount for which he is liable. If the debt exceeds the limit on the guarantee, the guarantor will merely be told that his guarantee is being fully relied upon.

The banker need not advise the surety of any change in the debtor's position: *National Provincial Bank Ltd. v. Glanusk* (1913). He may, however, insist on permission being given to him to do so on equitable grounds by threatening to call in the advance.

A guarantor who pays off the whole of the debt is entitled to claim from the banker any security which has been deposited against the debt. Also if the bank is obliged to sue the guarantor for payment of the guaranteed debt, the guarantor can claim the benefit of any counterclaim or set-off which the principal debtor may have had against the bank.

However, the rule that a person who has to make a payment for which another is primarily liable is entitled to be indemnified need not always be applied and the circumstances in which the guarantor acquires the obligation can be very significant. In *Owen v. Tate and Another* (1975) the guarantor assumed the responsibility not out of concern over the principal debtors, but in order to substitute his guarantee for another security belonging to a third person in whom he was interested. The substitution was as it turned out contrary to the wishes of the principal debtors as they protested when they heard about it. The circumstances in which the guarantor made the payment to the bank were also relevant. The principal debtors never wished to lose the benefit of the original security but had no choice as they had to accept the guarantee which without their authority or consent had been substituted for the security previously held with which they had fully agreed as acceptable. The Court of Appeal in this case did not support the guarantor in his action for an imdemnity because he had assumed the obligation without having first been asked so to do.

THE GUARANTOR

Normally any person with power to contract may bind himself by a guarantee.

Guarantee by Partnership

If one **partner** gives a guarantee in the name of the firm in accordance with the **usage of that firm** it will bind the other partners but there is no general authority implied by the law for one partner to bind his co-partners by giving a guarantee, and a partner in a professional firm has no implied power to bind the firm by a guarantee. In other words a **partner** has no implied authority to give a guarantee in the name of the firm unless it is connected with the firm's ordinary course of business or the partner has been specially authorised by the other partners to bind the firm.

As it may be difficult to prove such implied authority, all partners should sign a guarantee given by the firm.

Guarantee by Company

A company has no power to give a guarantee unless the power is expressly given in the objects clause of its Memorandum of Association. A trading company has implied power to borrow but there is no similarly implied power to give guarantees on the lines of those taken by banks.

Thus, the banker needs to check by referring to the Memorandum of Association whether the company has legal power to enter into such guarantees. Any power given by the Memorandum should be unambiguous and if the banker has any doubts he should ask the company to alter its Memorandum and if necessary the bank could provide the wording of a clause suitable for this purpose.

The Articles of Association next require examination to ascertain the extent to which powers have been delegated to the directors and whether the guarantee can be executed under hand or whether it has to be executed under seal.

The contract must be between the *company* and the bank and not between the directors of the company and the bank and the directors should pass a resolution authorizing the giving of the guarantee and specifying which officers of the company are to sign it. To avoid any later claim that the guarantee form signed was not that intended in the resolution, the copy resolution should be endorsed on the guarantee itself.

The directors passing the resolution should not be personally interested in that they might benefit personally from the giving of the guarantee. The implications of *Victors Ltd. v. Lingard* (1927) need to be borne in mind in this respect. If any directors have an interest in any contract in which the company is involved they must declare that interest under Section 199 Companies Act 1948 (Section 317 Companies Act 1985). Such directors may be interested because they have personally given security for the company's account, or may be directors of the company being guaranteed. Therefore it is usual for the articles to contain a provision that the directors who have interests may vote and form part of a valid quorum in a directors' resolution regarding the relevant contract. Unless there is such a provision, a director who has an interest may not validly vote on the relative resolution. If the articles state that a director who has declared an interest may vote, or where there clearly are no such interests, a directors' resolution may be taken. If the articles do not cover this point, then a members' resolution should be taken, but where this is impractical (due to the number of members) a directors' resolution, passed by a disinterested quorum, should be taken.

It is quite common for parent companies to guarantee the accounts of their subsidiary companies and vice versa, and quite often companies entering into bank guarantee arrangements do not have direct shareholding links but are associated with each other by virtue of common directors and shareholders. Whenever taking inter-company guarantees the banker should invite the directors of the guarantor company to examine whether they consider that it is in the interests of the guarantor company and of benefit to it, to enter into the guarantee. If they are of this opinion, then such opinion should be expressed in the board resolution authorising the giving of the guarantee. This could strengthen the bank's defence against any challenge made against the guarantee on the grounds of absence of benefit or commercial justification on the part of the guarantor company. The case *Charterbridge Corporation Ltd. v. Lloyds Bank Ltd.* (1969) is relevant to this issue.

When lending to a group of companies, bankers often are provided with what are usually referred to as "unlimited cross guarantees". This arrangment entails each of the companies comprising the group executing a guarantee, unlimited in amount, for the liabilities of each of the other companies which means that the banker can in practice allow any agreed credit limit to be utilised on a "net" basis between the accounts of the various companies. Care is needed should further companies joining the group be brought into a cross-guarantee arrangement and the hazards of a short cut were shown in *Ford and Carter Ltd. v. Midland Bank Ltd.* (1979).

A checklist of the steps to be taken when obtaining company guarantees is given in Chapter 10.

Guarantee by Joint Parties

Where two or more parties have undertaken to sign a guarantee the advance should not be made until all have actually signed. In *National Provincial Bank Ltd. v. Brackenbury* (1906) four parties had agreed to sign, thus forming the basis of the contract. Three signed and the bank made the advance in anticipation of the completion of the guarantee. The fourth party died before his signature could be obtained. It was held that the three who had signed were discharged.

A **joint guarantee** is one given by all the guarantors. Each is liable but all should be sued in a joint action, for, if some only are sued, the rest are discharged.

A **several guarantee** is one given by each of the guarantors. Each may be sued separately and judgement obtained against one does not discharge the others, subject of course, to the amount for which the guarantee is drawn to cover and to the fact that the banker can only obtain full payment of the debt.

A **joint and several guarantee** is one given by each and all of the guarantors. The parties may be sued in the way the banker deems fit, subject, of course, to the conditions stated above.

In bank guarantees, guarantors are made **jointly and severally liable**. If made only jointly liable it would be necessary to sue them all together if the complete remedy were required. If one were sued and not the others the judgement against the one would end the liability of all, and even judgement without satisfaction against one is a bar to proceedings against the others. Further, if the liability were merely joint and one died, his estate would be freed for the liability would fall upon the surviving guarantors. Hence the word "several" is necessary to enable the banker to sue one or all and give him the power to recover against the others if a judgement against one is unsatisfied, and to make the estate of a deceased guarantor liable. Thus the remedy against joint and several guarantors is cumulative until the whole debt is satisfied. If the creditors release one or more sureties whether they have contracted jointly, severally, jointly and severally, the others are discharged. This applies whether they are bound by the same or by different instruments. Relevant cases on this are *Ward v. National Bank of New Zealand* (1883), *Ellesmere Brewery Co. v. Cooper* (1896) and *Barclays Bank Ltd. v. Trevanion* (1933).

The form of guarantees used by banks are therefore worded so that they cover this contingency by giving the bank complete freedom of action to compromise with or release any guarantors without giving up its rights against the others.

INDEPENDENT LEGAL ADVICE

As was mentioned in the preceding chapter when third party charges over land and property were being discussed, it is very important that a surety should be a free agent when entering into the contract and should fully appreciate what contract is being entered into. Whereas it was generally the practice for banks to arrange for a woman guarantor to be separately advised (before she signed) by her own solicitor, it is no longer appropriate to assume that a woman guarantor is neither a free agent nor capable of appreciating the nature of the contract. Indeed since the Sex Discrimination Act 1975 the banks have reviewed their procedures in this sphere, and nowadays there is often no fixed procedure as to when independent legal advice must be automatically obtained, although each situation should be considered carefully from this aspect and decided accordingly. The question of a guarantor being seperately advised is not one to be overlooked lightly and whatever the sex of a relationship between the parties involved, the question should be given due consideration particularly in light of the *Lloyds Bank Ltd. v. Bundy* case — see below. Due to an increasing number of occasions of bank security being challenged over recent years, the banks are generally moving more towards the stance that all guarantees (and other third party forms of security) should be independently witnessed and it seems likely that this will become the general practice, with any exceptions being permitted only where a conscious decision to this effect has been made.

UNDUE INFLUENCE

This renders the contract voidable. It is presumed in the following cases:

(a) client guaranteeing solicitor;
(b) beneficiary guaranteeing trustree;
(c) ward guaranteeing guardian;

(d) child guaranteeing parent;
(e) patient guaranteeing doctor;
(f) disciple guaranteeing religious adviser.

There is no such presumption between husband and wife; *Howes v. Bishop* (1909) but undue influence may be proved as a fact — as in *Bank of Montreal v. Stuart and Another* (1911), where the wife was a confirmed invalid and guaranteed her husband's account, the contract was set aside on the grounds of undue influence.

Where any question of undue influence arises it is essential that the guarantor is independently advised and that the solicitor who advises the guarantor signs a statement on the guarantee form confirming that the terms and nature of the document have been fully explained to the guarantor.

A variation on the theme of undue influence occurred in *Lloyds Bank Ltd. v. Bundy* (1974).

In this case the defendant guaranteed the account of a company run by his son, and both Bundys and the company banked at the same branch of the plaintiff bank; the defendant charged his farm, his only asset, in support of the guarantee. Although at one earlier stage a solicitor was consulted, a larger replacement guarantee plus a further charge over the farm was taken by the assistant manager as a condition of continuing the company's account. It was held that (as the bank was in a position of undue influence, being relied on as the defendant's banker as well as the company's) the guarantee could not stand in the absence of independent legal advice to the guarantor before signature. There were special considerations to the case (for example, the guarantor's age and his actual reliance on the bank, and the very limited consideration as no new finance was provided). So it does not follow that every case would be so decided. Nevertheless any bank taking a guarantee should consider whether a duty is owed to the guarantor, and if in any doubt should ensure that appropriate independent legal advice is given to avoid any suggestion of undue influence.

BANK FORMS OF GUARANTEE

The surety usually guarantees the **whole debt** due from the principal debtor, either alone or jointly, with all charges, interest, etc., with a limitation of the amount for which he shall be liable.

Additionally, as otherwise it could be argued that the debt ceases to be one due from the principal debtor on his death or bankruptcy and becomes due from his estate, the guarantee provides that it shall be deemed to continue "due or owing" notwithstanding the death or bankruptcy of the principal debtor.

The "whole debt" clause used in bank forms of guarantee (usually supported by a clause in which the guarantor undertakes not to make any claim against the debtor or his estate whilst anything remains owing to the bank) is important in the event of the death or bankruptcy of the principal debtor as it prevents the guarantor from paying up the otherwise specified amount and proving on the estate with the bank being forced to reduce its claim accordingly.

Words are inserted in the guarantee form to ensure that it shall secure not merely a **specific** advance but all sums due or **which may become due**, i.e. all monies due at the time of determination of the guarantee. Some guarantees use the words "continuing security" but whatever the form the effect is to prevent the operation of the Rule in *Clayton's Case* and to make the guarantor responsible for the **ultimate** debt due to the bank (subject, of course, to any limitation of his liability).

Under Common Law a guarantor is a very favoured debtor and therefore a bank has to safeguard its position by expressly excluding the guarantor's normal rights by terms inserted in the form of guarantee.

As stated earlier, a guarantor is entitled to know the extent of his liability at any time. However, to prevent him from attempting to call for a copy of the borrower's account when steps are taken to enforce the guarantee, it is usual for the surety to agree to accept the statement of the bank as to the extent of his liability. In *Bache & Co. (London) Ltd. v. Banque Vernes et Commerciale de Paris* (1973) the bank gave a guarantee to the plaintiffs which included a provision that a notice of default submitted by the plaintiffs would be conclusive evidence of the liability. It was held that the clause was binding, and the bank could not raise a defence that the money was not due, except in extreme circumstances (such as a fraudulent claim) which did not arise here. Actions would be brought by the parties concerned to correct matters if the claim was wrong, but this did not prevent the guarantor from being liable meanwhile to honour the guarantee promptly.

A guarantor who has discharged his obligations has the right to be subrogated to all the rights of the creditor. Therefore the bank takes power to release, grant time or make other arrangements with the principal debtor. If the bank did not take such power, and if the bank gave time to the debtor by way of a binding contract, the guarantor's position would be prejudiced in that if he paid up the amount due under the guarantee his remedy against the principal debtor would be postponed. On similar ground, where a banker agreed to accept a composition under a Deed of Arrangement, a guarantor could try to deny his liability due to his rights against the principal debtor having been prejudiced.

If a guarantor pays off the whole of the indebtedness, the guarantor is entitled to any securities held by the bank, whether deposited by the debtor or third parties.

Where a surety has guaranteed only part of a debt, he is on repayment entitled to benefit "pro rata" from any securities held by the banker. This right, however, can be and is usually with bank guarantees excluded under the terms of the guarantee.

In the event of a joint and several guarantor paying up the full amount, the guarantor is entitled to appropriate contributions from his co-guarantors and any securities passing to the guarantors must be divided equally. Therefore if a banker released any security charged by either the principal debtor or by a third party, or released any other surety the rights of the guarantor would be prejudiced. The bank form of guarantor must therefore give the bank power to vary the security it holds and release any other sureties entirely at its own discretion.

There should also be a clause that a guarantee is to be in addition to, and without prejudice to, any securities of any kind then or thereafter held or to be held and full power restored to take, vary, exchange, or release such securities, renew bills and so forth. This is necessary, or it might be contended that other securities were taken in substitution for the security afforded by the guarantee, or, by merging or suspending the debt, affected the liability of the surety; for a guarantor who makes good the default of the customer is entitled to the benefit of other securities held by the creditor for the debt, whether they were held at the time the surety became bound or have been subsequently acquired, and whether the surety knew of them or not.

A further clause prevents a guarantor, having paid up under his guarantee liability, from claiming in bankruptcy, from enjoying the benefit of any securities held by the bank and sometimes from suing the debtor, until such time as the bank has been repaid in full. Additionally, the guarantor under a bank form of guarantee usually agrees not to take security from the debtor (or if he does to hold it in trust for the bank) and to be liable even if the customer is borrowing *ultra vires*.

GUARANTEE FOR THE ACCOUNT OF A PARTNERSHIP

Where the account or transaction guaranteed is that of a partnership the guarantee should provide that it shall not be affected by any change in the constitution of that partnership, for in the absence of agreement to the contrary any change in the constitution of the firm for or to which the guarantee is given revokes the guarantee as to future advances.

Notwithstanding such a provision, which would be fully effective against the **Guarantor**, it must not be overloooked that it will be necessary to break the Account to preserve recourse against the estate of a deceased or bankrupt partner as **principal debtor**.

It is normally the practice to advise the guarantor of such changed circumstances to give him an opportunity to determine his liability should he so desire.

GUARANTEES TO SECURE *ULTRA VIRES* BORROWINGS

It is a fundamental right of a surety who has discharged his obligation to stand in the shoes of the creditor and to exercise the rights of the creditor both against the principal debtor and against any security held. There must, therefore, be a legal debtor against whom proceedings may be taken: if there is not, then, apart from any express provision in the Guarantee, the surety is discharged. "If there is nothing due, the obligation to make that nothing good amounts itself to nothing".

Thus if a Guarantee is taken to secure the account of a minor or unincorporated body such as a Club, by reason of the fact that the bank could not itself recover against the principal debtor the Guarantee will be valueless: *Coutts & Co. v. Browne-Lecky* (1946). A similar situation arises when an advance has been made to a company in excess of its borrowing powers; any third party security could not normally be enforced. Where a guarantee for the account of a company is by the directors, they could still be held to be liable under the guarantee due to their particular relationship to the customer. This is however by no means certain and the possible exception should not be relied upon.

In order to overcome this difficulty, the form of guarantee should contain a clause which in effect makes the contract one of indemnity whereby the guarantor assumes responsibility as though he were principal debtor.

A suitable form of wording would be:

> "I agree that all sums of money which may not be recoverable from the principal by reason of any legal limitation, disability or incapacity on or of the principal, shall nevertheless be recoverable from me as sole or principal debtor."

The Consumer Credit Act 1974 does not invalidate indemnity clauses of this kind in respect of transactions which come within its purview.

DETERMINATION OF GUARANTEE

A guarantee may be determined in any of the following ways:

(a) By the guarantor giving appropriate notice and either paying off the amount owing or paying up the amount for which he is liable under the guarantee;
(b) By the bank making formal demand on the guarantor under the terms of the guarantee;
(c) By change of parties;
(d) By the death, mental disorder or bankruptcy of the parties.

DETERMINATION BY GUARANTOR

The guarantee document will set out the method by which the guarantee can be determined. This is usually effected by the guarantor or his personal representatives giving written notice to the bank, the period of notice being set out in the guarantee. Whether or not a banker who has received such notice of determination should permit fresh advances on the strength of the guarantee during the period of notice is arguable. There are differing views on this, some bankers maintaining that the principal debtor should be able to draw freely until the expiration of the notice, others arguing that only cheques actually outstanding should be met. In practice, the most equitable action would be for the banker to consult both with the customer and the guarantor, in order to try to arrange for outstanding cheques and any other commitments entered into on the strength of the existing overdraft facility to be honoured. When receiving notice of determination from a guarantor the banker should formally acknowledge the notice to terminate but in the acknowledgement the banker should make it clear that the guarantor's liability is not limited to the amount due at the time the guarantor gave notice. The banker should at all times in these circumstances try to adopt an equitable and responsible attitude and if a debtor insisted on drawing cheques up to the full amount of the guaranteed facility to a degree that the banker considered unreasonable or unnecessary, the banker could protect the guarantor's interests by calling in the facility (providing it is repayable on demand). This would mean stopping the account which would, of course, fix the guarantor's liability.

On the determination of a guarantee the account should be stopped to avoid the Rule in Clayton's Case operating adversely, and if a new account was opened and kept in credit, it need not be taken into account in calculating the guarantor's liability. Some bank forms of guarantee have a clause aimed at protecting the bank should it inadvertantly omit to break the account on determination of the guarantee. A clause of this nature held good in *Westminster Bank Ltd. v. Cond* (1940).

On receipt of a notice that one of three guarantors wishes to withdraw, the account should, subject to provisions previously discussed with regard to notice, be stopped and notice given to the customer and the other guarantors. If the retiring guarantor pays his share of the outstanding overdraft and the other guarantors sign a new guarantee and are good for the liability, the account may be continued.

It must not be overlooked, however, that a joint and several guarantor who wished to determine his liability is responsible to the extent of the limit of the guarantee: the bank is under no **obligation** to apportion the liability as between the guarantors.

It is doubtful if the liability of the co-guarantors for future advances is affected by the notice. Probably the co-guarantors would not be released, but it is safer to have a new guarantee.

If the remaining guarantors refuse to sign a new guarantee, the advance must be called in, for by **releasing** one surety the banker deprives the others of their rights to contributions in equity, and they will be released from liability on future advances. However, as mentioned earlier in this chapter the guarantee may expressly permit the banker to release one of the parties without the others being discharged and most bank forms of guarantee cover this contingency.

Where a bank advances an amount at once on the security of a guarantee, the guarantor cannot get out of his liability as the consideration is given once and for all. Additionally, say £5000 is placed to a customer's credit on the security of a £5000 guarantee and only £2500 has been drawn, the banker cannot return cheques on the second £2500 because the guarantor wishes to withdraw. The funds are advanced once and for all and the guarantor is liable.

PAYMENTS MADE BY A GUARANTOR

When a guarantor makes a payment to the bank (and when the principal debtor has not been made bankrupt) then in the absence of any special provisions in the form of guarantee, the intention of the guarantor should be ascertained. If the payment is intended to be in support of the guarantee it would be placed in a separate "suspense" type of account. If the guarantor intended the payment to be in discharge of his liability, strictly speaking the funds should be applied in reduction or full repayment of the principal debt. In the event of the principal debtor's bankruptcy, where the funds had been placed on separate account the banker could ignore this and prove for his full debt; where funds had been applied in reduction of the principal debt, the banker could prove only for the balance outstanding. This could clearly work to the banker's disadvantage and thus most bank forms of guarantee contain a clause covering this point as outlined earlier in this chapter. A situation could arise in practice where a guarantor wishes to clear up his position without delay and of course the principal debtor may never be made bankrupt. Where the funds received cover the full debt there is perhaps no real reason for the banker keeping them isolated but the guarantor should be made fully aware that if the funds are applied directly in repayment of the debt and the customer becomes bankrupt, the banker cannot then prove in the bankruptcy. When a payment from a guarantor (even if it represents full substantiation of the guarantee liability) does not fully repay the bank debt, the banker would always try to keep the funds isolated on a separate account.In such an instance, the banker could in writing confirm to the guarantor that the guarantor was under no further pecuniary liability to the bank. Interest would not continue to run against the guarantor as in practice the banker would allow full set-off rates of interest on the balance representing the monies received under the guarantee.

If a banker surrendered the guarantee to the guarantor when the guarantor's payment had not fully repaid the debt, this would almost certainly renunciate the bank's rights under the guarantee and enable the guarantor to prove in competition with the bank in the event of the customer's bankruptcy.

Most bank forms of guarantee include a clause to the effect that the guarantee document remains the property of the bank and therefore in practice even when the guarantor has discharged his liability the guarantee form remains with the bank. This clause can be particularly significant for the first six months after the date upon which the guarantor is released from pecuniary liability (and where the guaranator has not had to pay the full amount of the guarantee) in case it is held that a fraudulent preference occurred and the bank wishes to have its rights under the guarantee reinstated.

DEMAND BY THE BANK

The banker can at any time make formal demand under the terms of the guarantee for the guarantor to substantiate his liability. Where the guarantor does not have to make payment until demand has been made of him, the Limitation Act does not begin to run in his favour until such demand has been made: *Bradford Old Bank v. Sutcliffe* (1918). The relevant period is six years in the case of a guarantee under hand and twelve years for a guarantee under seal. Some practical aspects of the Limitation Act in relation to guarantees were discussed in Chapter 1.

CHANGE OF PARTIES

Bank forms of guarantee usually provide that the guarantee will not be affected by any change in the constitution of the bank, e.g. by a merger or take-over in which the bank is involved.

As mentioned earlier in this chapter, a similar provision should apply to a partnership which is secured by the guarantee. When the guarantee is for a company, a change of name by the company is immaterial as the company remains the same legal entity.

DEATH, MENTAL DISORDER OR BANKRUPTCY

Death

When the banker receives notice of the death of a guarantor, the steps he needs to take depend on whether or not the guarantor has bound his personal representatives to continue the guarantee. Most bank guarantees bind the personal representatives of the guarantor in order that notice of the guarantor's death will not determine the guarantee in respect of further advances. The relative provision in the guarantee usually stipulates a specified period of notice of determination to be given by the representatives.

Thus, the executors of the guarantor may at any time after the guarantor's death give notice to determine the guarantee as to future advances after the notice has expired. The fact that the guarantor has died does not terminate the guarantee but it can be terminated by the executors giving the prescribed notice. As soon as the banker becomes aware of the death of a guarantor, he should ensure that the legal personal representatives are aware of the guarantee liability and the terms under which they can give the bank notice of determination.

If the personal representatives are not bound by the guarantee, the banker should break the account upon receiving notice of the guarantor's death, opening a new and separate account through which all payments and receipts should be passed. This new account will not be secured by the guarantee but by taking these steps, the banker will prevent the operation of the Rule in Clayton's Case as, if the account is continued after notice of death, every payment out constitutes a fresh debt not covered by the guarantee.

If the principal debtor is also the sole executor, it is advisable to stop the account, notwithstanding any provision in the guarantee nor its continuance after the death of the guarantor, since there may be a conflict of interest. Similarly, the account should be stopped if the whole of the guarantor's estate is devised on trust: *Harris v. Fawcett* (1873) where the bank continued the advance knowing that there was no personal estate to answer the guarantee and it was held that the advances subsequent to the death were not covered.

With a joint and several guarantee, the death of one guarantor does not by itself release the co-guarantors: *Beckett v. Addyman* (1882).

The foregoing deals with the death of a guarantor; the death of the principal debtor will determine the guarantee and the debtor's account should be stopped, thereby fixing the extent of the guarantor's liability.

Bankruptcy

If a banker receives notice that a receiving order has been made against a guarantor, the principal debtor's account should be stopped and, assuming repayment is not forthcoming from the principal debtor, the banker should make formal demand for repayment from the guarantor.

If the guarantor is made bankrupt, the bank can prove against his estate for his contingent liability under the guarantee.

The bankruptcy of the debtor and his subsequent discharge do not release a guarantor for him. If a banker receives notice of a receiving order against the principal debtor, his account must be stopped immediately and completely, and the banker should make a formal demand on the guarantor for payment under the guarantee. This is necessary to start interest running against the guarantor under the terms of the guarantee. Due to the "whole debt" and some other clauses in bank guarantees (as explained previously in this chapter), any monies received from the guarantor, in response to the demand made, which are less than the entire indebtedness of the customer to the bank should be credited to a suspense account and can be ignored for purposes of proof.

Mental Disorder

As soon as as banker receives notice from a reliable source that a guarantor has become mentally disordered, he should stop the principal debtor's account as the mentally-disordered guarantor's estate is liable only for the balance then outstanding. The guarantee is terminated as to future advances by notice of mental disorder, and the effectiveness of any clause in the guarantee purporting to make it a continuing security until the Receiver of the mentally-disordered erson gives notice of determination to the bank is questionable. This specific point has not been tested in the courts but in *Bradford Old Bank Ltd. v. Sutcliffe* (1918) it was held, and not disputed on appeal, that a clause requiring notice of determination by the personal representatives on the death of the guarantor would not be applicable in the event of his mental disorder.

LAPSED GUARANTEES

When a guarantee is no longer relied upon, and the bank no longer requires the protection of any of its clauses, the action taken may depend on the terms of the guarantee. Generally the bank may wish to retain it, and may preserve this right in one of its clauses, but otherwise it may simply be destroyed or handed back to the guarantor.

CASH HELD IN SUPPORT OF GUARANTEE

As we have seen, frequently a cash sum received from the guarantor will be held on a separate account, in support of the guarantee. The tax position of such monies was considered in *Dunmore v. McGowan* (1976). The plaintiff had guaranteed a bank account and had transferred funds to a deposit account in the bank's name, to support the guarantee. The case was an action against the plaintiff's tax inspector, but the latter won in his contention that the interest must be regarded as taxable income of the plaintiff, notwithstanding that the funds were held by the bank.

LETTERS OF COMFORT

In practice, and often where larger companies (usually publicly-quoted or substantial overseas companies) are involved, the banker may meet resistance when trying to obtain a guarantee from such a company. Whilst the banker must decide on commercial and credit risk grounds whether or not he will insist on a formal guarantee from the parent company, bankers do in some instances dispense with a formal guarantee and accept instead what is usually called a "letter of comfort" or "comfort letter". This usually takes the form of a letter written by the parent company to the bank acknowledging the liability incurred by its subsidiary company to the bank and giving some sort of indication that it would not see the bank suffer any loss through granting the facility to its subsidiary. In practice, one letter of comfort may vary very considerably from another inasmuch that some such letters offer the banker the absolute minimum reassurance that the parent company is standing behind its subsidiary, whilst others can be much more explicit and indeed, occasionally letters of comfort are provided which are worded in such a way that arguably they may constitute contracts of guarantee and thus perhaps be legally enforceable. However, most "letters of comfort" would not be regarded by the prudent banker as constituting security in any real sense of the word, despite perhaps affording a degree of reassurance to the banker since at least the parent company is confirming its awareness of its subsidiary's liability, and therefore in those instances where the banker decides it must make the parent company legally liable (albeit secondarily) for the borrowing, it should insist on the parent executing a formal guarantee in favour of the bank, as it is generally regarded that a "letter of comfort" could not be readily enforced in the courts if the bank found it necessary to pursue the parent company in this way.

PERFORMANCE BONDS AND OTHER GUARANTEES/ BONDS/INDEMNITIES GIVEN BY BANKS

In this chapter, we have discussed guarantees in the context of these being given to secure the banking accounts of customers, but in many cases banks will themselves consider the giving of guarantees in approved cases, provided that they consider their customers as financially sound to reimburse the bank if the latter is called upon to pay. A counter-indemnity from the customer will be required, and often the bank will require security for the amount, in some cases insisting on full cash support.

A typical requirement is for a "performance bond" or guarantee, often called for by overseas governments and organisations particularly for large contracts; similar bonds are often required by local authorities in the U.K. when granting building contracts. Such a bond may well be for 5–10% of the amount of the contract or even more, and its effect is that the body awarding the contract has a ready source of remedy against the contractor if the latter defaults or if the work is unsatisfactory. Bankers are frequently asked to enter into Road Bonds in favour of a local authority where a builder customer is building houses. Such bonds mean that if the builder fails to complete roads and sewers, drains etc., then the local authority can make formal demand on the bank for the amount stipulated in the bond which the bank gave. The terms of the guarantee or bond may well oblige the bank to pay without any opportunity for the bank or its customer to challenge whether the claim is justified, and in such a case the bank will usually be obliged to pay, debiting its customer under the counter-imdemnity; the customer will then have to proceed through the Courts against the other party to the contract, if the payment is to be recovered.

A number of recent cases have highlighted the possible problems, a clear example being *R.D. Harbottle (Mercantile) Ltd. & Another v. National Westminster Bank Ltd. & Others* (1977). Acting on its customer's instructions, as part of the arrangments for an international transaction, the bank confirmed to Egyptian banks two guarantees for 5% of the purchase price of the goods being sold to Egyptian buyers; the Egyptian banks confirmed the guarantees to their own customers, the buyers. Under the guarantees, the bank was to make payment on "first demand".

Demand under the guarantees was subsequently made (the plaintiff customers denying that such demand was justified), and the bank succeeded in obtaining the discharge of an injunction which the plaintiffs had obtained to prevent them from paying. The Court held that — except possibly in clear cases of fraud — such obligations must be honoured, and the parties must then proceed through the courts for any redress, if they consider the end-result to be wrong.

Over recent years, bankers have been faced with requests for a whole range of bonds and guarantees. In addition to those mentioned above, a banker may be asked to provide tender or bid bonds for business customers who are seeking contracts, and if a customer has entered into a contract involving advance payments, the banker may be asked to provide a guarantee in favour of the customer's client undertaking to return an amount equivalent to the advance payment in the event of the customer's failure as defined in the terms of the documents.

For personal customers, a banker may be asked to underwrite or guarantee his customer who is seeking a duplicate share certificate, taking a car out of the country or applying for payment of money left to him by a deceased person without production of Probate or Letters of Adminstration. For customers who are involved in insurance underwriting by being members of underwriting syndicates in the Corporation of Lloyds, bankers often are asked to provide guarantees in favour of Lloyds, either as evidence of means when applying to join or so that in the event of the customer being asked to find moneys to contribute to an insurance claim made against the syndicate of which he is a member, Lloyds can call upon the bank to pay up if the customer does not.

Whenever asked to give bonds or guarantees for any of these purposes, it is important for the banker to ensure that the terms of the liability he is undertaking are clearly spelt out, both as to amount, duration and any other relative matters. In particular, the banker should ensure that the terms of the agreement would not allow the bank to be dropped into any dispute whereby on the one hand the banker could find himself pressed by the customer's client to pay over the monies, whilst on the other hand the customer could be attempting to stop the bank honouring the commitment. In other words, any form of contingent liability entered into by a banker, should be clear cut and unambiguous, so that the banker can pay up the agreed amount immediately he receives demand in the prescribed form. The banker can then debit the amount so paid, to the banking account of his customer, under the authority contained in the counter-indemnity the banker obtained from the customer at the outset, thus meaning that any remaining disagreements and disputes between the other parties are matters for them alone to resolve.

There have been several cases recently which have high-lighted the necessity to sustain the business community's confidence (particularly with regard to the international trading scene) in a bank's absolute obligation to pay up on demand under a performance bond. Two of the most recent cases are *Bolivinter Oil S.A. v. Chase Manhattan Bank S.A. and others* (1984) and *Potton Homes Ltd. v. Coleman Contractors Ltd.* (1984).

Chapter 9

Securities for Advances (cont.)

LIFE POLICIES

Generally speaking, life policies are regarded as good banking security; the advantages being that they are easy to charge, easy to realise and their value will increase all the time provided that the premiums are paid.

However, not all types of policy are suitable as security. In the main, the policies encountered by a banker are those in which the sum assured is payable on death (called "whole life" policies) and those payable at a fixed date, or at a fixed future date or previous death (called "endowment" policies). In each case the policies may or may not be entitled to participate in the profits of the life assurance company.

There are many variations in the terms under which policies are issued, and it is therefore very important that each policy should be carefully read before it is accepted as security.

The banker is usually concerned not so much with the capital sum assured, as with the surrender value of the policy, which is the amount that the insurance company will pay out at any particular time against the surrender of the policy.

A policy will have a surrender value after, usually, three years' premiums have been paid and it will increase as additional premiums are paid. The value at any time may be ascertained by reference to the company, or , in some cases, a table of surrender values may be set out in the Policy itself.

The capital sum has greater significance when a bank is lending without other security, and repayment of the advance depends upon the continued existence of the borrower; e.g. where the customer's income, which may perhaps be substantial, ceases upon death and the capital is held in trust, or, where the bank is lending, say, to a professional partnership and the firm's ability to repay rests on the continued existence of the partners. The question of life cover can be very significant when a banker is lending to a company whose chances of continued success rest substantially on the role(s) played by one or two key directors. This may arise because a director has particular skills which are vital to the company; the director may alternatively have all the personal contacts which may be crucial in the line of business carried out by the company, or more generally, a company may depend considerably upon one man as the "driving force" behind it. In such cases, a banker will usually in the terms on which he is prepared to finance the company, include a requirement that life cover for an amount bearing reasonable resemblance to the bank's exposure be taken out on the life of the party(ies) concerned and assigned to the bank. Many insurance companies nowadays offer policies specifically designed for this sort of situation. These are often referred to as "Keyman" policies.

As regards the standing of security afforded by life policies, if the policy has been issued by a first class British Company then obviously the bank need have no fear as to the ability of the company to pay out should the policy become a claim; this would usually be the case. The possibility of non-payment of a policy in an obscure office should, however, be kept in mind. Policies in companies domiciled abroad, with no English office, are not looked upon with enthusiasm because of the difficulties which can arise in collecting or surrendering such policies.

An insurance policy is a contract *uberrimae fidei* (of the utmost good faith), hence the insurance company may refuse to pay on the policy on the grounds of non-disclosure or misrepresentation of material facts at the time when the proposal was made.

There is little that can be done by the bank to protect itself but if the proposal declarations are embodied in the policy any obvious and material mis-statement should be the subject of enquiry.

In one respect, however, confirmation can be obtained. The banker should see that the age of the person insured has been admitted. If not, a birth certificate should be submitted to the company. This admission of age is important since a false statement of age may alter the amount recoverable under the policy.

There may be restrictive conditions in the policy — e.g. suicide within a stated period may avoid it, although usually there will be special provision for the rights of bona fide assignees for value. Since the Suicide Act 1961, suicide is no longer a crime, and so there are no considerations of public policy involved, but as it is a general principle of insurance that it does not cover a claim made on a policy where the insured has deliberately brought about the event insured against, the policy monies may still not be recoverable, in the absence of a suicide clause.

The clauses in the policy should be read very carefully to ascertain whether there are any onerous restrictions imposed on the life assured, relating perhaps to foreign travel or residence, occupation, abstinence from alcoholic drink, and if any such exist the bank should pay due regard to the customer's way of life relative to the restrictions.

The life assured need not be that of the policyholder as any person who has what is called an "insurable interest" in another person can insure that person's life. An insurable interest exists in the following situations:

- a man or woman can assure his or her own life;
- a man can assure the life of his wife and vice versa;
- a creditor can assure the life of his debtor;
- a company can assure the life of its director;
- a litigant can assure the life of the judge;
- an employer can assure the life of his employee and vice versa;
- a trustee can assure the interest of which he is trustee.

It is not necessary for an assignee to have an insurable interest.

When holding a life policy as security, it is essential that the policy remains in force and does not lapse through non-payment of premiums. Premium receipts should therefore be obtained and ideally the customer should arrange to pay the premiums through the bank by means of a standing order which will make for easy monitoring of the payment of premiums. Some insurance companies have come to an arrangement with the banks, whereby they will advise a banker who holds a policy as security if a premium is not received.

The bank must see that the policy itself contains no restriction on assignment and finally as the policy may be for the benefit of parties other than or in addition to the depositor (e.g. his wife and children), all persons interested as beneficiaries, if of full age, must join in the charge.

If any of the beneficiaries are minors no charge will be effective.

The Married Women's Property Act 1882, provides that a policy taken out by a husband on his own life for the benefit of his wife and/or children creates a trust in favour of the beneficiaries.

It was held in *Cousins v. Sun Life Assurance* (1932) that in such circumstances **where the wife was named** as the beneficiary and she predeceased the husband, her executors could claim the benefit of the surrender value of the policy.

In *Re Browne's Policy* (1903) where a Policy was taken out for the benefit of the wife and children, **without naming any of them** it was held that the second wife and her children were entitled to share with the children of the first marriage to the exclusion of the executors of the first wife.

Therefore, for a policy to be taken effectively as security where the beneficiaries are other than the assured they must be named clearly and they must join in the charge. Unless they are so specified the charge, although effective at the time of execution, may be avoided later if other beneficial interests are acquired.

Life policies can be given to a banker as "indirect" or "third party" security and, as with other third party security, the banker must when taking the security consider whether or not the assignor(s) should have the benefit of independent legal advice.

The smaller life policies known as "industrial" policies are those where the relatively small premiums are paid frequently, usually to a collector from the insurance company who acknowledges payment of the premiums in a policy passbook. These policies have their origins in the time prior to the welfare state when they were often taken out to provide for funeral expenses. As banking security they usually have the disadvantages of

(a) being often assignable only under certain restriction;
(b) carrying a relatively small surrender value;
(c) requiring frequent payments of premiums with difficulty in obtaining satisfactory proof of such payment.

CHARGING LIFE POLICIES AS SECURITY

Life Policies can be charged either by legal mortgage (i.e. legal assignment) or equitable mortgage (i.e. equitable assignment).

A legal charge is taken by way of assignment under seal (though, strictly, it need not be executed under seal, because the brief specimen assignment set out in the schedule to the Policies of Assurance Act 1867 is not a deed though it requires witnessing). The assignment will allow for redemption and contain power for the banker to surrender the policy for cash or for a fully paid policy, or to sell the policy, as a sale often realises more than the surrender value, and to pay premiums on behalf of the borrower to keep the policy alive.

The assignor usually covenants not to do anything to invalidate the policy (e.g. failing to observe any restrictive terms) and the mortgage will contain the usual banking provisions as to continuing security, power to consolidate, etc. The bank is also authorised to give an effective receipt to the Insurance Company for any monies payable under the policy.

Notice to Insurance Company

The Policies of Assurance Act 1867, provides that Insurance Companies must accept written Notices of Assignment giving the date and nature of the assignment and when the appropriate statutory fee is paid. Priority of assignments will be determined by the date upon which notice was received by the company unless an assignee has notice, whether actual or constructive, of the existence of a prior charge. In *Spencer v. Clarke* (1878) it was held that non-production of the policy constituted notice of a prior charge, and in such circumstances a legal assignee, even if he registers notice of his charge, could not gain priority over an equitable mortgage who had not given notice.

When taking a legal assignment, therefore, a bank should first obtain the policy and ascertain from the company whether there are any prior charges.

If any exist, the documents of charge, duly re-assigned, must then be executed but a notice is necessary in order to establish priority of the bank's charge and to enable the bank, if necessary, to sue on the policy.

The Notice is given in duplicate, one copy of which is returned, as an acknowledgement and is filed carefully with the policy. At the same time the bank obtains final confirmation that there is no prior charge.

In practice it is expedient to use a separate form of charge for each policy as this avoids complications should it become necessary to realise the security.

Notice should also be given of any re-assignment of a life policy in the normal way upon retirement of the advance and release of the security.

An equitable charge of a life policy is possible either by mere deposit of the policy, or deposit of the policy together with a memorandum of deposit. The weaknesses of an equitable charge, by comparison to a legal charge, are that insurance companies need not accept notice of equitable interests. Furthermore, whereas a legal mortgagee can sell or surrender a policy without reference to the depositor or recourse to the court, an equitable mortgagee cannot sue on the policy in his own name. Therefore, if the policy becomes a claim, the personal representatives will have to join in the discharge, and in the case of a chargor not co-operating in a forced realisation, the consent of the court will be required.

Most insurance companies are prepared to make loans within the surrender value of the policy and this method of obtaining repayment is frequently suggested by a bank which is carrying a "sticky" advance (i.e. where adequate reductions cannot be obtained). It has the advantage that the customer may still retain the cover whereas a surrender or sale results in the loss of all rights by the assured.

Second Assignment of a Life Policy

Where a second assignment of a policy is being taken, the original policy will not be able to be produced by the customer due to it being charged elsewhere. A duplicate policy (or full details of the existing one) can be obtained from the company and the bank will have its form of legal assignment completed and signed by the customer and will then give written notice of the assignment to the insurance company. The date upon which the notice is received will determine the priority of any claim against the proceeds; the notice being acknowledged by the return of the duplicate.

If the first assignment is in favour of the insurance company itself, the notice of the bank's interest will ensure that the policy and reassignment are sent to the bank if and when the policy is reassigned. If it was assigned elsewhere, the notice of the bank's interest must be addressed to the first lender to ensure a similar result. The notice should also contain a request to confirm the amount outstanding under the first assignment. The company should be asked to confirm the present surrender value and confirm that premiums are paid up to date. Thereafter the bank should make suitable arrangements to check that future premiums are paid.

Discharge of the Security

Normally a banker would be reluctant to surrender a policy charged to the bank except when the loan or advance was repaid but in some circumstances (e.g. where the customer has been made bankrupt) if repayment is not forthcoming, the banker may have to. As stated earlier, it may be possible to sell the policy through one of the companies specialising in this type of business but if this is impracticable the assurance company itself will have to be approached. When surrendering the policy to the company, the procedure is similar to that when collecting proceeds of a policy upon it maturing. The bank's form of assignment should be sent to the company with details of the position and the company will then forward its own form for completion. This form will incorporate a receipt for the monies due. On return of this form together with the policy itself, the company will pay over the proceeds to the bank. The bank would apply the proceeds in reduction or repayment of the borrowing, any surplus proceeds being held to the order of the customer or his Trustee in Bankruptcy, if he is bankrupt.

LENDING AGAINST PRODUCE: MERCHANDISE ADVANCES

Bank lending directly against security of produce and merchandise is not a particularly common occurrence, but nevertheless it does take place.

The drawbacks of produce and merchandise as security are:

(a) It is liable to depreciation; constant supervision is required and special storage facilities may be necessary; e.g. refrigeration.
(b) It is subject to varying market prices;
(c) It can only be realised by sale — often a forced sale;
(d) It is often subject to charges for freight or storage;
(e) The property in the goods does not pass unless documents of title have been delivered or the warehouse-keeper enters the goods in the bank's name. The fact that documents of title **are** available is no guarantee of the quality or value of the security. There is scope for fraud.
(f) The security is never perfect.

Due to these drawbacks a banker will make such advances only to customers of high standing and undoubted integrity and who are experienced in their particular trade. Additionally, the advances should be of a short term nature only such as to enable a customer to build up stocks in anticipation of seasonal requirements or to enable the customer to acquire goods or produce which is pre-sold to first class buyers. The bank would usually be looking for a margin in its security cover which will vary according to the type and realisability of the merchandise. The matter and method of valuing the security can be difficult and will need to recognise the condition and quality of the goods and whether they are liable to deteriorate. In practice the valuation placed on the security may well depend on information provided by the customer which emphasises that this sort of advance should be granted only to very reputable customers. Possibly shipping invoices would help to confirm values as would recent sales of the type of goods, and in some cases there may be relevant market quotations. Advances would usually be by way of loan, and a separate loan per consignment may be advisable to facilitate easier control and monitoring of the security cover.

Obviously this type of advance is usually required by importers who require financial assistance towards the cost of the goods imported. The import is usually financed by a documentary credit which is made available in the seller's country and which enables the seller to ship the goods knowing that prompt payment is effectively guaranteed from a reputable bank. The bank in the seller's country will pay the seller as soon as it has received from the seller all the necessary documents of title (see later) and has checked that these are in order. It is then reimbursed by the importer's bank which will check the documents again. If the importer can then pay the bank, the bank releases the documents to him so that he can collect the goods when they arrive at the home port and the importer's account is debited accordingly. Where the credit is not fully covered and the importer needs assistance on the strength of the goods, the bank will obtain a pledge of the goods. The documentary credit procedures entail the documents of title coming into the hands of the bank and then the pledge exists, but see below for further details.

TAKING DOCUMENTS OF TITLE AS SECURITY

The security is effected by taking a pledge of the documents of title, which are deposited with the banker, and this constitutes a constructive delivery of the goods themselves.

When taking documents of title, a banker should obtain the customer's signature to a memorandum of pledge (sometimes called a "letter of pledge") which in addition to providing evidence of the intention to pledge the goods, will give specific authority to the banker to store and insure the goods at the customer's expense and to realise them in the event of default. A memorandum or letter of pledge is in effect a form of Memorandum of Deposit.

Care needs to be exercised to differentiate between documents that actually give a title to the goods named in them (e.g. bills of lading, dock and warehouse-keepers' transferable warrants) and documents which merely constitute receipts acknowledging that the goods have been lodged in a warehouse. (e.g. warehouse-keepers' certificates and delivery orders).

BILLS OF LADING

A bill of lading is a document signed on behalf of the shipowning company in which goods are embarked acknowledging receipt of the goods and undertaking to deliver them at the port of destination to the consignee, provided that the freight and any other charges set out in the bill of lading have been paid.

It is both a contract of carriage of and receipt for goods and a document of title to those goods. Bills of lading are sometimes referred to as being "quasi negotiable" as they are transferable and thus may pass from hand to hand effecting change of ownership of the relative goods, by endorsement and delivery or mere delivery if the bill of lading has been endorsed in blank. Under the Bills of Lading Act 1855 a transferee can sue and be sued in his own name, but essentially cannot get a better title than that of his transferor.

When a banker is asked to lend against goods in transit represented by a bill of lading certain precautions are necessary and in practice a certain amount of expertise and familiarity with trade documentation is needed on the part of the banker. Such technical skill is called for so that the goods are suitably insured against damage and loss, and to enable them to be claimed if appropriate on their arrival. The banker may need to have the goods warehoused and insured against loss by fire. As mentioned earlier, evidence of intention to pledge the goods would be taken by way of the customer signing a Memorandum of Deposit. The possible flaws in bills of lading as security are that the title of the transferor may be defective, the goods may be of dubious value, the goods could be lost or damaged and insufficiently insured. A bill of lading could be forged and it is possible that the goods may be delivered to a holder of part of the bill of lading other than the banker.

The nature of the following documents should be noted:

- An **air consignment note** is evidence of a contract of affreightment and of receipt of goods, but it is not a document of title to the goods, and therefore cannot be considered as good security. It can be improved, however, by making arrangements with the bank's overseas correspondent so that the goods are consigned to that correspondent. When the goods arrive, they will be delivered to or to the order of the bank, which thus obtains possession of them.
- A **Charter Party** is the contract for the hiring of a ship, or part of a ship, for the conveyance of goods for a particular voyage or for a specified period. It is not a document of title to the goods and is of no value as security for an advance.
- A **Consular Invoice** is an invoice signed at the port of shipment by the Consul of the importing country certifying the correct value of the goods for customs duties purposes.
- A **Certificate of Origin** is similarly signed by the importing country's Consul and proves the source of goods where preferential import duties are in operation at the port of destination.

- The **Marine Insurance Policy** is the contract of the underwriter or company which covers the risk of loss during the voyage. It may usually be assigned by endorsement or by delivery alone if already endorsed in blank. Notice should be given to the underwriters.

DOCUMENTARY BILLS OF EXCHANGE

These are bills of exchange drawn by an exporter on the importer or his bank in respect of a shipment of goods of which the documents of title and other relative documents are attached. These documents may be surrendered to the importer or to the importer's bank on acceptance of the bill of exchange (a Documents on Acceptance or "D/A" bill) or on payment of the bill (a Documents on Payment or "D/P" bill). The documents are usually the bill of lading, the marine insurance certificate, the invoice, and perhaps a consular invoice and certificate of origin. The Documentary Credit opened by the importer's bank will stipulate the documentary requirements and conditions which the overseas exporter (i.e. the seller) must fulfil before he gets paid.

DOCK AND WAREHOUSE WARRANTS

These are documents issued by a dock company or warehouse company acknowledging receipt of goods and undertaking to deliver them to a specific party. They are not negotiable instruments but, if the issuing warehouse or dock company has statutory powers the warrants they issue may be legally transferable. The deposit of a transferable warrant would give a banker good title to the goods but in practice a memorandum of deposit should be taken to put the matter on a clear contractual basis. However, irrespective of whether a warrant is transferable or not, a safer course would be for the banker to have the goods placed in his own name and a new warrant issued in favour of the bank.

A WAREHOUSE RECEIPT OR CERTIFICATE

This is merely an acknowledgement of the receipt of specified goods from a named person. It is not transferable and the relative goods will be surrendered only on production of a properly signed delivery order. Therefore, if such a receipt is to be taken as security it must be accompanied by a signed delivery order and the banker then must have the goods held in his own name, with a new receipt being issued to him.

In all cases where documents of title are to be deposited as security, a Memorandum of Deposit should be taken as this, amongst other things, gives the banker authority to store and insure the goods at the customer's expense.

An effective pledge needs a constructive delivery of the goods, either:

(a) by deposit of a document of title, e.g. Bill of Lading or Transferable Dock or Warehouse warrant endorsed in blank; or

(b) by an acknowledgement by the warehouse company that they hold the goods to the order of the pledgee. Here the banker holds a certificate in the name of the bank.

RELEASE OF GOODS

When a banker holds goods or documents of title to goods as security for an advance it often becomes necessary to permit the depositor to obtain possession of the goods in order that he may realise them.

Upon **unconditional** release of the Documents of Title the pledge is no longer effective. Therefore, when releasing the Documents of Title to the customer, in order to ensure that the Bank has an effective title to the goods against a Liquidator or Trustee in Bankruptcy, it is essential to take a Trust Letter or a Trust Receipt. It must be realised that the taking of this Trust Letter or a Receipt has limitations insofar as the debtor has possession of the Documents of Title to the goods, and the Bank is entirely dependent upon the honesty of the customer to pay in the proceeds. Incidentally, the only really satisfactory way of getting a Charge over goods in a merchant's own factory is to have them transferred to another warehouse so that documents of title can be obtained and charged. If this is not done the alternative is to take a Conditional Bill of Sale, a method which does not appeal to bankers in view of the fact that when registered its publication usually does great damage to the credit of the person concerned.

The documents are given up to the customer on his signing a **Trust Letter** or **Trust Receipt** in which he undertakes to hold the goods and the proceeds **in trust for the banker**, to keep them stored apart from other goods (so that the banker may, if necessary, follow and resume possession of them) and to keep the goods insured, all at his own expense.

The advantage of this procedure is that an expert with a personal interest in securing a good return is selling the goods. The disadvantage is that it is an essential part of the idea that the customer shall have, at some time, control over the goods (i.e. the banker's security) although only as agent and trustee of the bank.

This provides the customer with an opportunity for fraud. Anyone who takes the goods or the documents of title with notice of the equitable charge constituted by the Trust Letter will be bound to hold in trust for the banker such proceeds as he has not already innocently paid to the pledgor (the customer). But a dishonest pledgor could prevent the buyer of the goods or a second banker with whom he has re-pledged the documents from becoming aware of the Letter of Trust until he had paid in full and the pledgor had misappropriated the proceeds which he undertook to hold in trust for the pledgee banker.

In *Lloyds Bank Ltd. v. Bank of America* (1938), Lloyds Bank surrendered documents of title to their customer against Trust Receipts but instead of selling the goods, their customer pledged the documents with Bank of

America who lent against them in good faith. The Court of Appeal held that the company had been constituted mercantile agents within the Factors Act 1889 and as such were unable to make a valid pledge to Bank of America, to whom judgement was accordingly given.

In practice therefore, great care is needed whenever advances are to be made against goods, especially if the documents of title are to be released against trust receipts. Such an arrangement should in any event, be contemplated only where the banker has full confidence in the customer's ability and integrity. Whilst the banker is lending against the warehoused goods, there is no reason why he should not make regular physical checks of the goods, and he should always ensure that they are adequately insured with the bank's interest having been noted and acknowledged. The banker should also be satisfied with the standing of the warehouse company and status enquiries should be made to assist in establishing this. Additionally, the banker may consider it appropriate to have a list of buyers and to satisfy himself about their creditworthiness.

Should the banker fear that a customer is abusing a trust where these have been released to the customer against trust receipts, the banker can write to the buyers giving notice of his charge and claiming the proceeds. If, however, any person buying bona fide and innocent of the banker's charge, is owed money by the bank's customer, he may exercise his right of set-off and pay over only the net amount to the banker.

AGRICULTURAL CHARGES AND FARMING ADVANCES

The Agricultural Credits Act 1928 authorises the creation of a charge known as an "agricultural charge" on farming stock and assets, which is available only to banks. An agricultural charge may be either **fixed** or **floating**, or a combination of both. A fixed charge covers such part of the farming stock and other agricultural assets belonging to the farmer at the date of the charge as may be specified therein, and may include, in the case of livestock, any progeny born after the date of the charge, and in the case of agricultural plant, any plant substituted for that specified in the charge. A floating charge covers the farming stock and other agricultural assets from time to time belonging to the farmer, or such part thereof as is mentioned in the charge.

A charge does not prevent the farmer from selling any of the property charged, but he is under an obligation forthwith to pay to the bank the proceeds of any such sale or any insurance or compensation monies received, except where the property is covered only by a floating charge, when the farmer may expend the monies on the purchase of other farming stock, which, on purchase, becomes subject to the charge. A fixed charge gives the bank the right to take possession of the property upon the death or bankruptcy of the farmer, or the dissolution of partnership, or default in repayment of the monies secured, and, after an interval of 5 clear days (or such less time as the charge provides) to sell the property. Upon the happening of the events just mentioned, a floating charge becomes fixed.

Bank forms of agricultural charge usually incorporate both a fixed and a floating charge. No stamp duty is required but the charge must be registered within 7 clear days after its execution otherwise it is void against any person other than the farmer. Registration is effected by completing Form A.C.1. (which requires signing by the farmer) and forwarding it with the relevant fee to the Agricultural Charges Superintendent at the Land Registry. Though the register is open for inspection, registration must not be published. A bank therefore, before taking a charge, will check that no prior charges have been created, by applying to the Land Registry on Form A.C.6. for an Official Search. Cancellation of an entry in the Register is effected by the bank completing and lodging Form A.C.3.

The type of finance provided by bankers for farmer customers varies quite considerably and the pattern of a farmer's bank account will to a large extent usually reflect the type of farming being undertaken. Farming customers can vary from a smallholder to a very large and sophisticated farming company and the banker will need to adapt his approach to any lending proposition accordingly.

The various natural cycles which occur in farming are of great significance to the lending banker just as in the case of other business customers where knowledge of the trading cycle is needed. The cycles arising with farmers will vary considerably according to the type of farming, e.g. eggs are laid daily and will therefore be turned into cash quickly, sales of milk to the Milk Marketing Board will be paid for monthly, pigs can be sold for cash after three months or so. Corn is gathered annually and then can be sold or stored for future use and arable farming generally will show a yearly cycle as the crops are grown and harvested. Sheep are sheared annually, lambs are produced annually and cattle raised for beef are usually sold only when over two years old.

The nature of a farmer customer's stock assumes rather different dimensions than in the case of many other customers. Normal commercial practice is to value stock at the lower of cost or market value and stock is regarded as being a liquid asset and is usually held for sale, either in its existing form or after processing. Plant and machinery which are agents of the business since they turn raw materials into finished stocks are considered to be fixed assets since the business would not in the normal course of its existing business sell the plant and machinery. However, a farmer's stock of animals can be both a fixed and liquid asset. The fact that a farmer's livestock can be disposed of easily through one of the many cattle markets held regularly throughout the country demonstrates the liquidity of the asset, but nevertheless it should be recognised that in many cases it is the product of the animals (e.g. meat, milk, wool) for which the animals are kept, and as such they are more properly regarded as fixed assets.

The stock of a farmer customer can obviously vary in value from time to time for a variety of reasons. Farmer customers are constantly changing their stocks which obviously affects the value but even ignoring the substantial changes in value which occur as the farmer replaces older cattle by young ones, it must be remembered that the farmer's stock will increase in value as the stock grows into more valuable and saleable assets. It is therefore very important when lending to farmer customers and when some reliance is being placed on stocks as security, for the banker to remain fully aware of the stock position and activities of the customers, and in particular to know at what stages of their farming cycles they are at.

Generally speaking, long-term lending would be avoided and may be more suitably directed towards the specialist organisations available to assist the farmer with this type of finance. The Agricultural Mortgage Corporation provides long-term finance for farmers as does the Land Improvements Company (another state sponsored institution) and two companies (Farming Loan Guarantees Ltd and the Agricultural Finance Federation) sponsored by the National Farmers' Union provide guarantees to banks to secure loans to finance a programme of agreed farm improvements. Specialist advice can often be usefully arranged and in some cases the banker may insist on the farmer receiving such advice which is available from the Agricultural Development and Advisory Service (ADAS) which is state sponsored and which came about as a result of the increased pace of technological and scientific innovation in farming which has occurred over recent years. Advisory services can also be provided by private consultants. Whilst traditionally, bankers would shy away from long term loans to farmers, banks do nevertheless adopt a flexible approach and often would therefore be willing to consider providing medium or longish-term loans for the purchase of additional land and/or buildings or for major farm improvements. In most cases, the bank will be lending to owner-occupiers and will normally as security require a legal charge over the farm buildings and land (or possibly a second mortgage where the farmer has raised mortgage finance on the farm). As additional security, the banker may take an Agricultural Charge, as described earlier, or this may of course be the only security available where the farmer is a tenant farmer. Medium or short-term lending, particularly purely seasonal lending would usually be granted by way of overdraft and may sometimes be agreed unsecured.

When considering lending to a farmer customer, the bank should see audited balance sheets and profit and loss accounts where available. However, in many cases the banker will wish to have a more up to date statement of the farmer's financial position and may achieve this by using the bank's own form of "farmer's balance sheet" which basically comprises a list of the farmer's assets and liabilities, the difference obviously representing the farmer's capital employed in the farm. Whilst often the farmer provides the details, the prudent banker will satisfy himself as to the values placed on the farming assets (and any other assets included) and may arrange to visit the farm at appropriate intervals in order to monitor and update the financial position. This can be particularly important when the bank is looking significantly to an agricultural charge as security for its lending.

The following is an example of the type of confidential statement or farmer's balance sheet which a banker should in many cases obtain from a farmer customer when considering a lending proposition or when reviewing an existing facility. Obviously the format can vary from bank to bank but essentially the following gives the formation which should be sought.

Assets £	**Liabilities** £
Livestock (to be specified) e.g. 75 dairy cows at £ each 30 heifers at £ each 60 pigs at £ each 200 sheep at £ each	Bank overdraft Rent, Rates owing
Growing Crops (to be specified) e.g. 90 acres barley at £ per acre 120 acres wheat at £ per acre	Creditors and other trade liabilities Hire Purchase Creditors Other Liabilities (e.g. loans from relatives or other "outside" sources)
Produce to be sold e.g. wheat barley (giving quantity and prices)	
Debtors (sundry and any special ones e.g. Milk Marketing Board)	
Land and Property (to be specified e.g. Farmhouse + Buildings valued at £............. 600 acres farmland at £ per acre)	
Machinery and Implements (to be specified e.g. 4 Tractors at £ 2 Land Rovers at £ 1 Harvester £ etc.)	Total Liabilities ________
Other Assets e.g. Cash at Bank Private Motor Cars Investments Life Policies (Surrender Value))	Balance (i.e. Estimated Capital)
£	£

A relatively recent development in farming has been the emergence of syndicates of farmers formed for joint ownership and use of farm machinery and equipment, such as combine harvesters, which are expensive and yet used only once a year. A system of syndicate credit has grown up, financed by county central organisations, registered as limited companies and themselves usually borrowing most of the required funds from banks. A further co-operative activity has been the formation of groups for buying their farming requirements in bulk and therefore at cheaper rates, and selling the produce to the market in bulk. The Agricultural Finance Federation (mentioned earlier) will lend for periods of up to three years to members of a co-operative.

HIRE PURCHASE AGREEMENTS AS SECURITY

When an article is sold on hire purchase a written agreement is entered into which specifies the amount borrowed, the number of payments to be made and the period over which the payments are to be made. The agreement also covers all other legal aspects of the contract between the hirer and the hire purchase company. The retailer who sold the goods is paid in full by the finance company, whose business it then is to see the contract through until the final payment is made. Obviously hire purchase finance companies therefore need access to sufficient funds to enable them to write a suitable amount of hire purchase business and sometimes such companies wish to borrow from their bankers for this purpose. Whilst many of the larger finance companies are either owned by banks which means they are funded on an in-house basis or are sufficiently large to warrant lending to unsecured, a banker may be asked to lend to lesser finance companies against the security of the hire purchase agreements they hold. The agreements of a company are constantly changing since older agreements are running off and being replaced by new ones the company enters into, and of course all the company's existing agreements will be being reduced as payments are made by the hirers under the agreements (except anywhere the hirer has defaulted).

When asked to lend to a finance company, a banker will be looking for the management of the company to have a good track record in that line of business and for the company to have a reasonable capital. The company needs to have a sound administration with good methods for monitoring their hire purchase agreements so that their records at all times show clearly the status of each hire purchase agreement. Thus the company can identify agreements in default and chase these up where appropriate, possibly in some cases resorting to repossession of the goods when other efforts at recovery have been abortive. The nature of the goods will indicate the desirability or otherwise of repossessing them. The bank will expect to find that the company's agreements are well-spread, are for normal amounts and normally short periods (usually 2 or 3 years), and that the company insists on hirers putting down reasonable deposits, has adequate credit and status enquiry procedures and checks also on the standing of all the retailers through whom the business comes.

When a banker is satisfied on these aspects, he may be prepared to lend up to a certain percentage of the total amount of instalments owing.

The relative agreements should be lodged with the bank and would usually be charged as security either by way of a specially drawn up equitable charge or by virtue of the company executing a debenture in the bank's favour. A search must be made against the company at Companies House and registration of the bank's charge would need to be effected under Section 95 of the Companies Act 1948 (now Section 395 of the 1985 Act).

The hire purchase agreements total will include interest, because the full amount of interest would have been added at the outset to the sum due under each agreement. It is therefore important for the bank to have a good margin in its security formula since otherwise the bank would in effect be lending practically the whole of the amount paid by the finance company to the retailer which would offend the normal prudent practice which says that the borrower should find something himself. Whilst in some cases a banker may lend up to 75% of amounts due under the agreements, in many cases (particularly for smaller or newer finance companies) the banker will restrict the bank's proportion to say 50% which means that the customer is having to find a reasonable contribution from its own resources. The security cover would need monitoring on a regular basis (say monthly with smaller companies and perhaps quarterly in many other cases) and the valuation would rely considerably on figures supplied by the customer. In particular, the company would need to advise the bank of any agreements in default so that these could be excluded from the bank's security. Often the bank would arrange that all agreements where payments were two months in arrears should be so excluded, and the relative agreements should be handed back to the company. The banker may strengthen his monitoring arrangement by being supplied say every six months with a certificate from the company's auditors verifying the amounts outstanding under the agreements and confirming that all those in arrears had been advised to the bank. Under the Consumer Credit Act 1974 it is necessary for the banker to check that his customer has the necessary licences to operate. Credit sale agreements (which may be called instalment trading agreements) can be taken as security in a similar way but here there would be no right of recovery by the finance company because the contract was one of sale whereas in a hire purchase agreement the contract is one of hire and the property does not pass to the hirer until the final payment has been made. However, under the terms of the credit sale agreement, the whole amount can be made to be immediately payable should one instalment fall into arrears, and a writ can then be issued and judgment obtained and the debtor's goods (including those which were the subject of the credit sale) sold to pay off the indebtedness. This relatively speedy remedy is an advantage to the finance company compared with the repossession route which is involved in the case of hire purchase agreements.

Chapter 10

Securities for Advances (cont.)

METHOD OF CHARGING SECURITY TO ENSURE THAT THE INTENDED LIABILITIES ARE EFFECTIVELY SECURED

In the case of non-corporate security it can be very important for the banker to ensure that the security taken is charged on the type of security charge form which will in fact achieve the secured position the bank is seeking to achieve.

Where an individual is giving security for his own liabilities, the matter is fairly straightforward but where a person is giving security which is intended to secure various liabilities to the bank, then care is needed.

Most banks will have both "own account" and "third party" forms, and the choice of form will depend upon (i) the person(s) giving the security and (ii) the liabilities to be secured. This is perhaps best illustrated by giving some examples. If Tom Jones signed an "own account" charge document the following liabilities would all be covered:

Private Account — Tom Jones.
Joint Account — Tom and Mary Jones
(Joint and Several Liability).
Partnership Account — Jones and Jackson
(Joint and Several Liability)
Sole Trader's Account — Tom Jones trading as Premier Autos.

It should be noted that if Tom Jones had signed a "third party" form to secure his joint account Tom and Mary Jones, only the joint liabilities are secured; the individual liabilities, partnership liabilities, sole trader's account, and guarantees would not be covered.

The following schedule sets out examples of the most common relationships, giving the type of security document to be used:

Person(s) giving security.	*Liabilities to be secured.*	*Form to be used and (if 3rd party) the liabilities to be secured.*
John Jones	John Jones	Own Account
John Jones	Ann Jones	3rd Party "Ann Jones"
John Jones	John and Ann Jones	Own Account
John Jones	Jenny's Bakery (Partnership)	3rd party or own account. (An own account can be used to secure partnership liabilities where joint and several liability exists, but it may be preferable to use a third party form as this covers any changes in the constitution of the partnership)
John Jones	Jenny's Cafe (John Jones trading as)	Own Account
John Jones	John Jones, and John and Janet Jones	Own Account
John Jones	John and Janet Jones. Fredart Bros. (Partnership, John and Gerald Jones)	Own Account
Janet Jones	John Jones	3rd Party "John Jones"
Janet Jones	John and Janet Jones	Own Account
Janet Jones	Janet Jones, John and Janet Jones	Own Account
John and Janet Jones	John and Janet Jones	Own Account

(continued overleaf)

Person(s) giving security.	*Liabilities to be secured.*	*Form to be used and (if 3rd party) the liabilities to be secured.*
John and Janet Jones	John Jones	3rd Party "John Jones"
John and Janet Jones	Jenny's Toy Shop (Partnership — John and Janet Jones)	3rd Party or Own Account
John and Janet Jones	John Jones, John and Janet Jones	3rd Party "John Jones"
John and Janet Jones	John Jones, Janet Jones, John and Janet Jones	When the security is given jointly to secure joint liabilities and sole liabilities of each of the parties, then a guarantee needs to be brought into the security arrangement. Either of the following alternatives would be effective: 3rd Party charge form securing the liabilities of John Jones, and a guarantee by John Jones to secure liabilities of Janet Jones; or 3rd Party Charge form securing the liabilities of Janet Jones and a guarantee by Janet Jones to secure liabilities of John Jones.
John and Peter Jones	Jones Furniture (Partnership of which John, Peter and Graham are partners)	3rd Party "Jones Furniture" (but remember the point mentioned earlier in respect of Jenny's Bakery, which applies here also)

VARIOUS SECURITIES CHECKLISTS

FIRST LEGAL CHARGE OVER REGISTERED LAND

- Obtain Land Certificate and Examine for title.
- Commence entry in the bank's security ledger.
- If leasehold property obtain any necessary permissions from Ground Landlord.
- Prepare charge form and authority to inspect the Register.
- If required, arrange for Independent Legal Advice to be obtained.
- Have the charge executed and the Authority to inspect the Register signed.
- If required, give notice to Ground Landlord.
- Send to Land Registry the Authority to Inspect the Register and an Application for a Search.
- Examine the search and investigate any adverse entries.
- Within priority period of search, register the charge by sending to the Land registry:
  Form A4
  Charge Form and Copy
  Land Certificate
  Fee
  Search Certificate
  Certificate under Land Registration Fee Order 1976.
- When charge certificate received from Land Registry check that the bank's charge is registered on the certificate, that the certificate has been compared to the Register after the date of registration and that there are no other charges registered on the certificate.
- Request Fire Policy from mortgagor and check for title, conditions and cover.
- Give notice and send the policy for endorsement to the Insurance company as necessary.
- If notice/endorsement not required, examine Last Premium Receipt.
- Ensure that Insurance company acknowledge notice or return policy duly endorsed.
- Make Local Search.
- Examine the Local Search.
- Complete entry in the bank's security ledger.
- Debit customer's account with any fees, commissions etc.

FIRST LEGAL CHARGE OVER UNREGISTERED LAND

- Obtain the Deeds and check them off to the schedule.
- Commence entry in the bank's security ledger.
- Obtain report on title if necessary.
- If leasehold property obtain necessary permissions from Ground Landlord.
- Prepare charge form.

- If required, arrange for Independent Legal Advice to be obtained.
- Have the charge executed.
- Give notice to Ground Landlord, if required.
- Search at Land Charges Department.
- Make Local Search.
- Examine Land Charges Department search and investigate any subsisting entries.
- Examine Local Search and investigate any unsatisfactory answers.
- Request Fire Policy from mortgagor and check for title, conditions and cover.
- Give notice and send the policy for endorsement to the Insurance company as required.
- If notice endorsement not required, examine Last Premium Receipt.
- Ensure that Insurance company acknowledge notice or return policy duly endorsed.
- Complete the entry in the bank's security ledger.
- Debit customer's account with any fees, commissions etc.

SECOND LEGAL CHARGE OVER REGISTERED LAND

- Obtain from the mortgagor an authority to approach the 1st Mortgagee and an authority to inspect the register.
- Send questionnaire to the 1st Mortgagee (accompanied by the mortgagor's authority).
- When questionnaire returned, check that information is as anticipated.
- If leasehold property, obtain any necessary permissions from Ground Landlord.
- Send off to Land Registry official search form (accompanied by the authority to inspect the Register).
- When received from Land Registry, check office copy to see that title is as expected and satisfactory.
- Prepare charge form and notice to 1st Mortgagee.
- If, required, arrange for Independent Legal Advice to be obtained.
- Have the charge executed.
- Send to Registrar, the office copy and the executed charge form with a copy of this.
- Send notice to 1st Mortgagee.
- Give notice to Ground Landlord, if required.
- When duplicate notice received back from 1st mortgagor, check that notice has been acknowledged satisfactorily.
- When charge certificate received from Land Registry, check details in this.
- Give notice to insurance company on fire cover.
- Enter details of the security in the bank's security ledger.
- Debit customer's account with any fees, commissions etc.

SECOND LEGAL CHARGE OVER UNREGISTERED LAND

- Obtain from the mortgagor an authority to approach the 1st mortgagee.
- Send to the 1st mortgagee the bank's form of questionnaire (together with the mortgagor's authority).
- When questionnaire received back from 1st mortgagee, check that the answers given are satisfactory.
- If leasehold property, obtain any necessary permissions from Ground Landlord.
- Prepare charge form and notice to 1st mortgagee.
- If required, arrange for Independent Legal Advice to be obtained.
- Have the charge executed.
- Have the charge registered at the Land Charges Registry and make official search.
- Send notice to the 1st mortgagee.
- Give notice to Ground Landlord, if required.
- When duplicate of notice received back from 1st mortgagee, check that all questions are answered.
- When certificate of Registration of charge and result of search received back, check details given.
- Give notice to Insurance Company on fire cover.
- Enter details of the security in the bank's security ledger.
- Debit customer's account with any fees, commissions etc.

DEBENTURE

- Obtain and check Memorandum and Articles of Association of the company.
- If land is to be included in charge, obtain the relative deeds or land certificates.
- If land registered, obtain company's authority to inspect the register.
- Obtain any necessary report on title for the land/properties.
- Obtain and check local searches.
- Prepare bank's form of debenture and forward this to company for execution and return.
- Obtain from company and check insurance policies covering any properties or other insurable assets.
- When debenture returned, check that it has been executed properly, checking in particular that the appropriate resolution has been passed.
- Give notice of bank's interest to insurance company and subsequently check that notice acknowledged.
- Send debenture to Companies House for registration under Section 95 Companies Act 1948 (registration must be effected within 21 days of creation of charge) (now Section 395 of the Companies Act 1985).
- When bank's charge registered, enter the security in the bank's security ledger.

- Debit customer's account with any fees, commissions etc.
- (Where land is concerned, it will be necessary to take all the steps that would be taken if the bank was taking only a specific charge over the land rather than a debenture.)

COMPANY GUARANTEE

- Obtain and check Memorandum and Articles of Association of the company.
- Make status enquiry on proposed guarantor company (where appropriate.)
- Prepare bank's form of guarantee and send to company for execution and return.
- When guarantee received back from customer, check that it has been properly executed, checking in particular that the appropriate resolution has been passed.
- Enter details of the security in the security ledger.
- Diary for renewal of status enquiry or for obtaining future balance sheets of guarantor company (where appropriate.)
- If guarantor company is customer of bank, ensure that the liability under the guarantee is recorded in guarantor company's records at branch.
- Debit customer's account with any fees, commissions etc.

Index